HOUGHTON MIFFLIN

Spelling and Vocabulary

Senior Author
Shane Templeton

Consultant
Rosa Maria Peña

 HOUGHTON MIFFLIN

Boston • Atlanta • Dallas • Geneva, Illinois • Princeton, New Jersey • Palo Alto

Acknowledgments

For each of the selections listed below, grateful acknowledgment is made for permission to excerpt and/or reprint original or copyrighted material as follows:

UPWORDS®, SCRABBLE®, and BOGGLE® are registered trademarks of Hasbro Inc. Used by permission of Hasbro Inc. All rights reserved.

Select definitions in the Spelling Dictionary are adapted and reprinted by permission from the following Houghton Mifflin Company publications. Copyright © 1994 THE AMERICAN HERITAGE FIRST DICTIONARY. Copyright © 1994 THE AMERICAN HERITAGE CHILDREN'S DICTIONARY. Copyright © 1994 THE AMERICAN HERITAGE STUDENT DICTIONARY.

Excerpt from *Dragon Stew,* by Tom McGowen. Copyright © 1969 by Tom McGowen. Adapted and reprinted by permission of the author.

Excerpt from *An Oak Tree Dies and a Journey Begins,* by Louanne Norris and Howard E. Smith, Jr. Copyright © 1979 by Louanne Norris and Howard E. Smith, Jr. Reprinted by permission of Crown Publishers, Inc.

Excerpt from *Through Grandpa's Eyes,* by Patricia MacLachlan, illustrated by Deborah Kogan Ray. Text copyright © 1980 by Patricia MacLachlan. Illustrations copyright © 1980 by Deborah Kogan Ray. Adapted and reprinted by permission of HarperCollins Publishers and Curtis Brown Ltd.

Excerpt from *When Winter Comes,* by Russell Freedman. Text copyright © 1981 by Russell Freedman. Reprinted by permission of the publisher, E.P. Dutton, a division of Penguin Books USA Inc.

ISBN: 0-395-85522-5

3456789-VH-03 02 01 00 99 98

Contents

Contents

Contents

Contents

Contents

Student's Handbook

How to Study a Word

1 **Look at the word.**

- What letters are in the word?
- What does the word mean?
- Does it have more than one meaning?

2 **Say the word.**

- What are the consonant sounds?
- What are the vowel sounds?

3 **Think about the word.**

- How is each sound spelled?
- Did you see any familiar spelling patterns?
- What other words have the same spelling patterns?

4 **Write the word.**

- Think about the sounds and the letters.
- Form the letters correctly.

5 **Check the spelling.**

- Did you spell the word the same way it is spelled in your word list?
- Do you need to write the word again?

Using Spelling Strategies

Sometimes you want to write a word that you are not sure how to spell. Follow these steps to work out the spelling.

1 Say the word softly. Listen to all the sounds. Then think about the letters and patterns that usually spell each sound.

I know that the |cr| sound at the beginning of a word is usually spelled **cr**. I've learned that the long e sound can be spelled **e** as in **we**, **ee** as in **keep**, or **ea** as in **clean**.

Also, I know that the final |k| sound can be spelled **k** or **ck**.

Matt liked fishing in the _____.

2 Have a go at the spelling! Write the word a few different ways to see which way looks right. Make a chart like the one shown. First, write the word one way. Then write the word another way.

Have a Go!		
First try	Second try	Correct
creak	creeck	

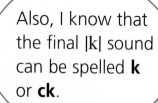

3 Does one spelling look like the right one? If you are not sure, check a dictionary. Look up your first try.

I looked up **c-r-e-a-k**, but it has a different meaning from the word I want.

4 If the word is not there, look up your second try.

Oh, here it is. It's spelled **c-r-e-e-k**. The long **e** is spelled **ee** and the |k| sound is spelled **k**.

5 Finish your chart by writing the word the right way. You might want to circle any parts you spelled wrong to help you remember.

Have a Go!

First try	Second try	Correct
cre(a)k	cree(c)k	creek

Spelling Strategies

1. Listen for sounds and patterns that you know.
2. Think of rhyming words that might be spelled with the same pattern.
3. Listen for word parts that you know—prefixes, suffixes, and endings.
4. Use a Have-a-Go chart.
5. Use a dictionary.

Short Vowels

Read and Say

READ the sentences. **SAY** each bold word.

|ĭ|
mix

Basic

1.	mix	*mix*	I will **mix** the eggs and water.
2.	milk	*milk*	The **milk** is very cold.
3.	smell	*smell*	The roses **smell** nice.
4.	last	*last*	Jeff is **last** in line.
5.	head	*head*	I have a hat on my **head**.
6.	friend	*friend*	Jemma is my best **friend**.
7.	class	*class*	I was late to **class** today.
8.	left	*left*	This is my **left** hand.
9.	thick	*thick*	That book is **thick**.
10.	send	*send*	Did you **send** the note?
11.	thin	*thin*	This cookie is very **thin**.
12.	stick	*stick*	He hit the ball with a **stick**.

Think and Write

Each word has the short *a*, *e*, or *i* sound. These sounds are shown as |ă|, |ĕ|, and |ĭ|. Each short vowel sound is followed by a consonant sound.

    |ă| l**a**st |ĕ| sm**e**ll |ĭ| m**i**x

How are the Elephant Words different?

A. Write **two** Basic Words with the |ă| sound.
B. Write **five** Basic Words with the |ĕ| sound. Remember the Elephant Words.
C. Write **five** Basic Words with the |ĭ| sound.

Review	Challenge
13. step **14.** dish	**15.** empty **16.** crisp

Independent Practice

💡 **Spelling Strategy**   A short vowel sound is usually spelled with one vowel followed by a consonant sound.

The |ă| sound is usually spelled *a*.
The |ĕ| sound is usually spelled *e*.
The |ĭ| sound is usually spelled *i*.

Phonics Use Basic Words in these exercises.

1–4. Write four words by adding the missing letters.

1. __ __ in
2. m __ __ __
3. __ end
4. __ ix

5–6. Write the two words that end with the same sounds as *pick* and *trick*.

Vocabulary: Classifying Both words in each group begin or end with the same two letters. Write the Basic Word that belongs in each group.

7. best, fist, _____
8. soft, lift, _____
9. clap, club, _____
10. tall, fill, _____

Elephant Words Write the Elephant Word that completes each sentence.

11. My best _____ Chris and I baked some muffins.
12. Maria bumped her _____ when she fell.

Challenge Words Write the Challenge Word that fits each meaning below. Use your Spelling Dictionary.

13. firm but breaks easily
14. having nothing in it

Dictionary

ABC Order Put words in ABC order by looking at the first letter of each word. Decide which of those letters comes first in the alphabet. If the first letters are the same, go to the first pair of letters that are different.

head	**sa**nd	**mil**k
left	**se**nd	**mix**

Practice 1–5. Write these words in ABC order.

step
dish
stick
left
last

Review: Spelling Spree

Letter Swap Write a Basic or Review Word by changing the first letter of each word.

6. fish   **10.** silk

7. bend   **11.** fast

8. fix   **12.** glass

9. dead

How Are You Doing?
Write each spelling word as a family member reads it aloud. Did you spell any words wrong?

Proofreading and Writing

Proofread for Spelling Proofread this journal page. Find seven spelling mistakes. Write each word correctly.

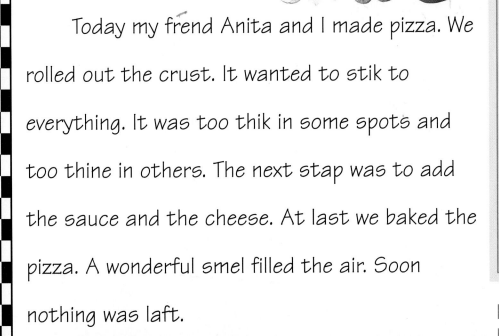

September 12

   Today my frend Anita and I made pizza. We rolled out the crust. It wanted to stik to everything. It was too thik in some spots and too thine in others. The next stap was to add the sauce and the cheese. At last we baked the pizza. A wonderful smel filled the air. Soon nothing was laft.

Basic
1. mix
2. milk
3. smell
4. last
5. head
6. friend
7. class
8. left
9. thick
10. send
11. thin
12. stick

Review
13. step
14. dish

Challenge
15. empty
16. crisp

Proofreading Marks
¶ Indent
∧ Add
ℐ Delete
≡ Capital letter
/ Small letter

Write a Description

Write a paragraph describing a tasty new food, such as Sun Soup. What does it look, taste, and smell like? Try to use three spelling words. Draw a picture of what you described. Share your description with a friend.

Proofreading Tip

To check your writing, read it over one line at a time.

Rhyming Riddles Rhyming words end with the same sounds, such as *milk* and *silk*. Write a word for each clue.

1. It rhymes with **smell**. It is found at the beach.

2. It rhymes with **thick**. It is used to build a house.

3. It rhymes with **thin**. It is part of your face.

4. It rhymes with **head**. You can eat it.

5. It rhymes with **class**. It grows outdoors.

Show What You Know! Use the words you wrote to finish this silly rhyme about Betty the Baker.

Betty the Baker shook her head.
She wanted to bake some tasty
___(6)___ .
The mix was so thin
It ran down her ___(7)___ .
When it baked it turned thick
And was hard as a ___(8)___ .

Home Economics

Baking All the words in the box have something to do with baking. Write those words to finish this recipe. Use your Spelling Dictionary.

Spelling Word Link

mix

flour
batter
oven
bread
stir

How to Bake a Loaf of Bread

Here's how to make a loaf of __(1)__.
Mix salt, baking powder, sugar, __(2)__,
and milk in a bowl. Then __(3)__
everything together, and pour the
__(4)__ into a pan. Bake it in a hot
__(5)__ for about an hour.

Try This

CHALLENGE

Yes or No? Is the underlined word used correctly? Write *yes* or *no*.
6. An <u>oven</u> will bake food.
7. Use a <u>batter</u> to mix the milk and the eggs.
8. Look at the red <u>flour</u> in the garden!

★★★ **Fact File**

In India and Pakistan, people make a flat bread called *chapati*. Chapati looks like a tortilla in size and shape.

More Short Vowels

|ŏ|

pond

Read and Say

READ the sentences. **SAY** each bold word.

Basic

1.	pond	*pond*	There are fish in the **pond**.
2.	luck	*luck*	Jamal has good **luck**.
3.	drop	*drop*	Do not **drop** the dish.
4.	lot	*lot*	We ate a **lot** of fish.
5.	rub	*rub*	Mom will **rub** my back.
🐘 6.	does	*does*	Maria **does** everything well.
7.	drum	*drum*	Jack beat the **drum**.
8.	sock	*sock*	I put my **sock** on my foot.
9.	hunt	*hunt*	Help me **hunt** for my dog.
10.	crop	*crop*	It was a good **crop** of corn.
11.	shut	*shut*	Did you **shut** the door?
🐘 12.	front	*front*	The car is in **front** of the house.

Think and Write

Each word has the short o sound or the short u sound.
These sounds are shown as |ŏ| and |ŭ|. Each vowel sound
is followed by a consonant sound.

|ŏ| l**o**t |ŭ| r**u**b

How are the Elephant Words different?

A. Write **five** Basic Words with the |ŏ| sound.
B. Write **seven** Basic Words with the |ŭ| sound.
Remember the Elephant Words.

Review
13. spot   14. much

Challenge
15. dodge   16. crumb

Independent Practice

Spelling Strategy A short vowel sound is usually spelled with one vowel followed by a consonant sound.

The |ŏ| sound is usually spelled *o*.
The |ŭ| sound is usually spelled *u*.

Phonics Use Basic Words in these exercises.

1–2. Write the words that start with the sounds you hear at the beginning of *shop* and *help*.

3–4. Write the two words that start with the sounds you hear at the beginning of *dress*.

5–7. Write the word that rhymes with each word.

    5. tub   **6.** duck   **7.** dot

Vocabulary: Classifying Write the Basic Word that belongs in each group.

    8. hat, shirt, _____

    9. farm, seed, _____

  10. stream, lake, _____

Elephant Words Write the Elephant Word that completes each sentence.

11. Where _____ Elena usually go fishing?

12. Meet me in _____ of the sporting goods store.

Challenge Words Write the Challenge Word that completes each sentence. Use your Spelling Dictionary.

13. Look at those fish _____ the rocks!

14. The ducks ate every _____ of bread.

Review: Spelling Spree

Hidden Words Write the Basic or Review Word hidden in each group of letters. Do not let the other words fool you.

Example: e t i p o n d p e *pond*

1. l o v d r u m k s
2. f o s h u s h u t
3. m u r m u c h o r
4. s p o f r o n t e
5. d o s s d r o p t
6. t r e n h u n t e
7. d e d o e s t o s
8. e b l b u r u b b

Code Breaker Use the code to figure out each Basic or Review Word below. Then write the word.

● = c	□ = l	⊥ = p	↑ = t
▲ = d	∞ = n	↕ = r	☆ = u
⊖ = k	⊠ = o	> = s	

Example: ▲ ↕ ⊠ ⊥ *drop*

9. □ ⊠ ↑
10. ● ↕ ⊠ ⊥
11. □ ☆ ● ⊖
12. ⊥ ⊠ ∞ ▲
13. > ⊥ ⊠ ↑
14. > ⊠ ● ⊖

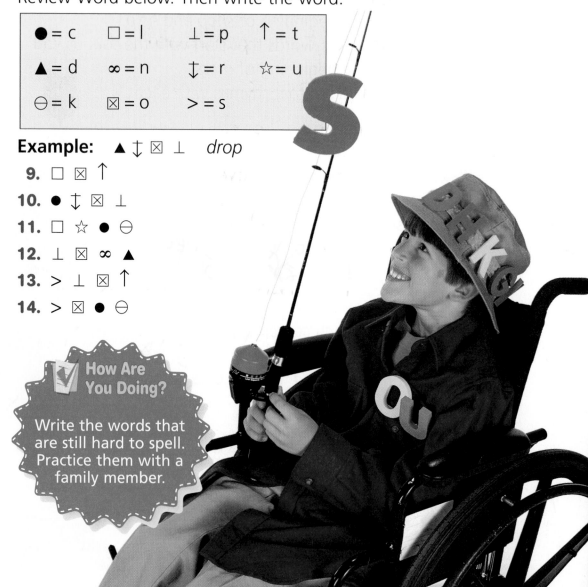

How Are You Doing?

Write the words that are still hard to spell. Practice them with a family member.

Proofreading and Writing

Proofread: Spelling and End Marks Use correct end marks.

STATEMENT: Lea went fishing.

QUESTION: Did she go to the lake?

Proofread Will's post card. Find three spelling mistakes and two missing end marks. Write the story correctly.

Dear Grandpa,

I fish every day at the pand I often hont for a new spot and just drap my line. How many fish do I catch I catch a lot!

Love,

Will

Proofreading Marks

¶ Indent
∧ Add
✌ Delete
≡ Capital letter
/ Small letter

Write a Post Card

Write a post card about a trip you took where you did something you enjoyed. What happened? Try to use three spelling words. Draw a picture on the front.

Proofreading Tip

Check that you used correct end marks for statements and questions.

Rhyming Words

Short o and Short u Words Match the letters on the fish with the letters on the signs. Write three *ock* words and three *ush* words.

Show What You Know! Write two sentences about fish. In each sentence, use one of the words you made.

Recreation

Fishing All the words in the box have something to do with fishing. Write those words to finish this page from a story. Use your Spelling Dictionary.

Spelling Word Link

pond

fishing rod
hook
nibble
river
bait

At last Kay found a fishing spot by the __(1)__. She threw the line of her __(2)__ into the air. The shiny __(3)__ at the end fell into the water. Then she waited eagerly for hungry fish to __(4)__ at the tasty __(5)__.

Try This CHALLENGE

Yes or No? Is the underlined word used correctly? Write *yes* or *no*.

6. Gulls <u>nibble</u> their fish in big gulps.
7. My dad uses <u>bait</u> to keep fish away.
8. My family goes rowing on the <u>river</u>.

 Fact File

Every year salmon leave the ocean. They fight swift rivers and may jump over ten-foot-high waterfalls to return to their place of birth.

Vowel-Consonant-e Pattern

Read and Say

READ the sentences. **SAY** each bold word.

|ō|
smo**ke**

Basic

1.	smoke	*smoke*	The **smoke** rose from the fire.
2.	huge	*huge*	What a **huge** hole it is!
3.	save	*save*	We will **save** for our trip.
4.	life	*life*	My cat has a good **life**.
5.	wide	*wide*	This shoe is too **wide** for me.
6.	come	*come*	Anna will **come** with us.
7.	mine	*mine*	This cup is **mine**.
8.	grade	*grade*	I am in the third **grade**.
9.	smile	*smile*	The joke made her **smile**.
10.	note	*note*	What does the **note** say?
11.	cube	*cube*	A **cube** has six sides.
12.	love	*love*	I **love** my dad.

Think and Write

Most of the words have the long *a, i, o,* or *u* sound. These sounds are shown as |ā|, |ī|, |ō|, and |yoo̅|. They are spelled vowel-consonant-*e*.

> |ā| s**ave** |ī| l**ife** |ō| sm**oke** |yoo̅| h**uge**

How are the Elephant Words different?

A. Write **six** Basic Words with the |ā| or |ī| sound.
B. Write **four** Basic Words with the |ō| or |yoo̅| sound.
C. Write **two** Basic Words with no long vowel sound.

Review
13. side   **14.** hope

Challenge
15. escape   **16.** explode

Independent Practice

Spelling Strategy
When spelling a word with a long vowel sound, remember that a long vowel sound is often spelled with the vowel-consonant-e pattern.

Phonics Use Basic Words in these exercises.

1. Write the word that ends with the same sound that you hear at the end of *page*.

2–5. Write four words by adding one or two consonants to these vowel-consonant-e patterns.

    2. __ ide   **4.** __ ube

    3. __ __ ade   **5.** __ __ ile

Vocabulary: Context Sentences Write the Basic Word that completes each sentence.

6. We saw the gray _____ from the fire.
7. The firefighters tried to _____ the animals.
8. A deer saved its _____ by standing in a lake.
9. Mateo wrote the firefighters a thank-you _____.
10. This drawing of the fire is not hers but _____.

Elephant Words Write the Elephant Word that matches each meaning.

11. to move toward
12. to have warm feelings for

Challenge Words Write the Challenge Word that fits each clue. Use your Spelling Dictionary.

13. Deer do this when they run from a fire.
14. People like to watch fireworks do this.

Dictionary

Parts of a Dictionary A dictionary lists words in ABC order. How could you find the word *cube* quickly? Turn to the beginning, where you will find the words starting with c.

BEGINNING	MIDDLE	END
abcdefg	hijklmnopq	rstuvwxyz

Practice Write *beginning*, *middle*, or *end* to tell the part of the dictionary where you would find each word below.

1. note   3. come   5. mine
2. save   4. wide   6. life

Review: Spelling Spree

Hink Pinks Write the Basic Word that fits each clue and rhymes with the given word.

Example: a burning wheel   **tire** _____   *fire*

7. a message carrier   _____ tote
8. a changed test score   _____ trade
9. a place for happy faces   _____ file
10. a square straw   _____ tube
11. a fancy, deep hole in the ground   fine _____
12. a daring rescue   brave _____

How Are You Doing?
Write your spelling words in ABC order. Practice with a family member any words you spelled wrong.

Proofreading and Writing

Proofread for Spelling Proofread this newspaper clipping. Find eight spelling mistakes. Write each word correctly.

Basic

1. smoke
2. huge
3. save
4. life
5. wide
6. come
7. mine
8. grade
9. smile
10. note
11. cube
12. love

Review
13. side
14. hope

Challenge
15. escape
16. explode

—Homes Saved—

A hugh cloud of smok rose into the sky. Firefighters were able to save the homes, but they could not stop the fire from climbing up the sid of a wid hill. People luv this land. They hopp it will com to lif again soon.

Proofreading Marks

¶ Indent
∧ Add
ℯ Delete
≡ Capital letter
/ Small letter

Write a List

Make a fire safety poster. Include a list of things to do and not to do around fire. Try to use three spelling words. Display your poster where your friends can read it.

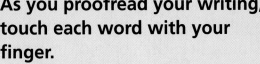
FIRE SAFETY

Proofreading Tip

As you proofread your writing, touch each word with your finger.

Rhyming Words

Long o and Long a Words Help the bears put out the fires. Follow each path of letters to make new words that rhyme with *smoke* and *save*. Hint: Not all the letters will work.

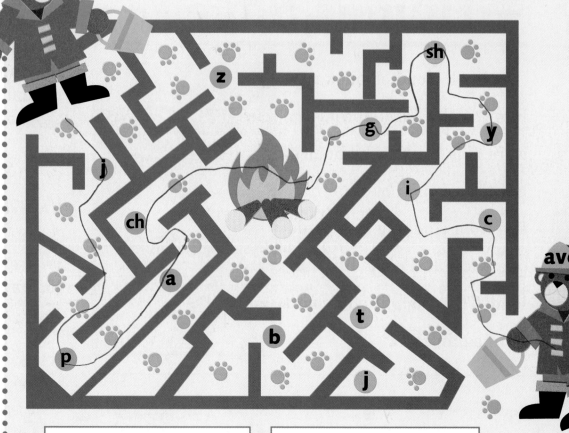

smoke		save	
1.	?	4.	?
2.	?	5.	?
3.	?	6.	?

Work Together Work with a partner to create a short skit about a forest fire. Use some of the rhyming words in your skit.

Vocabulary Enrichment

Unit 3 BONUS

Science

Forest Fires All the words in the box have something to do with forest fires. Write those words to finish this page from a park ranger's lookout log. Use your Spelling Dictionary.

Spelling Word Link

smoke

blaze
forest
animals
ranger
spark

From my lookout tower, I could see miles of green ___(1)___. No rain had fallen in weeks, and I was worried. Just one ___(2)___ from a match might start a ___(3)___. This would harm the woodlands and the ___(4)___ that live there. It's my job as a park ___(5)___ to protect them.

Try This CHALLENGE

Write an Ad What type of person would make a good forest ranger? Make a list of the types of things that a forest ranger does. Then write a help wanted ad for one. Try to use words from the lists in this unit.

Fact File

In 1950 a bear cub was saved from a forest fire. Now pictures of that bear, named Smokey, tell people to prevent forest fires.

29

More Long Vowel Spellings

Read and Say

|ā|
paint

READ the sentences. **SAY** each bold word.

Basic

1.	paint	*paint*	We will **paint** my house.
2.	clay	*clay*	We used **clay** in art class.
3.	feel	*feel*	Marie will **feel** better soon.
4.	leave	*leave*	I will **leave** the cat with you.
5.	neighbor	*neighbor*	Peter is my **neighbor**.
6.	eight	*eight*	Lin has **eight** friends.
7.	seem	*seem*	Does this **seem** big to you?
8.	speak	*speak*	I will **speak** to him now.
9.	paid	*paid*	We **paid** him for the milk.
10.	lay	*lay*	**Lay** the dress on the bed.
11.	need	*need*	The children **need** help.
12.	weigh	*weigh*	How much does it **weigh**?

Think and Write

Each word has the long *a* or the long *e* sound.

|ā| p**ai**nt, cl**ay** |ē| l**ea**ve, f**ee**l

What are two spelling patterns for the |ā| sound? What are two spelling patterns for the |ē| sound? How are the Elephant Words different?

A. Write **seven** Basic Words with the |ā| sound. Remember the Elephant Words.

B. Write **five** Basic Words with the |ē| sound.

Review		Challenge	
13. green	**14.** play	**15.** easel	**16.** crayon

Independent Practice

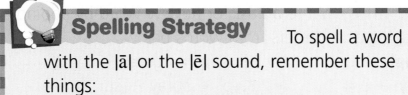

Spelling Strategy To spell a word with the |ā| or the |ē| sound, remember these things:

The |ā| sound can be spelled *ai* or *ay*.
The |ē| sound can be spelled *ea* or *ee*.

Phonics Use Basic Words in these exercises.

1. Write the word that ends with two consonant sounds.

2–3. Write the two words that end with the |ā| sound spelled *ay*.

4–6. Write the three words that have the |ē| sounds spelled *ee*.

Vocabulary: Synonyms A **synonym** is a word that means the same or almost the same as another word. Write a Basic Word that is a synonym for each word below.

7. talk   8. spent   9. go

Elephant Words Write the Elephant Word that completes each sentence.

10. Sid needs seven brushes, not _____.

11. This clay is heavy. It must _____ ten pounds.

12. My _____ Mrs. Ling is a famous painter.

Challenge Words Write the Challenge Word that fits each meaning. Use your Spelling Dictionary.

13. a coloring stick

14. a stand for painting

Review: Spelling Spree

Letter Math Write a Basic or Review Word by adding and taking away letters from words below.

Example: gray − ay + een = *green*

1. clay − c =
2. see + m =
3. p + maid − m =
4. f + heel − h =
5. leaf − f + ve =
6. pl + spray − spr =
7. n + weigh − w + bor =
8. p + rain − r + t =
9. w + sleigh − sl =

Silly Rhymes Write a Basic or Review Word to complete each silly sentence. Each answer rhymes with the underlined word.

10. Did you ever _____ from a mountain <u>peak</u>?
11. Have you ever <u>seen</u> a sky that is _____?
12. A turtle has a _____ to <u>speed</u>.
13. The blue <u>jay</u> is made out of _____.
14. Does your <u>weight</u> include the number _____?

How Are You Doing?

Write each spelling word as a partner reads it aloud. Did you spell any words wrong?

Proofreading and Writing

Proofread: Spelling and End Marks End a sentence with the correct mark.

COMMAND: Please clean the paintbrush now.

EXCLAMATION: Sue's painting won first prize!

Proofread this ad. Find three spelling mistakes and two missing end marks. Write the ad correctly.

Do you paint or pla with clay? Join the town art class You'll feal great To sign up, spek to Mr. Hanks.

Basic
1. paint
2. clay
3. feel
4. leave
5. neighbor
6. eight
7. seem
8. speak
9. paid
10. lay
11. need
12. weigh

Review
13. green
14. play

Challenge
15. easel
16. crayon

Proofreading Marks

¶ Indent
∧ Add
✂ Delete
≡ Capital letter
/ Small letter

Write Instructions

Instructions

Tell how to do something you learned in art class. Write step-by-step instructions. Try to use three spelling words. Let a friend try to follow your instructions.

Proofreading Tip Check each sentence to make sure you used the correct end mark.

Vocabulary Enrichment

Word Builder

Spelling
Word Link
lay

Using a Thesaurus Pages 251–252 will tell you how to use the **Thesaurus** in this book. Use your Thesaurus to find the best words to say what you mean. The entry below for *put* shows that *lay* might be used instead of *put*.

main entry word   part of speech   definition   sample sentence

put *v.* to cause to be in a certain place. **Put** *the spoons in the drawer*.
subentry ⋯⋯→ **lay** to put or set down. *He **lays** his coat on the bed*.

Write two words you could use in place of each of these words. Use your Thesaurus.

1–2. new   **3–4.** walk

Show What You Know! Find *hurry* in your Thesaurus. Write a sentence for each picture, using one of the subentries you found.

Art

Art Class All the words in the box have something to do with art class. Write those words to finish these instructions. Use your Spelling Dictionary.

Spelling Word Link

paint

picture
paste
poster
trace
marker

Here's how to make a big __(1)__ to tell people about your art show.

- First, cut out a __(2)__ of a famous painting from a magazine.
- Next, use glue to __(3)__ it on heavy paper.
- Then write in pencil the words that tell about your show.
- Last, use a bright __(4)__ to __(5)__ over the words that you wrote.

Try This CHALLENGE

Riddle Time Write a word from the box to answer each question.

6. What can you use to color?
7. What can make things stick together?
8. What can you make to announce a fair?

Fact File

The American painter Mary Cassatt studied in France. She often painted women and children in their everyday life.

Spelling the Long o Sound

Read and Say

READ the sentences. **SAY** each bold word.

|ō|
coach

Basic

1. coach	*coach*	She is the **coach** of this team.
2. blow	*blow*	I can **blow** my horn well.
3. float	*float*	Will this old boat **float**?
4. hold	*hold*	The box is too big to **hold**.
5. sew	*sew*	I need to **sew** my torn coat.
6. though	*though*	He ate even **though** he was full.
7. sold	*sold*	The store **sold** many toys.
8. soap	*soap*	Wash your hands with **soap**.
9. row	*row*	I sat in the front **row**.
10. own	*own*	Do you **own** that dog?
11. both	*both*	We should take **both** bags.
12. most	*most*	Who ate the **most** fish?

Think and Write

Each word has the long o sound. This sound is shown as |ō|. The |ō| sound can be spelled with the pattern *oa*, *ow*, or *o*.

|ō| c**oa**ch, bl**ow**, h**o**ld

How are the Elephant Words different?

A. Write **three** Basic Words with the |ō| sound spelled *oa*.
B. Write **three** Basic Words with the |ō| sound spelled *ow*.
C. Write **four** Basic Words with the |ō| sound spelled *o*.
D. Write **two** Basic Words with the |ō| sound spelled other ways.

Review	Challenge
13. cold **14.** slow	**15.** shallow **16.** program

Independent Practice

Spelling Strategy To spell a word with the |ō| sound, remember that this sound can be spelled *oa*, *ow*, or *o*.

Phonics Use Basic Words in these exercises.
1. Write the word that ends with the consonant sound you hear at the end of *each*.
2–3. Write the two words that rhyme with *cold*.

Vocabulary: Context Sentences Write the Basic Word that completes each sentence.
4. Do you sink in the water, or can you _____?
5. Jessie and Lianna are _____ good swimmers.
6. Carrie will _____ the boat beside the swimmer.
7. Can you _____ bubbles in the water?
8. Do you _____ this swimsuit, or is it Jason's?
9. Ms. Ling coaches _____ of these ten swimmers.
10. Please use _____ and warm water to wash your hands.

Elephant Words Write the Elephant Word that completes each sentence.
11. He needs a needle and thread to _____ this rip.
12. Nan tried to smile even _____ she was sad.

Challenge Words Write the Challenge Word that matches each meaning. Use your Spelling Dictionary.
13. not deep
14. a list of events and names

Dictionary

Guide Words **Entry words** are the main words in a dictionary. They are in ABC order. Two **guide words** at the top of each page help you find words quickly. They tell the first and last entry words on the page.

Practice 1–4. Write the four words that would be on the same page as the guide words *sky | sore*.

smell	spot
sew	slow
sold	soap

Review: Spelling Spree

Letter Swap Change the underlined letter in each word to make a Basic Word. Write the Basic Word.

Example: l<u>o</u>ad   *road*

5. ow<u>e</u>	**9.** soa<u>k</u>
6. <u>p</u>ost	**10.** s<u>a</u>w
7. sol<u>o</u>	**11.** b<u>a</u>th
8. bl<u>e</u>w	**12.** <u>l</u>ow

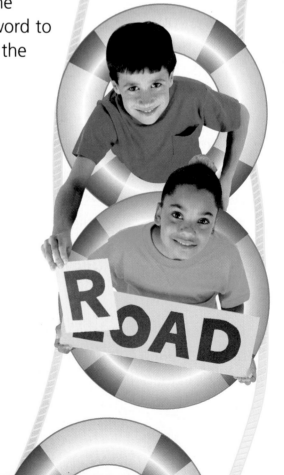

How Are You Doing? Write each spelling word in a sentence. Practice with a partner any words you spelled wrong.

Proofreading and Writing

Proofread for Spelling Proofread this diary entry. Find six spelling mistakes. Write each word correctly.

Last year I could hardly flot, but I

swam in a race today. I took holed of my

cap and walked up to the dock. The koach

yelled, "Go!" We all dived into the cald

water. I was too slo today, thow. Most of

my friends beat me.

Basic

1. coach
2. blow
3. float
4. hold
5. sew
6. though
7. sold
8. soap
9. row
10. own
11. both
12. most

Review

13. cold
14. slow

Challenge

15. shallow
16. program

Write an Opinion

Swimming Race

Would you like to be in a swimming race? If not, what kind of race would you like to enter? Why? Write a paragraph that explains your choice. Try to use three spelling words. Share your paragraph with a friend.

Proofreading Marks

¶   Indent
∧   Add
⌐   Delete
≡   Capital letter
∕   Small letter

Proofreading Tip

Check that your *o*'s and *a*'s are written clearly so they can be told apart.

Phonics and Spelling

Rhyming Words

Long o Words Which swimmer has the most fans? Match the letters on the fans' cards with the letters on the swimmers to make words that rhyme with *blow* and *most*. Write the new words you made.

p

cr

gl

t

fl

h

gh

_ow

_ost

blow	
1.	?
2.	?
3.	?
4.	?

most	
5.	?
6.	?
7.	?

1.

2.

Who has the most fans, Number 1 or Number 2?

Work Together Work in two small groups to have a word race. See how many words each team can create by changing one letter at a time for the word *row*.

Example: row − w + d = rod

Physical Education

Swimming Race All the words in the box have something to do with a swimming race. Write those words to complete this article from a school newspaper. Use your Spelling Dictionary.

Spelling Word Link

coach

whistle
goggles
meet
lane
scoreboard

San Jacinto Weekly

Volume 1

San Jacinto School Places First!
The last race of our final swim __(1)__ was about to begin. The San Jacinto racers pulled their __(2)__ over their eyes. The timer blew her __(3)__. Each racer dived into the pool and swam as quickly as possible down his or her __(4)__. In seconds it was over! The winning time was shown on the __(5)__. SJ's team had broken last year's record. They brought home the gold.

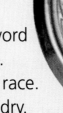

Try This
CHALLENGE

Yes or No? Is the underlined word used correctly? Write *yes* or *no*.
6. Do not eat <u>meet</u> before the race.
7. <u>Goggles</u> will keep your hair dry.
8. A red rope separated each <u>lane</u>.

Fact File
The butterfly stroke is often used in racing. As swimmers move, they arch their arms forward like wings.

6 Review: Units 1–5

|ĭ|
mix

| Unit 1 | Short Vowels | pp. 12–17 |

| last | head | friend |
| thin | left | class |

Spelling Strategy   In most words, the |ă| sound is spelled **a**, the |ĕ| sound is spelled **e**, and the |ĭ| sound is spelled **i**.

Write the word that is the opposite of each word below.
1. foot   **2.** right   **3.** first   **4.** fat

Write the word that completes each sentence.
5. Every Tuesday we have our music _____.
6. Uncle Mike, this is my best _____ Anna.

|ŏ|
pond

| Unit 2 | More Short Vowels | pp. 18–23 |

| luck | drop | does |
| sock | shut | front |

Spelling Strategy   In most words, the |ŏ| sound is spelled **o** and the |ŭ| sound is spelled **u**.

Write the word that rhymes with each word below.
7. but   **8.** knock

Write the word that completes each sentence.
 9. Be careful you do not _____ those dishes.
10. What _____ Mr. Wood do for a living?
11. Someone is ringing the _____ doorbell.
12. It was just _____ that Andy found his glasses.

Unit 3 Vowel-Consonant-e Pattern pp. 24–29

| save | smoke | come |
| cube | smile | love |

|ō|
smoke

Spelling Strategy   A long vowel sound is often spelled vowel-consonant-**e**.

Write the word that means the opposite of each word.
13. frown   **14.** hate   **15.** go

Write the word that completes each sentence.
16. Trisha needs another ice _____ for her juice.
17. Clouds of _____ came from the forest fire.
18. Chuck is trying to _____ money for a bike.

Unit 4 More Long Vowel Spellings pp. 30–35

| leave | clay | eight |
| paid | seem | weigh |

|ā|
paint

Spelling Strategy   In many words, the |ā| sound is spelled **ai** or **ay**. The |ē| sound may be spelled **ea** or **ee**.

Write the word that completes each sentence.
19. Where is the _____ for art class?
20. Nina has _____ cousins, not seven.
21. How much does your new baby brother _____?
22. Uncle Bob has already _____ for the tickets.
23. Eva and Li _____ to have lost their money.
24. Did Adam _____ the party already?

|ō|
coach

coach	sew	though
most	own	soap

Spelling Strategy   The |ō| sound can be spelled with the pattern **oa**, **ow**, or **o**.

Write the word that belongs in each group.

25. needle, cloth, _____

26. game, team, _____

Write the word that completes each sentence.

27. I hate _____ in my eyes when I wash my hair.

28. Who has the _____ baseball cards?

29. Teresa wants her _____ skateboard.

30. Lou likes to jog, _____ he is often too busy.

empty	crumb	escape
crayon	program	

Write the word that completes each sentence.

31. Dad, you have a _____ of toast on your tie.

32. Lee needs a purple _____ to color her picture.

33. Mary Ann's dog keeps trying to _____ from the yard.

34. Pam's piggy bank is _____ because she bought several gifts.

35. Look at the _____, and tell me which band will play next.

Spelling-Meaning Strategy

Word Forms

Like people, words have families. The words in a family look alike in some ways. They also have a common "family" meaning. They are related to each other. Read this paragraph.

Lisa collects **stickers**. She **sticks** some on her backpack, but she keeps most of them in books. Her favorite ones show boats.

Think How are *stickers* and *sticks* alike in meaning? How are *stickers* and *sticks* alike in spelling?

Here are some words in the *stick* family.

stick	stickier	stickers
sticky	stickiest	stickiness

Apply and Extend

Complete these activities on another piece of paper.

1. Look up the meaning of each word in the Word Box above in your Spelling Dictionary. Write six sentences, using one word in each sentence.

2. With a partner list words related to *thick*, *mix*, and *luck*. Then look in your Spelling-Meaning Index beginning on page 272. Add any other words in these families to your list.

A Story About Yourself

from

Through Grandpa's Eyes

by Patricia MacLachlan

John is visiting his grandfather. How can you tell that his grandfather is blind?

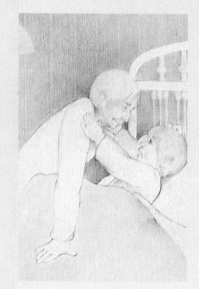

The sun wakes Grandpa differently from the way it wakes me. He says it touches him, warming him awake. When I look in the room, Grandpa is already up and doing his morning exercises, bending and stretching by the bed. He stops and smiles because he hears me.

"Good morning, John."

I exercise with Grandpa. Up and down. Then I try to exercise with my eyes closed.

"One, two," says Grandpa, "three, four."

"Wait!" I cry. I am still on one, two when Grandpa is on three, four.

I fall sideways. Three times. Grandpa laughs as he hears me falling on the floor.

Think and Discuss

1 What details tell you that Grandpa has a special way of seeing?

2 Why does the beginning of the story make you want to learn more about Grandpa?

3 Who is the *I* in the story? How do you know?

The Writing Process

A Story About Yourself

Write a story about yourself. Just follow the Guidelines and use the Writing Process.

1 **Prewriting**
- List interesting things you have done. Choose one to write about.

2 **Draft**
- Do not worry about mistakes—just write!

3 **Revise**
- Is your beginning interesting?
- Where could details make your story clearer?
- Use your Thesaurus to find exact words.

4 **Proofread**
- Does each sentence end correctly?
- Did you correct any misspelled words?

5 **Publish**
- Create a collage about you! Place your story on the collage.

• • • Guidelines for Writing a Personal Narrative

✓ Include a beginning, middle, and end.
✓ Include an interesting beginning.
✓ Use details that bring your story to life.

Composition Words
friend
last
does
come
huge
neighbor
most
own

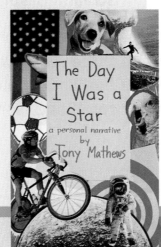

The Day I Was a Star
a personal narrative
by
Tony Mathews

Three-Letter Clusters

Read and Say

READ the sentences. **SAY** each bold word.

throw

Basic

1.	spring	*spring*
2.	throw	*throw*
3.	strong	*strong*
4.	three	*three*
5.	straight	*straight*
6.	scream	*scream*
7.	stream	*stream*
8.	spray	*spray*
9.	screen	*screen*
10.	street	*street*
11.	spread	*spread*
12.	string	*string*

Our flowers grow in **spring**.
I can **throw** the ball to Ana.
Kim is very **strong**.
I saw **three** baby ducks.
Lee rows in a **straight** line.
Bob let out a loud **scream**.
We fish in that **stream**.
Do not **spray** the car!
A bug is on the **screen**.
The truck is on our **street**.
The bird **spread** its wings.
I need **string** to fly my kite.

Think and Write

Each word begins with three consonants. You can hear their different sounds. When two or more consonants with different sounds are written together, they form a **consonant cluster**.

scream   **spr**ing   **str**ong   **thr**ow

A. Write **two** Basic Words that begin with *scr*.
B. Write **three** Basic Words that begin with *spr*.
C. Write **five** Basic Words that begin with *str*.
D. Write **two** Basic Words that begin with *thr*.

Review	Challenge
13. glad **14.** start	**15.** strength **16.** struggle

Independent Practice

Spelling Strategy When you are spelling a word that has a **consonant cluster**, say the word aloud and listen for the different consonant sounds. Remember, some words begin with the consonant clusters *scr*, *spr*, *str*, and *thr*.

Phonics Use Basic Words in these exercises.
1. Write the word that ends with the |ō| sound.
2. Write the word that rhymes with *long*.
3. Write the word that rhymes with *bread*.
4–5. Write the two words that have the |ā| sound.
6–7. Write the two words that have the |ē| sound spelled *ea*.

Vocabulary: Classifying Write the Basic Word that belongs in each group.
8. path, road, _____
9. ribbon, thread, _____
10. winter, fall, _____
11. one, two, _____
12. movie, theater, _____

Challenge Words Write the Challenge Word that completes each sentence. Use your Spelling Dictionary.
13. Two teams, the Screaming Eagles and the Fighting Tigers, are in a _____ for first place.
14. Does Victor have the _____ to pitch all nine innings?

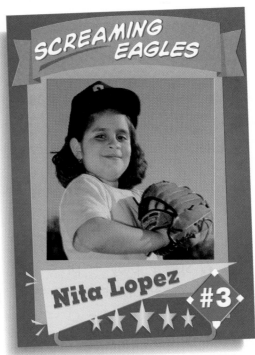

SCREAMING EAGLES

Nita Lopez #3

Dictionary

Definitions A dictionary entry has one or more **definitions**, or meanings, for the entry word. A **sample sentence** helps to make the meaning clear.

definition

street |strēt| *n. pl.* **streets** A road in a city or town: *I live on this street.*

sample sentence

Practice Use your Spelling Dictionary to complete the exercises.

1. Look up *strong*. Write the definition.

2. Look up *spread*. Write the sample sentence.

Review: Spelling Spree

Letter Math Write Basic or Review Words by solving the problems below.

Example: thr + bee − b = *three*

3. gl + had − h =

4. str + dream − dr =

5. spr + head − h =

6. st + dart − d =

7. spr + play − pl =

8. scr + green − gr =

9. str + cling − cl =

10. spr + thing − th =

How Are You Doing?

List the spelling words that are hard for you. Practice them with a family member.

thr   +   bee   −   b   =   three

Proofreading and Writing

Proofread for Spelling this part of Rashad's letter. Find six spelling mistakes. Write each word correctly.

May 14

Dear Uncle Devin,

The Smalltown baseball team is strog this spring. Our players thro hard! Bigtown hit first today. The team made thee strait outs. Then Smalltown scored a string of runs. Our fans really did screem! Mom heard them all the way up the streat!

Basic

1. spring
2. throw
3. strong
4. three
5. straight
6. scream
7. stream
8. spray
9. screen
10. street
11. spread
12. string

Review

13. glad
14. start

Challenge

15. strength
16. struggle

Proofreading Marks

¶ Indent
∧ Add
⌐ Delete
≡ Capital letter
/ Small letter

Write a Story

Pretend you are a baseball. Write a short story about a game you were in. How did it feel? What happened? Try to use three spelling words. You may also want to draw some pictures to show as you tell your story to a friend.

Proofreading Tip

As you proofread your writing, circle any word you are not sure of.

Phonics and Spelling

Rhyming Words

Rhyming Riddles Rhyming words end with the same sounds, such as *stream* and *cream*. Read the clues. Write a rhyming word for each spelling word.

1. It rhymes with *scream*. It happens during sleep.
2. It rhymes with *street*. It is a red vegetable.
3. It rhymes with *spray*. It is used in art class.
4. It rhymes with *spread*. It is used for sewing.

Show What You Know! Hit a home run! Write words that rhyme with the spelling word *throw*.

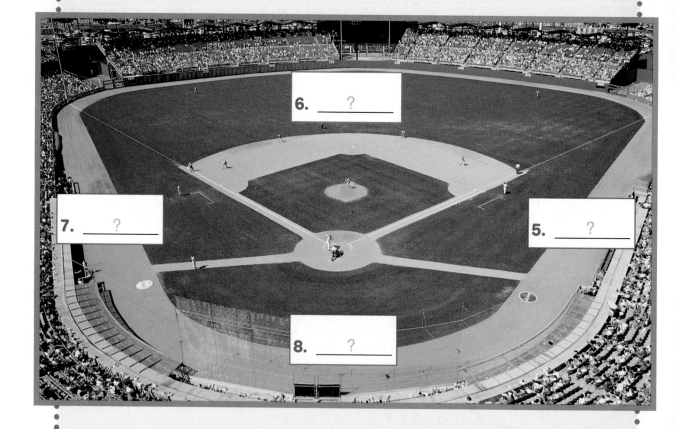

6. _____?_____

7. _____?_____

5. _____?_____

8. _____?_____

Vocabulary Enrichment

Unit 7 BONUS

Physical Education

Baseball All the words in the box have something to do with baseball. Write those words to complete this sports report. Use your Spelling Dictionary.

ON THE AIR

Rosa is a great baseball player. Today she hit Jim's first ___(1)___ beyond third ___(2)___. The fans in the ___(3)___ cheered. It was the first ___(4)___ this year! Later, Rosa caught a fly ball in her ___(5)___.

Try This CHALLENGE

Yes or No? Is the underlined word used correctly? Write *yes* or *no*.

6. Meg has a sore arm and cannot <u>pitch</u>.
7. Mikhail's <u>home run</u> tied the score.
8. The team used <u>bleachers</u> to clean their uniforms.

★★★ Fact File

One of the greatest players in baseball history was Roberto Clemente. Clemente was born in Carolina, Puerto Rico. He was famous for his fielding, throwing, and hitting. He won four National League batting titles during his baseball career.

Spelling the Long i Sound

Read and Say

READ the sentences. **SAY** each bold word.

|ī|
wild

|ī|
tie

Basic

1. wild	*wild*	These flowers grow **wild**.
2. bright	*bright*	My coat is a **bright** red.
3. die	*die*	The plant did not **die**.
4. sight	*sight*	That baby is a happy **sight**.
5. child	*child*	The **child** sat with her mother.
6. pie	*pie*	Jan baked a **pie**.
7. fight	*fight*	Even friends can have a **fight**.
8. lie	*lie*	I did not tell a **lie**.
9. tight	*tight*	This hat is too **tight** for me.
10. tie	*tie*	He wore a blue **tie**.
11. might	*might*	I **might** ride my bike.
12. mind	*mind*	You use your **mind** to think.

Think and Write

Each word has the long *i* sound. This sound is shown as |ī|. The |ī| sound can be spelled with patterns of one, two, or three letters.

|ī| br**igh**t, w**i**ld, d**ie**

A. Write **five** Basic Words with the |ī| sound spelled *igh*.
B. Write **three** Basic Words with the |ī| sound spelled *i*.
C. Write **four** Basic Words with the |ī| sound spelled *ie*.

Review	
13. find	**14.** night

Challenge	
15. lilac	**16.** delight

Independent Practice

Spelling Strategy When you hear the |ī| sound, think of the patterns *igh*, *i*, or *ie*.

Phonics Use Basic Words in these exercises.

1. Write the word that begins with the sound you hear at the beginning of *wide*.
2. Write the word that rhymes with *kind*.
3–4. Write the two words that begin with the sounds you hear at the beginning of *brave* and *chop*.

Vocabulary: Context Sentences Write the Basic Word that completes each sentence.

5. Use string to _____ the sunflowers to a stick.
6. Those fresh flowers are a beautiful _____.
7. I often _____ in the garden and look at the sky.
8. Plants _____ if they do not get enough water.
9. Those flowers look too _____ in that small vase.
10. If Jamie smells those flowers on your desk, he _____ sneeze.
11. Do not have a _____ over who will do the dishes.
12. These cherries will taste good in a _____.

Challenge Words Write the Challenge Word that completes each sentence. Use your Spelling Dictionary.

13. A _____ may be pink, purple, or white.
14. What a _____ to see such colorful flowers!

Dictionary

Pronunciation Key A dictionary entry has a
pronunciation that helps you say the entry word.

.... pronunciation

night |nīt| *n., pl.* **nights** The time between sunset
and sunrise, especially the hours of darkness.

The **pronunciation key** tells you what sounds the
symbols in the pronunciation stand for. It gives a sample
word for each sound. For example, *ice* has the vowel
sound shown by **ī**.

ī **i**ce

Practice Write the word in the key below that helps you
say the vowel sound in each pronunciation.

Example: |rŭb| *cut*

ā p**ay**   ē b**e**   ō g**o**   ŭ c**u**t

1. |lŭv| **2.** |nēd| **3.** |grād| **4.** |sōk|

Review: Spelling Spree

Hink Pinks Write the Basic or Review Word that fits the
clue and rhymes with the given word.

Example: you and two friends   **we** _____ *three*

5. a quiet little boy or girl   **mild** _____

6. a shining fighter for a king
_____ **knight**

7. a bedtime lamp
_____ **-light**

8. a gentle brain
kind _____

9. a crowded plane
_____ **flight**

10. a correct argument   **right** _____

**How Are
You Doing?**

Write each spelling
word as a partner
reads it aloud. Did
you spell any words
wrong?

Proofreading and Writing

Proofread for Spelling Proofread this diary page. Find eight spelling mistakes. Write each word correctly.

July 21

    I will fin some flowers for my mom's birthday. I can ti them with bright ribbon and put them in water so they won't diy. Then I mite pick wil berries to make piy. That will be a pretty site! When it's ready, I'll ly down and rest.

Proofreading Marks

¶ Indent
∧ Add
⤷ Delete
≡ Capital letter
/ Small letter

Write a Poem

Write a short poem about flowers, using pairs of rhyming words. Try to use three spelling words. Read your poem to a friend.

FLOWER

Proofreading Tip

Check for words that have silent letters.

Word Builder

Antonyms An **antonym** is a word that means the opposite. Which word is an antonym for *bright*: *dull* or *shining*? *Dull* is the antonym because it means the opposite of *bright*.

Write the antonym for each spelling word. Use the words from the box.

Spelling Word Link

bright

adult
loose
tame
truth
live
day

night
1. _____

tight
2. _____

wild
3. _____

lie
4. _____

die
5. _____

child
6. _____

Show What You Know! Write two sentences about flowers. Use at least one antonym pair.

Science

Flowers All the words in the box have something to do with flowers. Write those words to complete this page from a book about flowers. Use your Spelling Dictionary.

Spelling Word Link

lilac

April
May
daisy
tulip
violet

Spring flowers bloom in ___(1)___, the fourth month of the year. The tiny ___(2)___ is first, followed by the bright red ___(3)___. Next we see the white or yellow ___(4)___. Then it is the month of ___(5)___!

Try This

CHALLENGE

Make a Flower-Fact Card Make a card to give to someone special. Draw your favorite flower on the front of the card. On the back of the card, write some facts about the flower. Write your special greeting on the inside of the card and give it to that person.

★★★ Fact File

A sunflower looks like a giant daisy. It may grow to be ten feet tall, with a blossom one foot wide. Its seeds are a delicious snack!

The Vowel Sound in clown

Read and Say

READ the sentences. **SAY** each bold word.

|ou|
clown

Basic

1.	clown	*clown*
2.	crowd	*crowd*
3.	round	*round*
4.	sound	*sound*
5.	bow	*bow*
6.	would	*would*
7.	loud	*loud*
8.	ground	*ground*
9.	crown	*crown*
10.	count	*count*
11.	cloud	*cloud*
12.	mouth	*mouth*

We saw a **clown** at the party.

The **crowd** began to clap.

Is the moon **round** like a ball?

Did you hear that **sound**?

Take a **bow** after the play.

He **would** like to ride a bus.

What was that **loud** noise?

Sit on the **ground** by the tree.

Give the **crown** to the king.

I like to **count** my pennies.

I see a white **cloud** in the sky.

His **mouth** is full of food.

Think and Write

Most of the words have the vowel sound you hear in *clown*. This sound is shown as |ou|.

|ou| cl**ow**n, r**ou**nd

How is the Elephant Word different?

A. Write **four** Basic Words with the |ou| sound spelled *ow*.

B. Write **seven** Basic Words with the |ou| sound spelled *ou*.

C. Write **one** Basic Word that has the *ou* pattern but does not have the |ou| sound.

Review
13. town   14. out

Challenge
15. bounce   16. sprout

Independent Practice

Spelling Strategy   When you hear the
|ou| sound, as in *clown* and *round*, remember it is
often spelled with the pattern *ow* or *ou*.

Phonics Use Basic Words in these exercises.

1–2. Write the two words that begin with the same
consonant cluster as *creek*.

3–5. Write the three words that rhyme with *found*.

Vocabulary: Making Inferences Write the Basic
Word that matches each clue.

6. Sometimes the moon hides behind
this.

7. You do this when you say 1-2-3-4.

8. This part of the face smiles or
frowns.

9. You might do this if you met a
king or a queen.

10. This is the funny person in the
circus.

11. This is how a plane sounds
when it takes off.

Elephant Word Write the
Elephant Word that completes the
sentence.

12. Charleen _____ like to be a clown
in a circus or a play.

Challenge Words Write the Challenge
Word that completes each sentence. Use
your Spelling Dictionary.

13. Look at that little seal _____ a ball on its nose.

14. Flowers are starting to _____ in my garden.

Review: Spelling Spree

Finding Words Write the Basic or Review Word in each of these words.

1. clowning
2. outside
3. crowded
4. loudest
5. underground
6. counting

Silly Rhymes Write the Basic or Review Word that best completes each silly sentence. Each answer rhymes with the underlined word.

7. The king has a <u>brown</u> hat on top of his _____.
8. Would you be <u>proud</u> to sit on a soft white _____?
9. Listen to the happy <u>hound</u> make a sad _____.
10. I clapped for the <u>cow</u> that was taking a _____.
11. The bear looked <u>south</u> and opened its _____.
12. A circus <u>clown</u> is king of our _____.
13. If the pig <u>could</u> dance, it _____.
14. The lucky horse <u>found</u> a merry-go-_____.

How Are You Doing?

Write each spelling word in a sentence. Practice with a partner any words you spelled wrong.

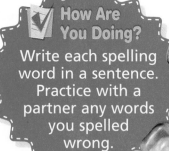

Proofreading and Writing

Proofreading: Spelling and Proper Nouns

A **proper noun** names a special person, place, or thing. Capitalize proper nouns.

Pablo Gomez   Maine   Big Top Circus

Proofread part of Ed's post card to Stacy. Find three spelling mistakes and two missing capital letters. Write the post card correctly.

Dear stacy,

There was a croud at the Ringling

Circus Galleries in the toun of sarasota.

You wood like the huge clown shoes.

Basic
1. clown
2. crowd
3. round
4. sound
5. bow
6. would
7. loud
8. ground
9. crown
10. count
11. cloud
12. mouth

Review
13. town
14. out

Challenge
15. bounce
16. sprout

Proofreading Marks

¶ Indent
∧ Add
↗ Delete
≡ Capital letter
/ Small letter

Write a Description

Describe the circus act you like best or would most like to see. Who is in it? How do they look? What do they do? Try to use three spelling words and some proper nouns. Draw a picture to go with your description.

Proofreading Tip   Check that you capitalized any proper nouns.

Vocabulary Enrichment

Word Builder

More Than One Meaning The word *bow* has different pronunciations and meanings.

a. **bow** |bou| to bend the body, head, or knee
b. **bow** |bou| the front part of a ship or a boat
c. **bow** |bō| a weapon for shooting arrows

Which meaning of *bow* is used in each sentence? Write the letter of the meaning.

Spelling Word Link

bow

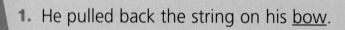

1. He pulled back the string on his <u>bow</u>.

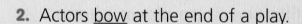

2. Actors <u>bow</u> at the end of a play.

3. Waves crashed over the <u>bow</u> of the ship.

Show What You Know! Write a sentence for each of the meanings of *bow*.

Recreation

The Circus All the words in the box have something to do with the circus. Write those words to complete this poster. Use your Spelling Dictionary.

Spelling Word Link

clown

elephant
trainer
roar
acrobat
juggler

COME TO THE CIRCUS!

See the circus parade led by an ___(1)___ walking on his hands! Hear the loud, angry ___(2)___ of a lion. Watch a huge gray ___(3)___ do tricks for its ___(4)___. Be amazed by a ___(5)___ throwing seven oranges into the air and catching them all!

Try This

CHALLENGE

Riddle Time Write a word from the box to answer each riddle.

6. What kind of bat does flips?
7. What animal carries a big trunk?
8. What can be heard but not seen?

⭐⭐⭐ **Fact File**

P. T. Barnum began the most famous circus in the world. One star was an elephant named Jumbo. *Jumbo* came to mean "very big."

JUMBO
THE CHILDREN'S GIANT PET

The Vowel Sound in lawn

|ô|
lawn

Read and Say

READ the sentences. **SAY** each bold word.

Basic

1.	lawn	*lawn*	We must mow the **lawn**.
2.	raw	*raw*	Don't eat **raw** meat.
3.	cloth	*cloth*	My coat is made of soft **cloth**.
4.	talk	*talk*	The vet will **talk** about dogs.
5.	straw	*straw*	The **straw** was in the barn.
6.	almost	*almost*	We **almost** lost the game.
7.	soft	*soft*	The puppy feels so **soft**.
8.	also	*also*	She **also** wants to go with us.
9.	wall	*wall*	We will paint this **wall** white.
10.	law	*law*	The judge knew the **law**.
11.	walk	*walk*	Do not **walk** too fast.
12.	cost	*cost*	How much does the bike **cost**?

Think and Write

Each word has the vowel sound you hear in *lawn*. The sound is shown as |ô|. The |ô| sound can be spelled with patterns of one or two letters.

|ô| l**aw**n, cl**o**th, **a**lmost

What consonant follows |ô| when it is spelled *a*?

A. Write **four** Basic Words with the |ô| sound spelled *aw*.
B. Write **three** Basic Words with the |ô| sound spelled *o*.
C. Write **five** Basic Words with the |ô| sound spelled *a* before *l*.

Review	Challenge
13. saw **14.** small	**15.** scald **16.** flaw

Independent Practice

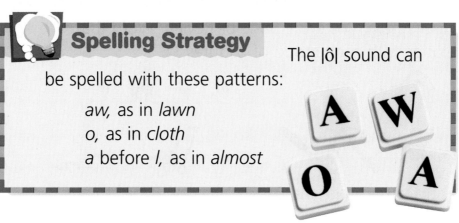

Spelling Strategy The |ô| sound can be spelled with these patterns:

aw, as in *lawn*
o, as in *cloth*
a before *l*, as in *almost*

Phonics Use Basic Words in these exercises.
1. Write the word that begins with a three-letter consonant cluster.
2. Write the word that ends with a double consonant.
3–4. Write the two words that have the |ō| sound.

Vocabulary: Context Sentences Write the Basic Word that completes each sentence.
5. Is there a _____ against burning leaves in town?
6. The cookout will be held on the back _____.
7. The potato salad will _____ less than a dollar.
8. Chen likes his steak well done, not _____.
9. Clean the picnic basket with a wet _____.
10. Carmen and Ellen are taking a _____ by the pond.
11. I will _____ to Frank about the cookout plans.
12. This thick grass feels very _____.

Challenge Words Write the Challenge Word that completes each sentence. Use your Spelling Dictionary.
13. I knitted a perfect sweater. There was not one _____ in it.
14. If I spill that hot soup, I might _____ myself.

Review: Spelling Spree

Classifying Write the Basic or Review Word that belongs with each group of pictures.

1.

2.

3.

4.

Questions Write the Basic or Review Word to answer each question.

5. What has doors or windows in it?
6. How does a rabbit like its carrot?
7. How does a pillow feel?
8. What is rude to do if your mouth is full?
9. What word means "nearly"?
10. What size shirt does a baby wear?
11. What is written on a price tag?
12. What word means "too"?
13. What is a rule everyone must obey?
14. What can you do if you are too tired to run?

How Are You Doing?
Write your spelling words in ABC order. Practice with a family member any words you spelled wrong.

Proofreading and Writing

Proofread: Spelling and Possessive Nouns
A **possessive noun** shows ownership. Add an **apostrophe**
(') and an *s* to a singular noun to make it possessive.

boy + 's = boy**'s** bike   Eli + 's = Eli**'s**

Proofread this page from a story. Find three spelling mistakes
and two missing apostrophes. Write the story correctly.

When I went to Toms cookout, I also

took my smal dog. It ate a mans strow

hat that cost allmost six dollars.

Proofreading Marks

¶ Indent
∧ Add
⌐ Delete
≡ Capital letter
/ Small letter

Write a Bulletin Board Note

FOUND

Imagine you are in charge of the Lost and Found
at school. Write a note about the things left
behind after a school cookout. Try to use three
spelling words. Share your note with a friend.

Proofreading Tip

**Check that you used an
apostrophe with each
possessive noun.**

Word Builder

Spelling Word Link

talk

gossip
answer
scold

Using a Thesaurus Which word more clearly tells that Tim and Sandy do not agree?

Tim and Sandy **talk**.   Tim and Sandy **argue**.

Argue means to "disagree." It is more exact than *talk*. Write the exact word for *talk* that best fits each sentence. Use your Thesaurus.

1. I _____ my little brother when he doesn't listen.
2. We never _____ about anyone.
3. Did he _____ you when you called?

Work Together Work with a partner to write a sentence for each picture. Use a different word for *talk* in each sentence.

Recreation

A Cookout All the words in the box have something to do with cookouts. Write those words to complete this invitation. Use your Spelling Dictionary.

Spelling Word Link

lawn

grill
hamburger
charcoal
apron
table

YOU'RE INVITED!

Uncle Marcus is ready to load the ___(1)___ with his special long-burning ___(2)___. He'll be wearing his funny cook's hat and ___(3)___. He will cook you a juicy ___(4)___ just the way you like it. There's always room at the ___(5)___. Please join us on Sunday at 1:00!

Try This CHALLENGE

Write a Recipe Write a recipe to tell someone how to make a hamburger or another one of your favorite foods. Try to use spelling words from this unit. Trade recipes with friends.

★★★ Fact File

One kind of cookout is a clambake. Rocks are heated in a pit and covered with seaweed. Then lobsters, clams, and corn are cooked on the rocks.

Unexpected Consonant Patterns

Read and Say

READ the sentences. **SAY** each bold word.

wr
write

Basic

1. knee	*knee*	I fell on my **knee**.
2. scratch	*scratch*	The cat gave her a **scratch**.
3. patch	*patch*	I need a **patch** for this hole.
4. wrap	*wrap*	We will **wrap** the box.
5. knot	*knot*	Please tie a **knot** in the bow.
6. wrong	*wrong*	This is the **wrong** book.
7. watch	*watch*	Did you **watch** a movie?
8. knife	*knife*	Use the **knife** to cut the cake.
9. write	*write*	Will you **write** to me?
10. knock	*knock*	I will **knock** on the door.
11. match	*match*	These socks do not **match**.
12. know	*know*	I **know** the way home.

Think and Write

Each word has an unexpected spelling for a consonant sound. One letter is "silent," or not pronounced.

|n| **kn**ee |r| **wr**ap |ch| scra**tch**

A. Write **five** Basic Words that begin with the |n| sound.
B. Write **three** Basic Words that begin with the |r| sound.
C. Write **four** Basic Words that end with the |ch| sound.

Review	Challenge
13. catch 14. two	15. stretcher 16. knuckle

Independent Practice

Spelling Strategy Remember, some words have unexpected consonant patterns.

A beginning |n| sound may be spelled *kn*.
A beginning |r| sound may be spelled *wr*.
A final |ch| sound may be spelled *tch*.

Phonics Use Basic Words in these exercises.

1. Write the word that ends with |ē| spelled *ee*.
2. Write the word that ends with |ō| spelled *ow*.
3–4. Write the two words with |ī| spelled *i*-consonant-*e*.

Vocabulary: Context Sentences Write the Basic Word that completes each sentence.

5. With a broken hand, Dad cannot tie the

   _____.
6. The nurse checked the time on his _____.
7. Did you _____ the sick cat in a warm blanket?
8. The cat made a big _____ on my hand.
9. Just _____ on the nurse's door.
10. The burn from a _____ can be very painful.
11. It is _____ to put anything greasy on a burn.
12. After Dina walked through a _____ of poison oak, her legs itched.

Challenge Words Write the Challenge Word that completes each sentence. Use your Spelling Dictionary.

13. The two men carried the hurt girl on a _____.
14. Ali scraped the _____ of her thumb.

Dictionary

Choosing the Correct Meaning If an entry word has more than one meaning, the meanings are numbered. A sample sentence may be given to make the meaning clear.

wrong |rông| *adj.* **1.** Not correct. **2.** Bad: *It is wrong to lie.* **3.** Not working correctly.

Practice Write the meaning of *wrong* that is used in each sentence.
1. It is <u>wrong</u> to steal.
2. Two names on the map were <u>wrong</u>.
3. Is something <u>wrong</u> with Billy Joe's radio?

1. _____

2. _____

3. _____

Review: Spelling Spree

Word Web 4–11. Find eight Basic or Review Words by matching the letters. Write the eight words.

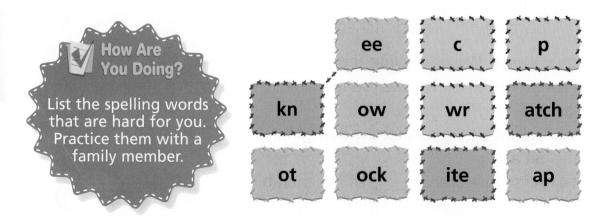

How Are You Doing?

List the spelling words that are hard for you. Practice them with a family member.

Proofreading and Writing

Proofread for Spelling Proofread this journal entry. Find six spelling mistakes. Write each word correctly.

February 15

　　Everything went rong today. First, I broke too shoelaces. I had to use ones that were too long and did not mach. Then I did not wach where I was going. I tripped and knocked a nife off the table. I was lucky that I got only a scrach on my knee.

Basic

1. knee
2. scratch
3. patch
4. wrap
5. knot
6. wrong
7. watch
8. knife
9. write
10. knock
11. match
12. know

Review

13. catch
14. two

Challenge

15. stretcher
16. knuckle

Write a List of Rules

Play It Safe

It is no fun to hurt yourself. Think of ways people get hurt at home or in school. Then list at least five safety rules. Try to use three spelling words. Post your rules where your friends can read them.

Proofreading Marks

¶ Indent
∧ Add
˞ Delete
≡ Capital letter
/ Small letter

Proofreading Tip

When you do your writing on a computer, be sure to use a spell checker before you print.

Vocabulary Enrichment

Words That Begin with wr Long ago the *w* in *wrap* was pronounced. Now it is silent. Add *wr* to the word endings to build new words. Write the new words.

Spelling Word Link

wrap

1.　　　？

2.　　　？

+ eath

+ ench

wr

+ ing

+ en

3.　　　？

4.　　　？

OUCH!

Show What You Know! Write the meaning of each new word from the web. Use your Spelling Dictionary.

Vocabulary Enrichment

Health

First Aid All the words in the box have something to do with first aid. Write those words to finish the letter. Use your Spelling Dictionary.

Spelling Word Link

scratch

bandage
sling
splint
blood
breathe

December 28, 1998

Dear Mom and Dad,

Yesterday morning, Tim got hurt skiing. He had a broken arm and ___(1)___ on his face from a cut. The ski patrol put a ___(2)___ on his cut and a ___(3)___ on his arm to keep it straight. They told Tim to ___(4)___ slowly. When I saw Tim this morning, his arm was in a ___(5)___ tied around his neck. He said he's going to be fine.

Love,
Jaime

Try This CHALLENGE

Yes or No? Is each underlined word used correctly? Write *yes* or *no*.

6. Can you <u>splint</u> the cloth into two pieces?
7. Cover a cut with a clean <u>bandage</u>.
8. I have a cold, so it is hard to <u>breathe</u>.

 Fact File

There are four blood types: A, B, AB, and O. If someone needs blood, it must come from a person with the correct blood type.

12 Review: Units 7–11

throw

throw	spring	straight
screen	street	spread

Spelling Strategy   Some words begin with the consonant clusters **scr**, **spr**, **str**, and **thr**.

Write the word that means the opposite of each word.
1. crooked
2. catch
3. autumn

Write the word that completes each sentence.
4. Mrs. Brink put a new _____ in this window.
5. We brought a blanket to _____ out on the sand.
6. Take a right turn at the next _____.

|ī| |ī|
wild   tie

die	wild	bright
fight	lie	mind

Spelling Strategy   The |ī| sound can be spelled with the pattern **igh**, **i**, or **ie**.

Write the word that matches each clue.
7. A full moon may look this way on a dark night.
8. Crops do this if they do not get enough rain.
9. A person may tell this instead of the truth.
10. This is what jungle animals are.
11. You use this when you think.
12. Cats and dogs may do this.

Unit 9   The Vowel Sound in clown   pp. 60–65

crowd	sound	would
count	crown	ground

|ou|
clown

Spelling Strategy   The |ou| sound, as in *clown* and *round*, is often spelled with the pattern **ow** or **ou**.

Write the word that completes each sentence.

A huge __(13)__ of people had come to see Queen Ann. There were too many people to __(14)__. Many of them were sitting on the __(15)__. One person said that the queen __(16)__ come in a horse-drawn coach. Then people heard the __(17)__ of a cannon. Queen Ann arrived, wearing a long dress and a __(18)__.

Unit 10   The Vowel Sound in lawn   pp. 66–71

almost	straw	cloth
walk	soft	law

|ô|
lawn

Spelling Strategy   These patterns can spell the |ô| sound: **aw**, as in *lawn*; **o**, as in *cloth*; **a** before **l**, as in *almost*.

Write the word that completes each sentence.

19. Mom made me a skirt out of some red _____.
20. This soup is so hot I _____ burned my mouth.

Write the word that belongs in each group.

21. grass, hay, _____
22. crawl, run, _____
23. judge, court, _____
24. fluffy, fuzzy, _____

write
wr

| Unit 11 | Unexpected Patterns | pp. 72–77 |

| knot | scratch | wrong |
| write | knife | watch |

Spelling Strategy   Some words have unexpected consonant patterns.

|n| → **knee** |r| → **wrap** |ch| → scra**tch**

Write the word that belongs in each group.

25. fork, spoon, _____

26. cut, burn, _____

Write the word that completes each sentence.

27. Read the question, and then _____ your answer.

28. Please tell me the time if you have a _____.

29. Is this answer right or _____?

30. Janice cannot get the _____ out of her ribbon.

| Challenge Words | Units 7–11 | pp. 48–77 |

| strength | delight | |
| bounce | stretcher | scald |

Write the word that means the opposite of each word.

31. freeze

32. weakness

Write the word that completes each sentence.

33. No one was badly hurt in the accident, so a _____ is not needed.

34. Going for a swim is a _____ on a hot day.

35. That window may break if you _____ a ball against it.

Spelling-Meaning Strategy

Word Forms

You have learned that words belong to families. The words in a family are spelled alike in some ways. They are also related in meaning. Read this paragraph.

> One of my favorite sights is a **bright** full moon in a coal black sky. Its **brightness** lights my way in the dark.

Think How are *bright* and *brightness* alike in meaning? How are *bright* and *brightness* alike in spelling?

Here are some words in the *bright* family.

bright	brighten	brighter
brightness	brightly	brightest

Apply and Extend

Complete these activities on another sheet of paper.

1. Look up the meaning of each word in the Word Box above in your Spelling Dictionary. Write six sentences, using one word in each sentence.

2. With a partner list words related to *child, mind,* and *count.* Then look in your Spelling-Meaning Index beginning on page 272. Add any other words in these families to your list.

based on

Finn McCool

by May Lynch

Lisa wants to make puppets to act out the play *Finn McCool*. She used these steps for making a puppet.

Making a puppet from a cardboard tube can be easy! First, find a cardboard tube from a roll of paper towels or toilet tissue. Cut the tube to the size you want. Next, use crayons or markers to draw your puppet's eyes and mouth. Then make paper ears, nose, hair, arms, and clothes. Finally, glue them to the tube.

Now bring your puppet to life. Just put your middle fingers inside the tube. Then wiggle your fingers, and your puppet will move.

Think and Discuss

1 What **steps** for making a puppet are given in the first paragraph?

2 Which sentence in the first paragraph tells the **main idea** of the paragraph?

3 What **order words**, such as *first* and *next*, are used?

The Writing Process
Instructions

Write instructions for something you like to do. Follow the Guidelines. Use the Writing Process.

1 **Prewriting**
- Make a list of things you do well. Choose a topic.
- List all materials and steps.

2 **Draft**
- Think about what you're telling how to do.
- Put the steps in correct order.

3 **Revise**
- Are the steps in order? Did you forget any?
- Did you use order words?

4 **Proofread**
- Did you use commas in a series correctly?
- Did you correct any misspelled words?

5 **Publish**
- Draw illustrations to go with your instructions and make an activity card.

•••••• **Guidelines for Writing Instructions**

✓ Begin with a topic sentence.
✓ Include all materials that are needed.
✓ Include all steps in the correct order.
✓ Use order words like *first*, *next*, and *finally*.

Composition Words
three
straight
tight
round
soft
walk
wrap
knot

Vowel + |r| Sounds

Read and Say

READ the sentences. **SAY** each bold word.

|ôr|
storm

Basic

1.	storm	*storm*	The **storm** had strong winds.
2.	clear	*clear*	The sky is **clear** now.
3.	dark	*dark*	Rain fell from a **dark** cloud.
4.	star	*star*	I can see a bright **star**.
5.	fourth	*fourth*	We sat in the **fourth** row.
6.	door	*door*	Please shut the **door**.
7.	smart	*smart*	Keisha is a **smart** baby.
8.	art	*art*	We painted in **art** class.
9.	near	*near*	Your house is **near** mine.
10.	north	*north*	He went **north** on his trip.
11.	ear	*ear*	The loud noise hurt her **ear**.
12.	March	*March*	It can be cold in **March**.

Think and Write

Each word has a vowel sound + *r*. These sounds are shown as |är|, |îr|, and |ôr|.

|är| d**ar**k |îr| cl**ear** |ôr| st**or**m

How are the |ôr| sounds spelled in the Elephant Words?

A. Write **five** Basic Words with the |är| sound.
B. Write **three** Basic Words with the |îr| sound.
C. Write **four** Basic Words with the |ôr| sound.
Remember the Elephant Words.

Review
13. hard   **14.** short

Challenge
15. tornado   **16.** argue

Independent Practice

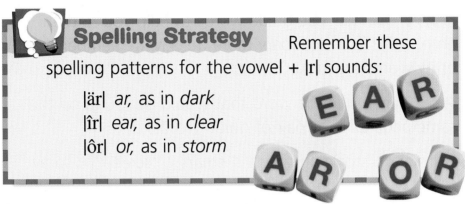

Spelling Strategy Remember these spelling patterns for the vowel + |r| sounds:

|är| *ar,* as in *dark*
|îr| *ear,* as in *clear*
|ôr| *or,* as in *storm*

Phonics Use Basic Words in these exercises.
1. Write the word with the |ch| sound.
2–3. Write the two words that begin with *st*.
4–5. Write the two words that rhyme with *part*.

Vocabulary: Context Sentences
Write the Basic Word that completes each sentence.
6. The wind is blowing from the _____.
7. Today will be cool, sunny, and _____.
8. Look at those huge, _____ rain clouds!
9. The cold air made Jason's _____ hurt.
10. I hear thunder, so a storm must be _____.

Elephant Words Write the Elephant Word that completes each sentence.
11. This rainstorm is the _____ one in two weeks.
12. The strong wind blew open the _____.

Challenge Words Write the Challenge Word that fits each meaning. Use your Spelling Dictionary.
13. disagree   14. a twisting, dangerous storm

Dictionary

Guide Words Use guide words to help you find an entry word in a dictionary more quickly. Remember that entry words are in ABC order.

Practice Write the word that would be found on the same page as each pair of guide words.

> star   storm   short   smart   screen   spray

1. stir | stun   **3.** shirt | shy   **5.** spike | spy

2. scarf | scuba   **4.** sly | smell   **6.** squash | step

Review: Spelling Spree

Letter Change Change the order of the letters in each word. Write a Basic Word that begins with the underlined letter.

Example: rea<u>d</u>   *dear*

7. ear<u>n</u>   **9.** o<u>d</u>or   **11.** <u>t</u>ar

8. rat<u>s</u>   **10.** ar<u>e</u>   **12.** thor<u>n</u>

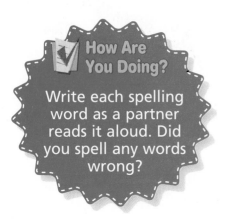

How Are You Doing?

Write each spelling word as a partner reads it aloud. Did you spell any words wrong?

Proofreading and Writing

Proofread for Spelling Proofread this weather report. Find eight spelling mistakes. Write the words correctly.

Basic

1. storm
2. clear
3. dark
4. star
5. fourth
6. door
7. smart
8. art
9. near
10. north
11. ear
12. March

Review

13. hard
14. short

Challenge

15. tornado
16. argue

Weather Report

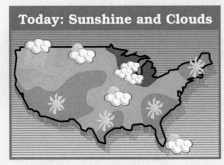

Today: Sunshine and Clouds

The sky is cleer now, but expect a strom after darck. It will rain for a shot time, and a hrd wind will blow from the north. This will be the forth day of rain this Mach. Be smat, and carry an umbrella!

Write a Weather Report

What do you think the weather will be like tomorrow? Will it be rainy, cloudy, or sunny? Write a weather report. Try to use three spelling words. Discuss your report with a friend. What clothes would you wear for the weather you wrote about?

Proofreading Tip

When proofreading your writing, say each word out loud to yourself.

Proofreading Marks

¶ Indent
∧ Add
⌐ Delete
≡ Capital letter
/ Small letter

Rhyming Words

Words with Vowel + |r| Match the letters on the raindrops with the letters on the clouds to build words that rhyme with *clear* and *dark*. Write four words that rhyme with *clear* and four words that rhyme with *dark*.

1. _____
2. _____
3. _____
4. _____

5. _____
6. _____
7. _____
8. _____

Show What You Know! Write two rhyming sentences about a rainy day. Use two of the rhyming words you made.

Science

Weather All the words in the box have something to do with weather. Write those words to finish this page from a travel magazine. Use your Spelling Dictionary.

Spelling Word Link

storm

fog
sleet
heat
cool
damp

Travel Monthly 61

Forget the snow and icy __(1)__ of winter. Say good-by to chilly spring days with __(2)__ winds. No more __(3)__ raincoats and clouds of __(4)__! Come to Florida, where you can lie on the beach and feel the __(5)__ from the sun.

Try This CHALLENGE

Write an Ad What if you had a machine that could control the weather? People would probably line up to buy it! Write an ad for a weather machine. Tell people how it works and what it can do. Try to use words from the box to tell about the machine.

★★ Fact File

Weather satellites fly over the clouds with cameras that take pictures of the earth. The pictures are used to predict weather.

The Vowel + |r| Sounds in first

|ûr|
g**ir**l

Read and Say

READ the sentences. **SAY** each bold word.

Basic

1.	girl	*girl*	I met a **girl** in a red dress.
2.	turn	*turn*	Please **turn** around.
3.	first	*first*	Meg is in the **first** grade.
4.	her	*her*	Rosa lost **her** book.
5.	were	*were*	The clowns **were** funny.
6.	work	*work*	I **work** hard in school.
7.	hurt	*hurt*	I fell and **hurt** my knee.
8.	bird	*bird*	Look at that **bird** fly!
9.	word	*word*	Did I spell a **word** wrong?
10.	third	*third*	This is my **third** try.
11.	dirt	*dirt*	We put the seeds in **dirt**.
12.	serve	*serve*	Who will **serve** the food?

Think and Write

Each word has the vowel + |r| sounds that you hear in *her*. These sounds are shown as |ûr|.

|ûr| h**er**, f**ir**st, t**ur**n, w**or**k

A. Write **three** Basic Words with |ûr| spelled *er*.
B. Write **five** Basic Words with |ûr| spelled *ir*.
C. Write **two** Basic Words with |ûr| spelled *ur*.
D. Write **two** Basic Words with |ûr| spelled *or*.

Review
13. any   **14.** been

Challenge
15. perfect   **16.** sturdy

Independent Practice

Spelling Strategy Remember these spelling patterns for the |ûr| sounds:

er, as in *her*   ur, as in *turn*
ir, as in *gir*   or, as in *work*

Phonics Use Basic Words in these exercises.

1. Write the word that begins with *th*.

2–4. Write *work*. Then write two other words that begin with the same sound.

5–8. Write four words by adding a vowel and *r* to the letters below.

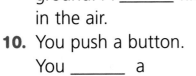
   5. s __ __ ve   **7.** h __ __
   6. g __ __ l   **8.** h __ __ t

Vocabulary: Word Pairs Write the Basic Word that completes each pair of sentences.

9. A snake crawls on the ground. A _____ flies in the air.

10. You push a button. You _____ a steering wheel.

11. You rake leaves on a lawn. You shovel _____ into a hole.

12. The caboose is the last train car. The engine is the _____ train car.

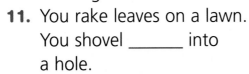
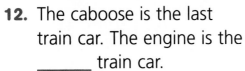

Challenge Words Write the Challenge Word that fits each meaning. Use your Spelling Dictionary.

13. strong   14. without any mistakes

Review: Spelling Spree

Word Maze 1–8. Begin at the arrow and follow the Word Maze to find eight Basic or Review Words. Write the words in order.

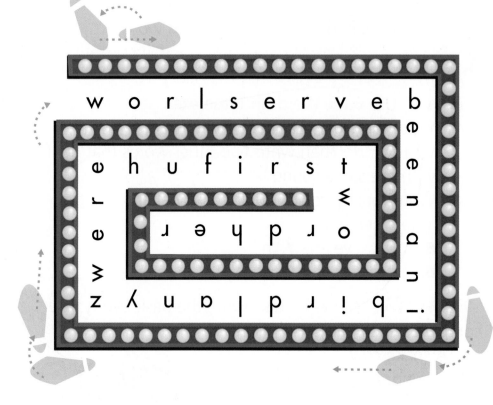

Letter Math Write a Basic Word by solving each problem below.

Example: worry − ry + d = word

9. worst − st + k =
10. d + shirt − sh =
11. t + burn − b =
12. g + twirl − tw =
13. hurry − ry + t =
14. thirst − st + d =

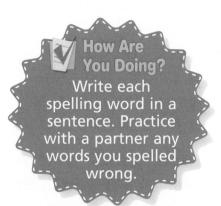

How Are You Doing?
Write each spelling word in a sentence. Practice with a partner any words you spelled wrong.

Proofreading and Writing

Proofread: Spelling and Using good **and** bad

Use *good* and *bad* correctly.

	good	**bad**
COMPARING TWO:	better	worse
COMPARING MORE THAN TWO:	best	worst

Proofread this journal entry. Find three spelling mistakes and two wrong forms of good or bad. Write the paragraph correctly.

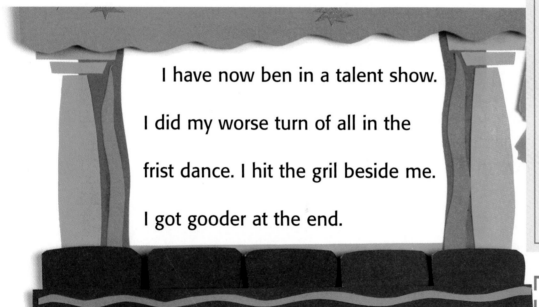

I have now ben in a talent show.

I did my worse turn of all in the

frist dance. I hit the gril beside me.

I got gooder at the end.

Proofreading Marks

¶ Indent
∧ Add
ℱ Delete
≡ Capital letter
/ Small letter

Write an Invitation

Write an invitation to a show performed by your dance class. Tell when and where it will be held. Make it sound exciting. Try to use three spelling words and at least one form of *good* or *bad*.

Dance

Proofreading Tip

Check that you used the correct forms of good and bad.

Word Builder

Using a Thesaurus Which sentence is more exact?

The **bird** flew at night.   The **owl** flew at night.

The second sentence is more exact because *owl* tells what kind of bird flew at night.

Write one of the words from the box in place of *bird* in each sentence. Use your Thesaurus.

1. That <u>bird</u> has such a pretty red breast.
2. Look at that <u>bird</u> dive into the ocean!
3. I love to hear my yellow <u>bird</u> sing.
4. That black <u>bird</u> makes such a loud noise.

Show What You Know! Write two or three sentences about what the birds in the picture are doing. Try to use one or two of the words from the box.

Spelling Word Link

bird

sea gull
crow
robin
canary

Performing Arts

Dance Class All the words in the box have something to do with dance class. Write those words to finish this page from a book about dance. Use your Spelling Dictionary.

> A dancer and his or her ___(1)___ should move together easily. They must be able to ___(2)___ across the stage or to ___(3)___ from side to side in time to the ___(4)___. Each hand or body ___(5)___ should be beautiful to watch.

Spelling Word Link

turn

music
partner
movement
sway
skip

Try This CHALLENGE

Yes or No? Is the underlined word used correctly? Write *yes* or *no*.

6. Trees often <u>sway</u> in the wind.

7. I watched the dancer's every <u>movement</u>.

8. Did he <u>skip</u> up the tree to get the cat?

 Fact File

Edgar Degas was a great French artist. Some of his works show dancers practicing or relaxing after a class.

The Vowel Sound in coin

Read and Say

READ the sentences. **SAY** each bold word.

|oi|
coin

Basic

1.	coin	*coin*
2.	soil	*soil*
3.	noise	*noise*
4.	boy	*boy*
5.	oil	*oil*
6.	toy	*toy*
7.	spoil	*spoil*
8.	point	*point*
9.	boil	*boil*
10.	join	*join*
11.	joy	*joy*
12.	foil	*foil*

I will not spend this old **coin**.
Flowers grew in the soft **soil**.
Do not make any **noise**.
The **boy** ran home.
My mom put **oil** in the car.
The baby played with a **toy**.
The food did not **spoil**.
Can you **point** to your boat?
Please **boil** some water.
Did you **join** a club?
Friends give us much **joy**.
Please wrap this food in **foil**.

Think and Write

Each word has the vowel sound you hear in *coin*. This sound is shown as |oi|.

|oi| c**oi**n, b**oy**

A. Write **nine** Basic Words with |oi| spelled *oi*.
B. Write **three** Basic Words with |oi| spelled *oy*.

Review	Challenge
13. are **14.** give	**15.** moist **16.** destroy

Independent Practice

Spelling Strategy The |oi| sound, as in *coin* and *boy,* is spelled with the pattern *oi* or *oy*.

Phonics Use Basic Words in these exercises.

1. Write the word that begins with a consonant cluster.
2–3. Write *coin*. Then change the first letter to write another spelling word.
4–6. Write *boy*. Then write two other words that rhyme with *boy*.

Vocabulary: Making Inferences Write the Basic Word that matches each clue.

7. This part of a pin is sharp.
8. This is a way to cook eggs.
9. This is what you hear on a busy street.
10. You can wrap food in this to keep it fresh.
11. A car needs this.
12. Seeds are planted in this.

Challenge Words Write the Challenge Word that completes each sentence. Use your Spelling Dictionary.

13. Remove the stain with a _____ cloth and some soap.
14. This hot weather will _____ the crops if it does not rain soon.

Dictionary

Words That Look the Same Some words are spelled the same but have different meanings. The words are numbered and listed separately in a dictionary. What are two meanings of *foil*?

> **foil¹** |foil| *v.* **foiled, foiling** To keep from success: *The alarm foiled the thief.*
>
> **foil²** |foil| *n., pl.* **foils** A thin sheet of metal: *Wrap the meat in foil.*

Practice Which meaning of *foil* is used in each sentence? Write *foil¹* or *foil²*.

1. The rain will <u>foil</u> our wish to go camping.
2. Please cover the leftovers with <u>foil</u>.
3. Wrap the corn in <u>foil</u>, and then roast it.
4. How did Meg <u>foil</u> your plan to win the game?

Review: Spelling Spree

Missing Letters Each missing letter fits in ABC order between the other letters. Write the missing letters to spell a Basic or Review Word.

Example: r __ t n __ p h __ j k __ m *soil*

5. o __ q n __ p h __ j m __ o s __ u
6. r __ t o __ q n __ p h __ j k __ m
7. e __ g n __ p h __ j k __ m
8. a __ c n __ p h __ j k __ m
9. f __ h h __ j u __ w d __ f
10. n __ p h __ j k __ m
11. s __ u n __ p x __ z
12. i __ k n __ p x __ z

> **How Are You Doing?**
> Write your spelling words in ABC order. Practice with a family member any words you spelled wrong.

Proofreading and Writing

Proofread for Spelling Proofread this ad. Find six spelling mistakes. Write each word correctly.

SUDSY LAUNDROMATS

Sudsy Laundromats ar lively places with a lot of noize and fun. Humming machines wash out sol. You might find a loose coyn in a dryer. Even a little boi or girl can use the washing machines. It's easy. Come joyn the fun!

Write Instructions

Write instructions that tell how to wash clothes. What do you do first? When is the soap added? Try to use three spelling words. Then have a friend pretend to wash clothes, using your instructions.

Soap

Proofreading Marks

¶ Indent
∧ Add
ᵍ Delete
≡ Capital letter
/ Small letter

Proofreading Tip

When proofreading your writing, put a check mark on each word.

More Than One Meaning *Spoil* has several meanings.

a. to make less perfect or useful
b. to become unfit for use
c. to give someone too much

Which meaning of *spoil* is used in each sentence?
Write the letter of the meaning.

1. Milk will <u>spoil</u> if you don't put it in the ice box.
2. Uncle Don will <u>spoil</u> me with lots of presents.
3. The post will <u>spoil</u> our view of the ball game.

Show What You Know! Write a sentence for each picture.
Use one of the meanings of *spoil* in each sentence.

Life Skills

The Laundromat All the words in the box have something to do with the laundromat. Write those words to finish this note. Use your Spelling Dictionary.

Spelling Word Link

soil

laundry
washer
soak
load
fold

Teresa,

    Please wash and dry a __(1)__ of dark-colored clothes. Remember to __(2)__ the stains in your jeans. Pour only a cup of soap into the __(3)__ before you put the clothes in. Please __(4)__ the clean __(5)__, and put it away. Thanks.

                  Mom

Try This CHALLENGE

Yes or No? Is the underlined word used correctly? Write *yes* or *no*.

6. <u>Soak</u> the socks to dry them.
7. A <u>washer</u> dries clothes.
8. There is another <u>load</u> of light-colored shirts to wash.

★★ Fact File

Wool and cotton cloth are made from animal and plant products. Some kinds of cloth, such as nylon, were created by scientists.

101

Spelling the |j| Sound

Read and Say

READ the sentences. **SAY** each bold word.

large jeans

Basic

1. jump	*jump*	Do not **jump** on the bed.
2. stage	*stage*	A clown is on the **stage**.
3. gym	*gym*	We had a class in the **gym**.
4. large	*large*	I own a **large** cat.
5. jeans	*jeans*	Becky wore her **jeans**.
6. judge	*judge*	Who will **judge** the art show?
7. page	*page*	Please read that **page**.
8. jar	*jar*	She put the jam in a **jar**.
9. age	*age*	The baby is big for his **age**.
10. June	*June*	We took a trip in **June**.
11. orange	*orange*	He used an **orange** crayon.
12. giraffe	*giraffe*	We saw a **giraffe** at the zoo.

Think and Write

Each word has the consonant sound you hear at the beginning of *jump*. This sound is shown as |j|. When *g* spells the |j| sound, it is followed by *e*, *i*, or *y*.

|j| **j**ump, lar**ge**, **gi**raffe, **gy**m

How are the |j| sounds spelled in the Elephant Word?

A. Write **one** Basic Word with |j| spelled two ways.
B. Write **four** other Basic Words with |j| spelled *j*.
C. Write **seven** other Basic Words with |j| spelled *g* followed by *e*, *i*, or *y*.

Review	Challenge
13. job **14.** brother	**15.** plunge **16.** courage

Independent Practice

 Spelling Strategy   The |j| sound can be spelled with the consonant *j* or with the consonant *g* followed by *e, i,* or *y.*

Phonics Use Basic Words in these exercises.

1. Write the word that has the |ĭ| sound spelled *y.*

2–3. Write a word that rhymes with each word below.
   2. charge   **3.** car

4–6. Write the three words with the |ā| sound spelled *a*-consonant-*e.*

Vocabulary: Classifying Write the Basic Word that belongs in each group.

   7. red, blue, _____
   8. hop, skip, _____
   9. April, May, _____
   10. shoes, coat, _____
   11. elephant, hippo, _____

Elephant Word Write the Elephant Word to complete the sentence.

12. Who will _____ the three o'clock race in the gym?

Challenge Words Write the Challenge Word that completes each sentence. Use your Spelling Dictionary.

13. Jason likes to watch divers who can _____ into a pool from a high board.

14. Who has the _____ to run against Speedy Sue in the next race?

Review: Spelling Spree

Hink Pinks Write the Basic or Review Word that fits the description and rhymes with the given word.

Example: what a washer does   cleans _____ *jeans*

1. a song for the month after May   _____ **tune**
2. a list of birth dates   _____ **page**
3. a tearful task   **sob** _____
4. a kangaroo's bruise   _____ **bump**
5. a big cost   _____ **charge**
6. a glass container for an auto   **car** _____
7. a home for a bird in a play   _____ **cage**

Comparisons Write the Basic or Review Word that completes each comparison.

8. This hose is longer than the neck of a _____.
9. This robe is as comfortable as a pair of _____.
10. Mrs. Lyon is as wise as a _____ in a court.
11. This desk is as shiny as a waxed _____ floor.
12. This drink is as tasty as fresh _____ juice.
13. Stan is as helpful as an older _____.
14. Jan's face is as readable as a _____ in a book.

How Are You Doing?

List the spelling words that are hard for you. Practice them with a family member.

Proofreading and Writing

Basic
1. jump
2. stage
3. gym
4. large
5. jeans
6. judge
7. page
8. jar
9. age
10. June
11. orange
12. giraffe

Review
13. job
14. brother

Challenge
15. plunge
16. courage

Proofread: Spelling and Introductory Words Use a comma after words such as *first* or *next* when they begin a sentence.

First, step up to the starting line.

Proofread this page from a story. Find three spelling mistakes and two missing commas. Write the paragraph correctly.

Pablo's brouther went to the jym for Sports Day. First he gave a juge his name and age. Next he showed how far he could jump. He won a giraffe puppet!

Proofreading Marks
¶ Indent
∧ Add
ᕱ Delete
≡ Capital letter
/ Small letter

Write a Story

Write a story about being in a race. Tell what happened. Remember to use commas. Try to use three spelling words. Share your story with a friend.

FINISH

Proofreading Tip

Check that you used commas after words like *first* or *next* when they begin a sentence.

Vocabulary Enrichment

Word Builder

Spelling
Word Link

giraffe

mosquito
octopus
walrus
skunk

Words from Other Languages Did you know that *giraffe* comes from the Arabic word *zirafah*? Many English words come from other languages.

Write the word from the box that fits each clue. Use your Spelling Dictionary.

1. a Greek word for an animal with eight arms
2. a Native American word for a small animal that sprays when scared
3. a Spanish word for a biting bug
4. a Dutch word for a sea animal with big tusks

Show What You Know! Look at the pictures. Write what the animals are saying.

5. _____ ?

6. _____ ?

7. _____ ?

8. _____ ?

Physical Education

Field Day All the words in the box have something to do with a field day. Write those words to finish this article from a school newspaper. Use your Spelling Dictionary.

Spelling Word Link

jump

field
track
medal
prize
contest

Field Day Tomorrow!

Everything is ready for tomorrow. Ropes mark the dirt __(1)__ circling the baseball __(2)__. Once again a crowd will watch Carlota and Ahmed race for the title of fastest runner. They each have two wins in this __(3)__. Who will finally win first __(4)__ and receive the gold __(5)__?

Try This CHALLENGE

Word Groups Write the word from the box that belongs in each group.

6. game, race, _____
7. path, course, _____
8. meadow, lawn, _____

Fact File

Wilma Rudolph could not walk until she was eight because of polio. She went on to become the first American female runner to win three Olympic gold medals.

Spelling the |k| and |kw| Sounds

Read and Say

|kw|
queen

READ the sentences. **SAY** each bold word.

Basic

1. park	*park*	We walked in the **park**.
2. queen	*queen*	The **queen** bee was hungry.
3. skin	*skin*	I felt the cold air on my **skin**.
4. picnic	*picnic*	We had a **picnic** in the yard.
5. quick	*quick*	The cat was too **quick** to grab.
6. school	*school*	I do well in **school**.
7. quart	*quart*	This jar can hold one **quart**.
8. week	*week*	I was at home all **week**.
9. quit	*quit*	She **quit** playing at bedtime.
10. squeeze	*squeeze*	Don't **squeeze** the balloon.
11. second	*second*	He is **second** in line.
12. crack	*crack*	Did you **crack** the egg?

Think and Write

Each word has the |k| sound, as in *park*, or the |kw| sounds, as in *queen*.

|k| par**k**, qui**ck**, pi**c**ni**c** |kw| **qu**een

How is the |k| sound spelled in the Elephant Word?

A. Write **one** Basic Word with the |kw| and the |k| sounds.
B. Write **four** other Basic Words with the |kw| sounds.
C. Write **seven** other Basic Words with the |k| sound. Remember the Elephant Word.

Review	Challenge
13. black **14.** coat	**15.** insect **16.** freckles

Independent Practice

Spelling Strategy The |k| sound can be spelled with the pattern *k, ck,* or *c*. The |kw| sounds can be spelled with the *qu* pattern.

Phonics Use Basic Words in these exercises.
1. Write the word that has the |k| sound spelled both *c* and *ck*.
2–5. Write the four words with the |ĭ| sound.

Vocabulary: Context Sentences Write the Basic Word that completes each sentence.
6. Ty and I visited Mr. Day, a beekeeper, last _____.
7. We saw some bees _____ through a tiny hole.
8. One bee landed on a flower. Then a _____ bee landed beside it.
9. "The most important bee is the _____ bee, " I said.
10. Tim asked, "Do bees live in trees in the _____?"
11. At lunch Mr. Day shared a _____ of milk with us.

Elephant Word Write the Elephant Word to complete the sentence.
12. Sarah and I are learning about bees in _____.

Challenge Words Write the Challenge Word that completes each sentence. Use your Spelling Dictionary.
13. The bee is an _____ that is related to the ant.
14. You cannot see where a bee stung Robert because he has so many _____ on his arm.

Dictionary

Part of Speech A dictionary entry shows if a word is a noun, a verb, or another **part of speech**. Abbreviations are used.

n. = noun

v. = verb

park |pärk| *n., pl.* **parks** An area of land used for recreation: *We play in the park.* *v.* **parked, parking** To stop and leave a car for a time: *Where did you park the car?*

Practice Write *noun* or *verb* to tell how *park* is used in each sentence.

1. Many children play in the park on Saturday.
2. Teachers park their cars behind the school.
3. Jim's baseball team practices in the park.

Review: Spelling Spree

Classifying Write the Basic or Review Word that belongs in each group.

4. mittens, hat, _____
5. month, day, _____
6. hair, fingernails, _____
7. snap, break, _____
8. pint, gallon, _____
9. king, princess, _____
10. library, bank, _____

11. stop, finish, _____
12. red, green, _____

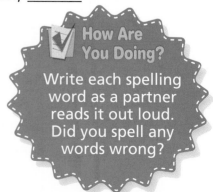

How Are You Doing?

Write each spelling word as a partner reads it out loud. Did you spell any words wrong?

Proofreading and Writing

Proofread for Spelling Proofread this page from a magazine article about bees. Find six spelling mistakes. Write each word correctly.

Have you ever been in a parck

and had a tiny blak and yellow bee

visit your picknick? Don't squeez it if it

crawls on your skin or coat. Don't be quik to

scare it away. It is a tiny wonder! Watch its

wings. They beat about 250 times a sekund.

Bees

Basic
1. park
2. queen
3. skin
4. picnic
5. quick
6. school
7. quart
8. week
9. quit
10. squeeze
11. second
12. crack

Review
13. black
14. coat

Challenge
15. insect
16. freckles

Write a Description

Pretend that you are a bee. How do you spend your days? How do you have fun? When are you in danger? Write a description of your life. Try to use three spelling words. You may want to draw a picture of how a flower looks to you. Share your description and picture with a friend.

Proofreading Marks

¶ Indent
∧ Add
⌐ Delete
≡ Capital letter
/ Small letter

Proofreading Tip

Spell each letter in a word out loud to make sure there are no missing letters.

Vocabulary Enrichment

Word Builder

Spelling Word Link

quart

cup
pint
quart
gallon

Measurements Do you usually buy a quart or a gallon of milk? *Quart* and *gallon* are measurements, or amounts.

Write the word that fits each meaning. Use your Spelling Dictionary.

1. a measurement equal to two cups
2. a measurement equal to four quarts
3. a measurement equal to sixteen tablespoons
4. a measurement equal to two pints

Work Together Work with a partner to brainstorm some other types of measurements. Write them to complete the web below.

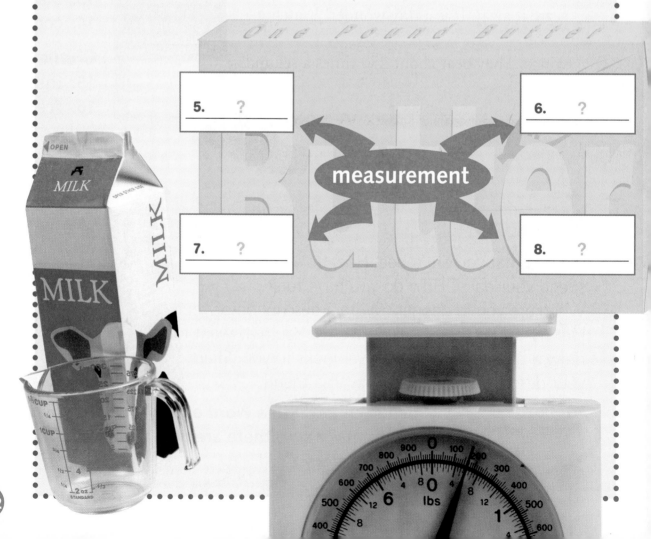

5. ?

6. ?

measurement

7. ?

8. ?

Science

Bees All the words in the box have something to do with bees. Write those words to finish this page from a field guide. Use your Spelling Dictionary.

Spelling Word Link

queen

bumblebee
buzz
honey
hive
sting

The black and yellow ___(1)___ makes its home in thick grass or in the ground, not in a ___(2)___. This bee will ___(3)___ as it gathers food from flowers to make golden ___(4)___. Be careful if a bee is near you! It can ___(5)___ if you scare it.

Try This

CHALLENGE

Make a Poster Make a safety poster about how people should act around bees. Try to use words from the box above. Draw pictures for your poster, and post it where others can see it.

★★★ **Fact File**

Bees gather pollen for food. As bees go from plant to plant, some pollen drops into each flower, and new flower seeds begin to grow.

18 Review: Units 13–17

|ôr|
storm

Unit 13 Vowel + |r| Sounds pp. 84–89

clear	fourth	door
north	near	March

Spelling Strategy Remember these spelling patterns for the vowel + |r| sounds:
|är| *ar,* as in d**ar**k |îr| *ear,* as in cl**ear**
|ôr| *or,* as in st**or**m

Write the word that fits each group.
1. east, south, _____
2. second, third, _____
3. January, February, _____

Write the word that completes each sentence.
4. I see the lake bottom when the water is _____.
5. Remember not to slam the _____ when you leave.
6. Patsy's house is _____ the old shoe factory.

Unit 14 Vowel + |r| Sounds in first pp. 90–95

turn	first	were
word	third	serve

|ûr|
girl

Spelling Strategy The |ûr| sound can be spelled *er, ir, ur,* and *or.*

Write the words to complete the paragraph.
Today we had a surprise party for my brother Ben. The lights __(7)__ out when he came in. Dad jumped up to __(8)__ them on, and we all yelled the __(9)__ *surprise!* The __(10)__ thing we did after that was __(11)__ the cake. Then we gave Ben presents. He opened mine __(12)__, after Mom's and Dad's.

Unit 15   The Vowel Sound in coin   pp. 96–101

toy	soil	noise
joy	point	spoil

|oi|
coin

Spelling Strategy   The |oi| sound, as in *coin* and *boy*, is spelled with the patterns *oi* or *oy*.

Write the word that means the same as each word.
13. dirt   **14.** ruin

Write the word that completes each sentence.
15. Will you _____ out the park as we drive by it?
16. Grandma says it is a _____ to watch the baby.
17. Sam gave Tony a _____ truck for his birthday.
18. You will wake Dad if you make too much _____.

Unit 16   Spelling the |j| Sound   pp. 102–107

large	jeans	judge
giraffe	June	orange

**large
jeans**

Spelling Strategy   The |j| sound can be spelled with the consonant *j* or with the consonant *g* followed by *e*, *i*, or *y*.

Write the word that matches each clue.
19. These pants are usually blue.
20. The first day of summer is in this month.
21. An elephant is this size.
22. This person is in charge of a courtroom.
23. This animal can eat leaves from tall trees.
24. You make this color by mixing red and yellow.

|kw|
queen

picnic	quick	school
week	second	squeeze

Spelling Strategy   The |k| sound can be spelled with the pattern *k*, *ck*, or *c*. The |kw| sounds can be spelled with the *qu* pattern.

Write the word that completes each sentence.

25. There is only one _____ left until vacation!

26. I will miss all my _____ friends this summer.

27. Maybe we should all go on a _____ together.

28. I should make some _____ plans before vacation.

29. Dad says we can all _____ into his car.

30. Maybe we can even get together a _____ time.

Challenge Words   Units 13–17   pp. 84–113

insect	perfect	
plunge	tornado	moist

Write the word that belongs in each group.

31. fish, bird, _____

32. wet, damp, _____

Write the word that completes each sentence.

33. I only had one wrong answer on the test, but Ann got a _____ score.

34. Shelley likes to _____ into the cool lake on a hot day.

35. Dad says we should stay in the basement until the _____ has passed.

Spelling-Meaning Strategy

Word Forms

Words belong to families, just as people do. The words in a family are spelled alike in some ways. They are also related in meaning. Read this paragraph.

I heard shouts of **joy** and ran downstairs. Our favorite uncle had arrived. Uncle Bob is very funny, and we always **enjoy** his stories.

Think How are *joy* and *enjoy* alike in meaning? How are *joy* and *enjoy* alike in spelling?

Here are some words in the *joy* family.

joy	joyous	joyful
enjoy	enjoyable	enjoyment

Apply and Extend

Complete these activities on another sheet of paper.

1. Look up the meaning of each word in the Word Box above in your Spelling Dictionary. Write six sentences, using one word in each sentence.

2. With a partner list words related to *serve*, *large*, and *quart*. Then look in your Spelling-Meaning Index beginning on page 272. Add any other words in these families to your list.

Literature and Writing

from

Dragon Stew

by Tom McGowen

A young man wants to make his fortune. What does this story beginning tell about him?

A shabby young man came trudging up the road toward the castle. He had patched knees and elbows, and the feather in his worn hat was bedraggled. But he had a merry grin, and he was whistling a cheerful tune. When he saw the long line of people, he asked a soldier standing nearby, "What's going on? Why are all these people lined up around the castle?"

"The king's looking for a new royal cook!" the soldier replied. "The cook with the most unusual recipe will get the job and will live in the palace off the best of the land!"

"I'm just the sort of cook the king wants," the young man answered, "and I have the most unusual recipe he's ever heard of !"

Think and Discuss

1 How does the young man look and act? What do you learn about this character?

2 This story beginning makes you want to read more. Why?

3 Where and when do you think the story takes place?

The Writing Process
A Story

Write a story of your own! Just follow the Guidelines and use the Writing Process.

1 Prewriting
- Brainstorm story ideas with a partner. Choose one for your story.

2 Draft
- Tell your story in pictures first. Make three drawings that show the beginning, middle, and end.

3 Revise
- Did you include all the parts of your story you wanted to?
- Would more details or dialogue make it better?

4 Proofread
- Did you capitalize all proper nouns?
- Did you correct any misspelled words?

5 Publish
- Make a picture book out of your drawings and a clean copy of your final draft. Add a title and a fun cover.

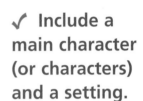

····Guidelines for Writing a Story

✓ Include a main character (or characters) and a setting.
✓ Include a problem that the main character has to solve.
✓ Include details and use dialogue.

Composition Words

dark
storm
girl
noise
boy
large
crack
squeeze

A Trip to the Moon

The Vowel + |r| Sounds in hair

Read and Say

READ the sentences. **SAY** each bold word.

|âr|
bear

Basic

1.	hair	I will cut your **hair**.
2.	care	Please take **care** of my sick cat.
3.	chair	She sat in a big **chair**.
4.	pair	I need a **pair** of socks.
5.	bear	We saw a **bear** in the woods.
6.	where	Do you know **where** he is?
7.	scare	That big bug gave me a **scare**.
8.	air	A kite floats in the **air**.
9.	pear	I ate a **pear** from that tree.
10.	bare	I put my **bare** foot in the water.
11.	fair	We saw pigs at the **fair**.
12.	share	I will **share** my toys with you.

Think and Write

Each word has the vowel + |r| sounds that you hear in *hair*.

|âr| c**are**, h**air**, b**ear**

A. Write **four** Basic Words with |âr| spelled *are*.

B. Write **five** Basic Words with |âr| spelled *air*.

C. Write **two** Basic Words with |âr| spelled *ear*.

D. Write **one** Basic Word with |âr| spelled another way.

Review	
13. buy	14. could

Challenge	
15. flair	16. compare

Independent Practice

Spelling Strategy The |âr| sounds can be spelled with these patterns:

are, as in *care*
air, as in *hair*
ear, as in *bear*

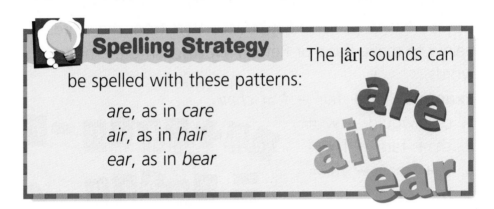

are air ear

Phonics Use Basic Words in these exercises.

1. Write the word that begins with the |sh| sound.

2–3. Write *care*. Then add a letter to *care* to write another word.

4–6. Write the word that sounds like each word below but is spelled differently.

    4. bear   **5.** pear   **6.** fare

Vocabulary: Classifying Write the Basic Word that belongs in each group.

7. table, stool, _____

8. orange, apple, _____

9. land, sea, _____

10. deer, fox, _____

11. fur, feathers, _____

Elephant Word Write the Elephant Word to complete the sentence.

12. Melissa, _____ do you get your hair cut?

Challenge Words Write the Challenge Word that completes each sentence. Use your Spelling Dictionary.

13. Ben goes to different shops to _____ haircut prices.

14. Kate has a _____ for cutting hair.

Review: Spelling Spree

Letter Math Add and subtract letters from the words below to make Basic or Review Words. Write the new words.

Example: ch + fair − f = *chair*

1. c + would − w =
2. sh + fare − f =
3. p + chair − ch =
4. b + scare − sc =
5. c + stare − st =
6. sc + stare − st =
7. wh + there − th =
8. f + hair − h =
9. p + wear − w =

Silly Sentences Write a Basic or Review Word to complete each silly sentence.

Example: Apples and a _____ grew on a tree. *pear*

10. I had a friendly talk with a big brown _____.
11. I saw a puppy comb its long _____.
12. Alexander saw a book rising into the _____.
13. An elephant likes to sit in a _____.
14. The dog has money to _____ a snack.

How Are You Doing? Write each spelling word in a sentence. Practice with a partner any words you spelled wrong.

Proofreading and Writing

Proofread for Spelling and Commas in a Series
Use commas to separate a series of three or more words in a sentence.

   Ethan, Joe, and Kendra had their hair cut.
Proofread this ad. Find three spelling mistakes and two missing commas. Write the ad correctly.

Good Care for Your Hair

Get your hair washed

cut and dried for a fare

price! Come to

Sylvia's Shop, were you

always get a great by.

Proofreading Marks

¶ Indent
∧ Add
⌐ Delete
≡ Capital letter
/ Small letter

Write a Comic Strip

Draw two or three small pictures that show you getting a funny haircut. Write a caption for each picture. Try to use spelling words.
Example: I went to get my hair washed, cut, and dried.

Proofreading Tip   **Check that you used commas to separate words in a series.**

Phonics and Spelling

Rhyming Words

The |âr| Final Sound *Hair*, *pear*, and *care* rhyme, even though the final sounds are spelled differently. Here are more rhyming words.

fare   repair   square   rare   beware   wear

Write the word above that completes each sentence. Use your Spelling Dictionary.

2. I want to _____ my new hat to school.

1. These coins are very old and _____.

4. Tim told me to _____ of the dog.

3. Dad will _____ my broken bike.

FEROCIOUS DOG

5. She packed her books in a big _____ box.

6. Nancy saves all her change for bus _____.

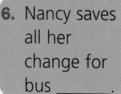

Show What You Know! Write rhyming sentences using some of the rhyming words.

Careers

Hairdresser All the words in the box have something to do with hairdressing. Write those words to complete this interview with a movie star. Use your Spelling Dictionary.

Spelling Word Link

hair

shampoo
trim
style
brush
dryer

Interviewer: How do you keep your hair so fresh and clean looking?

Gloria Glamoure: I use a good ___(1)___ to wash my hair. It dries so fast that I do not need a ___(2)___. Every month I have Todd, a hairdresser, ___(3)___ my hair because it grows fast. He uses a comb and a soft ___(4)___ to fix it in a new ___(5)___.

Try This CHALLENGE

Yes or No? Is the underlined word used correctly? Write *yes* or *no*.

6. <u>Shampoo</u> makes hair dirty.
7. Anna uses a <u>brush</u> to cut her hair.
8. You can <u>trim</u> hair that gets too long.

★ Fact File

Fashions often seem odd once they are out-of-date. For example, some people once wore long, curled wigs that were powdered white.

Homophones

Read and Say

READ the sentences. **SAY** each bold word.

our **reading** hour

Basic

1. *hear* Tell me what sound you **hear**.
2. *here* Please sit **here**.
3. *new* We have a **new** house.
4. *knew* My cat **knew** how to find me.
5. *its* The dog is in **its** house.
6. *it's* I think **it's** time to leave.
7. *our* Do you like **our** yard?
8. *hour* We read for an **hour**.
9. *there* He is over **there** by the tree.
10. *their* They have **their** bikes with them.
11. *they're* Dad and Mom know **they're** right.

Think and Write

Each word is a homophone. **Homophones** are words that sound alike but have different spellings and meanings.

HOMOPHONE	MEANING
|nōō| **n**ew	not old
|nōō| **kn**ew	understood

How are the homophones in each pair or group different?

A. Write the **four pairs** of homophones.
B. Write the **three words** that are homophones.

Review	
12. eye	**13.** I

Challenge	
14. seen	**15.** scene

Independent Practice

Spelling Strategy **Homophones** are words that sound the same but have different spellings and meanings. When you spell a homophone, think about the meaning of the word you want to write.

Vocabulary: Context Sentences Write the Basic Word that completes each sentence.

1. Mom says (its, it's) okay to have a snack.
2. The church bells ring every (hour, our).
3. The car is so clean because it is (knew, new).
4. Come (hear, here) and listen to this record.
5. I like tacos if (they're, their, there) very spicy.
6. My sister and I think of (our, hour) uncle's farm when we smell newly cut grass.
7. Look how the car glows with (its, it's) new coat of paint!
8. Jamie, do you (here, hear) those dogs growling?
9. Shawna and Paul always eat (they're, their, there) spinach.
10. Jeffrey (knew, new) that he should be home before dark.
11. Did Melissa leave her glasses at the park when she was (their, they're, there)?

Challenge Words Write the Challenge Word that completes each sentence. Use your Spelling Dictionary.

12. Have you ever (scene, seen) a rainbow?
13. The first (seen, scene) in that play was so sad that I almost cried.

Dictionary

Homophones Look at the dictionary entry below. Notice the ✦ in the last line. This points out the homophone for *it's*.

> **it's** |ĭts| Contraction of "it is" or "it has."
> ✦ *These sound alike* **it's, its.**

Practice Look up each word in your Spelling Dictionary. Write its homophone.

1. seem   **2.** blue   **3.** know
4. week   **5.** main   **6.** sale

Review: Spelling Spree

Puzzle Play Write a Basic or Review Word for each clue. Circle the letter that would be in the box.

Example: in this place __ __ ☐ __   *here*

  7. belongs to it __ ☐ __
  8. belongs to them __ ☐ __ __ __
  9. what we see with __ __ ☐
10. belongs to us __ __ ☐
11. not old __ ☐ __

Write the letters you circled in order. They will spell a Basic Word that completes this sentence.

12. Curtis said that _____ was plenty of chili left.

HERE

How Are You Doing?
Write your spelling words in ABC order. Practice with a family member any words you spelled wrong.

Proofreading and Writing

Proofread for Spelling Proofread this journal entry. Find seven spelling mistakes. Write each word correctly.

I love to here birds! They started to sing an our ago. There are more birds hear this year. Eye never new they could be so loud! Wow--its as if their cheering!

Basic
1. hear
2. here
3. new
4. knew
5. its
6. it's
7. our
8. hour
9. there
10. their
11. they're

Review
12. eye
13. I

Challenge
14. seen
15. scene

Proofreading Marks

¶ Indent
∧ Add
⌐ Delete
≡ Capital letter
/ Small letter

Write a Description

What is your favorite food? How does it look, smell, and taste? Write a paragraph describing it. Try to use three spelling words. Share your paragraph with a friend.

Proofreading Tip

If you use the computer to check your spelling, remember that it cannot tell you whether you have used the correct homophone.

129

Vocabulary Enrichment

More Homophones Which shines–a sun or a son? These two words are homophones.

sun a large star   **son** a male child

Write a homophone from the box to complete each sentence. Use your Spelling Dictionary.

Spelling Word Link

hear
here

fair
fare
pail
pale
sail
sale

1. Lee's face turned _____ with fright.

2. Use this _____ to carry water from the well.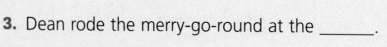

3. Dean rode the merry-go-round at the _____.

4. You must have exact change for the bus _____.

5. That store is having a big _____ next week.

6. It's hard to _____ when there is no wind.

Work Together Write a sentence for each homophone. Read your sentences to a partner. Have your partner write the correct homophone for each sentence.

Unit 20
BONUS

Language Arts

Using Your Senses All the words in the box have something to do with using your senses. Write those words to complete this diary entry. Use your Spelling Dictionary.

Spelling Word Link

hear

bumpy
shiny
burnt
squeaky
sour

February 22, 1998

Dear Diary,
    Today my senses told me that I had a bad day! First, I had ___(1)___ toast for breakfast. Then the milk on my cereal was ___(2)___. This afternoon I fell off my bike on a ___(3)___ dirt road. Now my new shoes don't look ___(4)___ anymore, and my bike sounds ___(5)___.

Try This
CHALLENGE

Yes or No? Is the underlined word used correctly? Write *yes* or *no*.

6. The meat was <u>burnt</u> by the flames.
7. The <u>squeaky</u> door made no sound.
8. The lemon tasted <u>sour</u>.

★★★ **Fact File**

Braille is an alphabet that blind people can read with their fingers. There is a different pattern of tiny bumps for each letter.

Read and Say

READ the sentences. **SAY** each bold word.

air | plane

Basic

1.	airplane	We rode in an **airplane**.
2.	inside	We should go **inside** now.
3.	grandmother	My **grandmother** hugged me.
4.	sometimes	I set the table **sometimes**.
5.	himself	He went shopping by **himself**.
6.	nothing	I have **nothing** to do.
7.	birthday	We had a party for my **birthday**.
8.	herself	She will fix the car **herself**.
9.	outside	Can you play **outside**?
10.	grandfather	I spoke with my **grandfather**.
11.	baseball	When is the **baseball** game?
12.	something	I saw **something** on the hill.

Think and Write

Each word is a compound word. A **compound word** is made up of two or more shorter words.

air + plane = airplane   **him + self** = himself

How do you say the Elephant Word? How do you say the two words that form the Elephant Word?

Write the **twelve** Basic Words. Draw a line between the two words that make up each compound word.

Review
13. someone 14. cannot

Challenge
15. suitcase 16. everybody

Independent Practice

Spelling Strategy To spell a **compound word**, think about the spellings of the shorter words that make up the compound word.

Phonics Use Basic Words in these exercises.

1–6. Each word below is part of two compound words. Write the six compound words.

1–2. grand   **3–4.** self   **5–6.** side

Vocabulary: Context Sentences Write the Basic Word that completes each sentence.

7. Marcos took an _____ instead of a train to Chicago.
8. We played a lot of games at the _____ party.
9. There is always _____ fun to do at Uncle Ben's.
10. Maria usually goes to her grandparents' house on Sundays, but _____ she goes to her aunt's.
11. Elena saw her favorite _____ team play at Candlestick Park.

Elephant Word Write the Elephant Word to complete the sentence.

12. My family will let _____ spoil our trip.

Challenge Words Write the Challenge Word that completes each sentence. Use your Spelling Dictionary.

13. Each person may take only one _____ on the weekend trip.
14. The trip leader told _____ to meet at the train station.

Review: Spelling Spree

Compound Clues Write a Basic or Review Word to answer each question.

1. What word means the opposite of *nothing*?
2. What day is the day you become a year older?
3. What is in your backpack if it is empty?
4. What word means the opposite of *inside*?
5. What is a name for your father's father?
6. What does a pilot fly?
7. What word means the opposite of *no one*?
8. What game do you play with a bat?

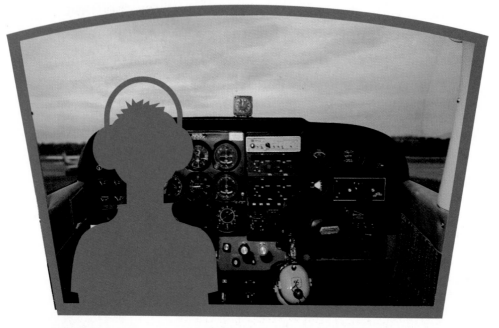

Compound Words Each word is part of a Basic or Review Word. Write those Basic and Review Words.

9. mother
10. can
11. her
12. times
13. in
14. him

How Are You Doing?

List the spelling words that are hard for you. Practice them with a family member.

Proofreading and Writing

Proofread for Spelling and Quotation Marks

Put quotation marks around a speaker's exact words.

Eric asked, "May I go?"

Proofread this story. Find three spelling mistakes and two missing quotation marks. Write the story correctly.

It was pouring

outside. I said, I canot see

anything. Then I saw

somone. There was my

granmother!

1. airplane
2. inside
3. grandmother
4. sometimes
5. himself
6. nothing
7. birthday
8. herself
9. outside
10. grandfather
11. baseball
12. something

Review
13. someone
14. cannot

Challenge
15. suitcase
16. everybody

Proofreading Marks

¶ Indent
∧ Add
ℱ Delete
≡ Capital letter
/ Small letter

Write a Conversation

"Hi!"

Think of a conversation you would like to have with a friend or family member. Maybe you want to invite a friend for a visit. Write what you would say to each other. Use quotation marks. Try to use three spelling words.

Proofreading Tip

Check that you used quotation marks correctly.

Vocabulary Enrichment

Word Builder

Spelling
Word Link
outside

More Compound Words You can make new compound words by putting together two shorter words. The compound word will have the meanings of the shorter words that form it.

out + side = outside **"the side that is out"**

Form six compound words by matching the words on the baggage to the words on the tags. Use your Spelling Dictionary.

time

web

sand

flag

foot

pole

soap

suds

cob

day

print

box

Show What You Know! Now write one of the compound words for each of the meanings.
1. the time of day between sunrise and sunset
2. a pole for a flag
3. the bubbles in soapy water
4. the mark left by a foot
5. the web spun by a spider
6. a play area filled with sand

Vocabulary Enrichment

Social Studies

Going for a Visit All the words in the box have something to do with going for a visit. Write those words to finish this page from a personal narrative. Use your Spelling Dictionary.

Spelling Word Link

airplane

visit
aunt
pajamas
slippers
bathrobe

MONARCHS of NEW YORK CITY

My uncle and __(1)__ invited me to __(2)__ them in New York. They said, "Our house gets cold! You will need warm __(3)__ for sleeping." I took a __(4)__ to wear over my pajamas and __(5)__ for my feet.

Try This CHALLENGE

Make a Travel Poster Make a poster for somebody's house you like to visit. Draw a picture of the place. Write words on the poster to describe the things you like about visiting there.

★★★ Fact File

Most of the United States lies in four time zones. At 3:00 P.M. in Oregon, it is 4:00 P.M. in Utah, 5:00 P.M. in Iowa, and 6:00 P.M. in New York.

Words That End with -ed or -ing

chopped

Read and Say

READ the sentences. **SAY** each bold word.

Basic

1.	chopped	Mom **chopped** the tree down.
2.	tapping	Who is **tapping** on the door?
3.	saving	The boy is **saving** his coins.
4.	cared	We **cared** for the lost kitten.
5.	rubbed	I **rubbed** my sore knee.
6.	fixing	She is **fixing** her bike.
7.	smiled	The baby **smiled** at me.
8.	joking	He was only **joking**.
9.	dropped	I **dropped** a pencil on the floor.
10.	grinning	Why is she **grinning**?
11.	wrapped	I **wrapped** the gift in red paper.
12.	patted	The girl **patted** the dog.

Think and Write

Each word has a base word and *-ed* or *-ing*. A **base word** is a word to which an ending may be added.

care − e + ed = car**ed**   rub + b + ing = ru**bbing**

How is the Elephant Word different?

A. Write **four** Basic Words that drop the final *e*.
B. Write **seven** Basic Words that double the final consonant.
C. Write **one** Basic Word that does not change its spelling.

Review
13. making 14. stopped

Challenge
15. propped 16. framed

Independent Practice

Spelling Strategy   When a base word ends with *e*, drop the *e* before adding *-ed* or *-ing*.

When a base word ends with one vowel and one consonant, the consonant is usually doubled before *-ed* or *-ing* is added.

Phonics   Use Basic Words in these exercises.

1–4. Write four words by adding *-ed* or *-ing* to each base word.

   1. grin   **3.** care

   2. wrap   **4.** save

Vocabulary: Context Sentences   Write the Basic Word that completes each sentence.

   5. Dad _____ wood for the tree house.

   6. I liked to hear the hammer _____ the nails.

   7. Melissa _____ the doorknob until it shined.

   8. Dad shouted when he _____ a hammer out of the window.

   9. Dad _____ me on the back when we finished.

 10. Luis _____ happily when he saw the tree house.

 11. He was only _____ when he said he hated trees.

Elephant Word   Write the Elephant Word to complete the sentence.

 12. Mom will be _____ the door today.

Challenge Words   Write the Challenge Word that fits each meaning. Use your Spelling Dictionary.

 13. enclosed   **14.** supported

Dictionary

Base Words How can you find out how to spell a word that ends with *-ed* or *-ing*? Look up its base word in a dictionary.

> **pat** |păt| *v.* **patted, patting** To touch gently with the open hand: *Don't pat the dog.*

Practice Write the base word you would look up in a dictionary to find each word below.

1. joking

2. smiled

3. fixing

4. stopped

5. making

6. chopped

Review: Spelling Spree

Ending Match Write eight Basic or Review Words by adding *-ed or -ing.* Remember to double the final consonant or drop the final e.

7. tap

8. make

9. drop

10. grin

11. care

12. save

13. joke

14. wrap

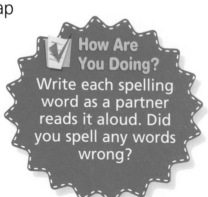

How Are You Doing?
Write each spelling word as a partner reads it aloud. Did you spell any words wrong?

Proofreading and Writing

Proofread for Spelling Proofread this journal page. Find six spelling mistakes. Write each word correctly.

March 14

    Uncle Rafe dropped by and saw that I was fiksing my new tree house. He stoped, smild, and pated my back. I told him that Dad had choped and sawed the wood. I had rubed the edges with sandpaper. His praise left me grinning from ear to ear.

Basic
1. chopped
2. tapping
3. saving
4. cared
5. rubbed
6. fixing
7. smiled
8. joking
9. dropped
10. grinning
11. wrapped
12. patted
Review
13. making
14. stopped
Challenge
15. propped
16. framed

Proofreading Marks

¶ Indent
∧ Add
ℛ Delete
≡ Capital letter
/ Small letter

Write Instructions

Write some instructions on how to build something fun but simple, such as a snowman, a sandcastle, or a paper airplane. Try to use three spelling words. Draw a picture to go with your instructions.

Proofreading Tip

Watch out for letters that have been left out of words.

Phonics and Spelling

Word Builder

Double Consonants and Vowels When you double the consonant before adding *-ed* or *-ing*, the vowel sound is usually short. When you drop the e and add *-ed* or *-ing*, the vowel sound is usually long.

Read the words on the wooden ladder rungs. Match the words on the ladder rungs to the correct tree house.

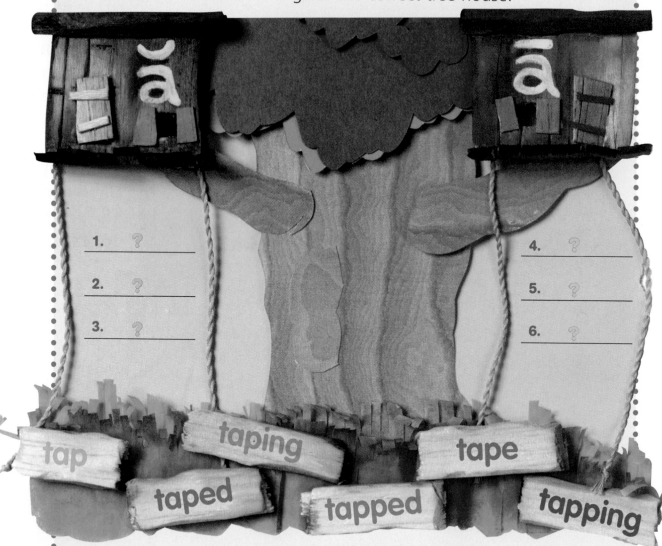

1. ?

2. ?

3. ?

4. ?

5. ?

6. ?

tap

taping

tape

taped

tapped

tapping

Show What You Know! Work with a partner to write sentences, using the words that you made.

Industrial Arts

Building a Tree House All the words in the box have something to do with building a tree house. Write those words to complete this letter. Use your Spelling Dictionary.

March 1, 1998

Dear Tío Julio,

Mom came up with a great __(1)__ to __(2)__ a tree house. First, we chose the biggest __(3)__ of the tree. Then Mom climbed up the __(4)__. We handed her the tools, nails, and __(5)__. When the house was done, we all painted it. I can't wait for you to see it!

Love,
Julia

**Try This
CHALLENGE**

Write a Description What kind of tree house would you build? Draw a picture and write a paragraph describing it. What would it look like? What would be in it? Try to use words from the box in your description.

★★ **Fact File**

In the rain forest in French Guiana, scientists work in the treetops on a "raft" that stretches over the top of the forest. The scientists study plants, animals, and insects.

Changing Final y to i

Read and Say

READ the sentences. **SAY** each bold word.

pony + ies
= pon**ies**

Basic

1.	babies	The **babies** are learning to walk.
2.	puppies	My dog had three **puppies**.
3.	cried	I **cried** when I fell down.
4.	carried	Dad **carried** my little brother.
5.	stories	We will read five **stories**.
6.	dried	Has the wet paint **dried**?
7.	hurried	She **hurried** across the street.
8.	ponies	There are **ponies** in the barn.
9.	flies	That bird **flies** fast.
10.	tried	He **tried** to win the game.
11.	parties	I like to go to **parties**.
12.	pennies	Can we count the **pennies** now?

Think and Write

Each word is made up of a base word and the ending
-*es* or -*ed*. The spelling of the base word changes when
-*es* or -*ed* is added.

baby − y + ies = bab**ies**   cry − y + ied = cr**ied**

Does a consonant or a vowel come before the final *y* in
each base word? How do *baby* and *cry* change when
-*es* or -*ed* is added?

A. Write **seven** Basic Words that end with -*ies*.
B. Write **five** Basic Words that end with -*ied*.

Review		Challenge
13. lady	**14.** very	**15.** canaries **16.** libraries

Independent Practice

Spelling Strategy   Remember, when a base word ends with a consonant and *y,* change the *y* to *i* before adding *-es* or *-ed.*

Phonics   Use Basic Words in these exercises.

1–4. Each word below is missing a double consonant. Write the four words.

1. hu __ __ ied
2. pe __ __ ies

3. ca __ __ ied
4. pu __ __ ies

5–7. Add the ending *-ed* to each base word below. Write the three new words.

5. cry
6. try
7. dry

Vocabulary: Making Inferences
Write the Basic Word that matches each clue.

8. People often read these in books.
9. Children often have these on their birthdays.
10. These often buzz around food at picnics.
11. Children often ride these at fairs.
12. These are very young children.

Challenge Words   Write the Challenge Word that completes each sentence. Use your Spelling Dictionary.

13. Jason has two yellow _____ for pets.
14. Siri looked for facts on pet care at two _____.

Review: Spelling Spree

Alphabet Dash Write the Basic or Review Word that goes in ABC order between each pair of words.

1. easy, _____, goose
2. gray, _____, ice
3. joke, _____, milk
4. use, _____, wait

5. band, _____, cone
6. cool, _____, cub
7. paint, _____, paste
8. swing, _____, trot

Sentence Pairs Write the Basic Word that best completes each pair of sentences.

Example: A bee cannot swim. It only _____. *flies*

9. I do not see any big horses. I see only _____.
10. My sisters are not grownups. They are _____.
11. I do not have any dimes. I only have _____.
12. Dad does not sing songs. He tells _____.
13. I do not have grown dogs. I have only _____.
14. We did not wash the dishes. We only _____ them.

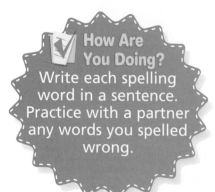

How Are You Doing?
Write each spelling word in a sentence. Practice with a partner any words you spelled wrong.

Proofreading and Writing

Proofread for Spelling and End Marks in Quotations Put quotation marks around a speaker's exact words. Put the end mark inside the quotation marks.

Alex cried, "Hurry!" Kate answered, "I am."

Proofread this page from a story. Find three spelling mistakes and a missing end mark. Write the page correctly.

I visited a lade and her puppies. She said, "They cryed all night " Doesn't she know that puppies are babys?

Proofreading Marks

¶ Indent
∧ Add
𝓇 Delete
≡ Capital letter
/ Small letter

Write a Story

Write a story about a baby animal that is separated from its parents and is raised by a different kind of animal. What will the baby say when it learns what kind of animal it really is? Use quotation marks around a speaker's exact words. Try to use three spelling words. Then share your story with a friend.

Proofreading Tip

Check that you put end marks inside quotation marks.

Vocabulary Enrichment

Word Builder

Animal Sounds Some words, such as *cried* and *howled*, name special sounds that animals make.

The dogs **cried**.   The wolves **howled**.

Write the word that best completes each sentence. Use your Spelling Dictionary.

2. The mouse _____ when it saw the cat.

1. The hen _____.

4. The snake _____.

3. The guard dog _____. behind the fence.

5. The duck _____.

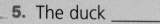

6. The canary _____.

Work Together Work with a friend. Imagine you are the animals in the pictures. Act out the sound each animal makes.

Science

Baby Animals All the words in the box have something to do with baby animals. Write those words to complete this page from a magazine article on baby animals. Use your Spelling Dictionary.

Spelling Word Link

puppies

calf
fawn
cub
chick
duckling

The baby and grown-up names for animals are sometimes related. A young chicken is a __(1)__, for example. A baby duck is a __(2)__. The baby and grown-up names for animals may also be very different. A baby bear is a __(3)__, a young bull is a __(4)__, and a baby deer is a __(5)__.

Try This
CHALLENGE

Yes or No? Is the underlined word used correctly? Write *yes* or *no*.

6. The mother cow looked for its <u>calf</u>.

7. The <u>fawn</u> trotted after the other deer.

8. A bear usually has one <u>chick</u> or twins.

⭐ **Fact File**

A baby kangaroo is a *joey*. It is less than an inch long when it is born. A joey lives in its mother's pouch for six to eight months.

24 Review: Units 19–23

|âr|
bear

Unit 19   Vowel + |r| sounds in hair **pp. 120–125**

bear	chair	where
pear	fair	scare

Spelling Strategy   The |âr| sounds can have these patterns: *are*, as in c**are**; *ear*, as in b**ear**; *air*, as in h**air**.

Write the words to complete the paragraph.
Bonnie and I went to the county ___**(1)**___ yesterday.
I bought a ___**(2)**___ to eat, and Bonnie bought a fuzzy
___**(3)**___. Bonnie saw a strong man break a ___**(4)**___ in half
with one hand. The most fun was the House of Horrors,
___**(5)**___ we had a really good ___**(6)**___!

our
reading
hour

Unit 20   Homophones   pp. 126–131

its	hear	our
it's	here	hour

Spelling Strategy   **Homophones** sound the same but have different spellings and meanings.

Write the word that completes each sentence.
7. If it snows, we will wear (hour, our) boots.
8. My dog really likes (its, it's) bath.
9. Dinner will be ready in an (our, hour).
10. Do you (hear, here) those birds singing?
11. Dad says that (its, it's) going to rain today.
12. Carla will meet us (here, hear) at noon.

Unit 21   Compound Words   pp. 132–137

grandmother	himself	nothing
outside	birthday	baseball

air | plane

Spelling Strategy   A **compound word** is made up of two or more shorter words.

Write the word that belongs in each group.

13. myself, herself, _____   **14.** soccer, hockey, _____

Write the word that completes each sentence.

15. Debby will have her _____ party tomorrow.

16. The box had _____ in it.

17. Tina is going _____ to water the garden.

18. Jud's _____ is coming to visit on Sunday.

Unit 22   Words with -ed or -ing   pp. 138–143

cared	tapping	fixing
joking	wrapped	smiled

chopped

Spelling Strategy   The spelling of some base words changes when **-ed** or **-ing** is added.

care − e + ed = **cared**
tap + p + ing = **tapping**

Write the word that rhymes with each word below.

19. trapped   **20.** napping

Write four spelling words by adding *-ed* or *-ing* to each base word below.

21. smile   **22.** joke   **23.** fix   **24.** care

**pony + ies
= ponies**

Unit 23	Changing Final y to i	pp. 144–149

carried	stories	dried
ponies	pennies	tried

Spelling Strategy   When a base word ends with a consonant and **y**, change the **y** to **i** before adding **-es** or **-ed**.

Write the word that completes each sentence.

25. We played outside while the wet paint _____.

26. Irene _____ to open the door, but it was stuck.

Write four spelling words by adding -es or -ed to each base word below.

27. pony   **29.** story

28. carry   **30.** penny

Challenge Words	Units 19–23	pp. 120–149

libraries	framed	seen
everybody	compare	scene

Write two spelling words by adding -es or -ed to each base word below.

31. frame

32. library

Write the word that completes each sentence.

33. At the Science Fair, the judges will _____ the projects and choose a winner.

34. We have already _____ that movie.

35. An actor forgot his lines in the first _____.

36. Our teacher says that _____ is going on the trip.

Spelling-Meaning Strategy

Word Forms

Knowing the meanings and spellings of pairs of homophones will help you spell the other words in their families. Read these sentences.

> This **week** I will go skiing on the **weekend**.
> "I am **weak** from the flu," Jo said **weakly**.

Think How are *week* and *weekend* alike in meaning and spelling? How are *weak* and *weakly* alike in meaning and spelling?

Here are words in the *week* and *weak* families.

week	weekly	weak	weakly
weekend	biweekly	weakness	weaker

Apply and Extend

Complete these activities on another sheet of paper.

1. Look up the meaning of each word in the Word Box above in your Spelling Dictionary. Write **eight** sentences, using one word in each sentence.

2. With a partner list words related to *bear* and *bare* and to *son* and *sun*. Then look in your Spelling-Meaning Index beginning on page 272. Add any other words in these families to your list.

Literature and Writing

from

An Oak Tree Dies and a Journey Begins

by Louanne Norris
and Howard E. Smith, Jr.

These paragraphs describe an oak tree. Which words help you picture the tree in your mind?

A big, old oak tree grew on the bank of a river. During the summer its green leaves hid many of its branches. Other branches were dead and bare. Light gray bark covered most of its trunk. Once the oak had had firm, pale brown wood under its bark, but over the years parts of it had rotted and turned gray. The tree had a few large holes in its trunk, and some of its branches had broken off.

One autumn night, the biggest storm in years shook the old oak tree. Strong winds whipped away many of its yellow and brown leaves. The tree swayed and creaked, and the wind pulled at its roots. Some of the roots that were rotten broke, and the oak tree fell to the riverbank.

Think and Discuss

1 Which words tell how the tree looked? How did it sound during the storm?

2 Which details describe what the big storm did to the old tree?

The Writing Process

A Description

Write a description of something you like. Follow the Guidelines and use the Writing Process.

1 Prewriting
- Look through magazines or family photographs. Do you see someone or something to describe?

2 Draft
- Write as much as you can. Don't worry about mistakes right now!

3 Revise
- Can you use more sense words or details?
- Use your Thesaurus for exact words.

4 Proofread
- Did you use commas with words in a series?
- Did you correct misspelled words?

5 Publish
- Make a card with your description. Decorate the cover. Put your description inside!

••• Guidelines for Writing a Description

✓ Begin with an interesting sentence that tells about the topic.

✓ Use sense words and details that describe your topic.

✓ Use exact words and comparisons to create a clear picture.

Composition Words

bare
hear
outside
patted
tapping
smiled
dried
cried

The Prefixes re- and un-

Read and Say

READ the sentences. **SAY** each bold word.

unhappy

Basic

1.	unfair	That rule is **unfair**.
2.	unhappy	She looked **unhappy**.
3.	rewrite	I am going to **rewrite** my story.
4.	unkind	Was he **unkind** to you?
5.	remake	I must **remake** my clay pot.
6.	untie	This knot is hard to **untie**.
7.	unlike	This glass is **unlike** the others.
8.	unclear	It is **unclear** who won the race.
9.	unhurt	He was **unhurt** after his fall.
10.	retell	I like to **retell** this story.
11.	unwrap	Which box did you **unwrap**?
12.	reuse	Wash that dish and **reuse** it.

Think and Write

Each word has a prefix and a base word. A **prefix** is a word part added to the beginning of a base word.

PREFIX		BASE WORD		NEW WORD	MEANING
re	+	write	=	**re**write	to write again
un	+	happy	=	**un**happy	not happy
un	+	tie	=	**un**tie	opposite of *tie*

A. Write **four** Basic Words that have the prefix *re-*.
B. Write **eight** Basic Words that have the prefix *un-*.

Review
13. do 14. have

Challenge
15. unimportant 16. review

Independent Practice

Spelling Strategy   A **prefix** is a word part added to the beginning of a base word. It adds meaning to the base word.

The prefix *re-* means "again."
The prefix *un-* means "not" or "opposite of."

Phonics Use Basic Words in these exercises.

1. Write the word that ends with a double consonant.
2–5. Write the four words with a long vowel sound spelled with the vowel-consonant-*e* pattern.

Vocabulary: Context Sentences Write the Basic Word that completes each sentence.

6. Josh tripped over a rock, but he was _____.
7. The baby was _____ until she got her bottle.
8. If your shoe is wet, _____ it and take it off.
9. Dad told Sue that she could _____ her presents.
10. Do not be _____ to animals.
11. He thought that the judge's ruling was _____.
12. He got lost because the directions were very _____.

Challenge Words Write the Challenge Word that fits each meaning. Use your Spelling Dictionary.

13. to study again
14. having little meaning or value

Dictionary

Syllables A **syllable** is a word part with one vowel sound. The dictionary uses dots (•) to separate the syllables of an entry word.

> **un•hap•py** |ŭn hăp′ ē| *adj.* **unhappier, unhappiest** Not happy; sad.

Practice Write each word below. Draw a line between the syllables. Use your Spelling Dictionary.

1. picnic   **5.** outside
2. almost   **6.** circus
3. balloon   **7.** invite
4. neighbor

Review: Spelling Spree

Puzzle Play Write the Basic Word that matches each clue. Circle the letter that would appear in the box. Write the circled letters in order. They will spell something you can do to brighten a bad day.

Example: not fair __ __ ☐ __ __ __   *un⟨f⟩air*

 8. to open a present __ __ ☐ __ __ __
 9. not bruised __ __ ☐ __ __ __
10. to loosen __ __ __ ☐ __
11. to use again __ __ __ ☐ __
12. to write again __ __ __ __ __ ☐ __
13. to tell again __ __ __ __ __ ☐
14. to make again __ ☐ __ __ __ __

Mystery Word: __ __ __ __ __ __ __

> **How Are You Doing?**
> Write your spelling words in ABC order. Practice with a family member any words you spelled wrong.

Proofreading and Writing

Proofread for Spelling Proofread this note. Find six spelling mistakes. Write each word correctly.

Dear Tamika,

It is unlik you to be anhappy.

Maybe your thoughts are unkleer, but do

not think that life is uncind and unfare.

If you have a bad day, think about

something funny, or retel a good joke!

Your friend,

Cassie

Proofreading Marks

¶ Indent
∧ Add
⌐ Delete
≡ Capital letter
/ Small letter

Write a Story

Write a story about a bad day you have had. Try to use three spelling words. You may want to draw some pictures to go with your story.

Bad Day
March 14 was a really bad day for me. It was my birthday. I know

Proofreading Tip **Say aloud each letter in a word to make sure there are no missing letters.**

Word Builder

Adding Prefixes Different prefixes can be added to a base word to build new words with different meanings.

Spelling Word Link

unwrap

fold
done
used

wrap   "to put a covering on"
unwrap   "to take off a covering"
rewrap   "to wrap again"

Unscramble the letters to form the words from the box. Then add *re-* and *un-* to each word to make two new words. Match each new word with one of the definitions below.

1. not used
2. to be used again
3. not done
4. done again
5. to undo the folds of
6. to fold again

Show What You Know! Write a sentence for each of the words you made.

Life Skills

A Bad Day All the words in the box have something to do with a bad day. Write those words to complete this page from a story. Use your Spelling Dictionary.

Spelling Word Link

unhappy

trouble
oversleep
quarrel
mistake
angry

This morning, Lisa's dad thought she might __(1)__, so he woke her. Lisa got __(2)__ and started to __(3)__ with him. Lisa's dad just smiled and asked, "What's the __(4)__?"

"I'm just tired," said Lisa. "It was a __(5)__ to fight with you." She gave him a hug.

Try This CHALLENGE

Yes or No? Write *yes* or *no* to answer each question.

6. If you got up early, did you oversleep?
7. Might people quarrel if they don't agree?
8. Will a perfect test have a mistake?

★★★ Fact File

When people say, "Every cloud has a silver lining," they mean that something good can come out of trouble or bad luck.

The Suffixes -ful, -ly, and -er

Read and Say

READ the sentences. **SAY** each bold word.

Basic

1.	teacher	Our **teacher** reads to us.
2.	friendly	He is very **friendly**.
3.	useful	This jar is so **useful**.
4.	careful	Be **careful** with that knife.
5.	slowly	Little children walk **slowly**.
6.	helper	Who will be my **helper**?
7.	quickly	Please come here **quickly**.
8.	farmer	Does the **farmer** grow corn?
9.	hopeful	I am **hopeful** that we will win.
10.	singer	She is a good **singer**.
11.	thankful	I am **thankful** for your help.
12.	sadly	We left the playground **sadly**.

Think and Write

Each word is made up of a base word and a suffix. A **suffix** is a word part added to the end of a base word.

BASE WORD		SUFFIX		NEW WORD	MEANING
care	+	ful	=	care**ful**	full of care
slow	+	ly	=	slow**ly**	in a slow way
help	+	er	=	help**er**	one who helps

A. Write **four** Basic Words that have the suffix -*ful*.
B. Write **four** Basic Words that have the suffix -*ly*.
C. Write **four** Basic Words that have the suffix -*er*.

Review	Challenge
13. of **14.** said	**15.** listener **16.** calmly

Independent Practice

Spelling Strategy   A **suffix** is a word part added to the end of a base word. It adds meaning to the base word.

The suffix *-ful* can mean "full of" or "having."
The suffix *-ly* can mean "in a way that is."
The suffix *-er* can mean "a person who."

Phonics Use Basic Words in these exercises.

1–3. Write the word that names the person who does each job.

   1. help   **2.** sing   **3.** farm

4–5. Write the two words with the |ō| sound spelled *ow* or *o*-consonant-*e*.

Vocabulary: Word Clues

Write the Basic Word that fits each clue.

  6. the opposite of *useless*
  7. the opposite of *careless*
  8. the opposite of *unfriendly*
  9. how people feel at Thanksgiving
10. the opposite of *slowly*
11. a person who helps others learn how to read, write, and spell
12. the opposite of *happily*

Challenge Words Write the Challenge Word that means the opposite of each word below. Use your Spelling Dictionary.

13. nervously   **14.** speaker

Review: Spelling Spree

Hidden Words Write the Basic or Review Word that is hidden in each group of letters. Do not let the other words fool you.

Example: l a l s l o w l y *slowly*

1. a s i n g e r e t
2. a f t e a c h e r
3. t h o p e f u l e
4. c o h e l p e r t

5. h o s a i d e s t
6. s t e f a r m e r
7. f u t e t o f
8. s i s a d l y a t

Comparisons Write the Basic Word that best completes each comparison.

9. Tina can run as _____ as a frightened deer.
10. This tool is as _____ as a lamp in the dark.
11. Mr. Jensen felt as _____ as a person whose life had been saved.
12. That baby is as _____ as a puppy that is wagging its tail.
13. Emma is as _____ as someone carrying eggs.
14. Kurt moves as _____ as a sleepy turtle.

How Are You Doing?
List the spelling words that are hard for you. Practice them with a family member.

Proofreading and Writing

Proofread: Spelling and Book Titles Begin the first, last, and each important word of a book title with a capital letter. Underline the book title.

Toni read <u>The Farmer and the Singer of Tales</u>.

Proofread this page from Mia's book report. Find three spelling mistakes, a missing capital letter, and a missing underline. Write the book report correctly.

Title   Miss Nelson Is missing!

Author Harry Allard

About the Book   Miss Nelson leaves, and her class kwikly misses her. They hope for the return af their frendly teacher.

Basic
1. teacher
2. friendly
3. useful
4. careful
5. slowly
6. helper
7. quickly
8. farmer
9. hopeful
10. singer
11. thankful
12. sadly

Review
13. of
14. said

Challenge
15. listener
16. calmly

Write a Book Report

Write two or three sentences about a book you have read. Tell a little about what happened in the book. Try to use three spelling words.

Proofreading Marks
¶ Indent
∧ Add
⌐ Delete
≡ Capital letter
/ Small letter

Proofreading Tip Check that you began the first, last, and each important word of a book title with a capital letter. Did you underline the book title?

Vocabulary Enrichment

Word Builder

Adding Suffixes You can build new words by adding suffixes to a base word. Each suffix adds to the meaning of the base word.

care + ful = careful   "full of care"
care + ful + ly = carefully   "in a careful way"

Add suffixes to the words *help* and *play* to make four new words. Then look up each new word in your Spelling Dictionary. Write the correct meaning next to each new word.

HELP + FUL = (1.)   + LY = (2.)

1.   ?

2.   ?

5.   ?

6.   ?

PLAY + FUL = (3.)   + LY = (4.)

3.   ?

4.   ?

7.   ?

8.   ?

Show What You Know! Write a sentence about school for each new word you made.

Careers

Teaching All the words in the box have something to do with teaching. Write those words to complete this page from a mystery story. Use your Spelling Dictionary.

Summer was over. The month of __(1)__ was here. I waited in my empty classroom for the school year to begin. Suddenly in walked sixteen new __(2)__. They were smart and eager to __(3)__. Should I give them a __(4)__ about their summer reading? I had a better idea. I'd start things slowly. I sent them to the playground for __(5)__.

Spelling Word Link

teacher

students
recess
September
test
learn

Try This CHALLENGE

Write a List Imagine you were teacher for a day. What would you have your class do? Write a list of things to do. Use words from the box.

★★★ **Fact File**

When Sequoya invented an alphabet for the Cherokee language, thousands of Cherokee learned to read vond write their language.

The VCCV Pattern

READ the sentences. **SAY** each bold word.

win | dow

Basic

1.	*invite*	Did you **invite** her to the party?
2.	*Monday*	School starts on **Monday**.
3.	*enjoy*	What games does he **enjoy**?
4.	*until*	We can play outside **until** dark.
5.	*forget*	Did you **forget** your lunch?
6.	*napkin*	My **napkin** fell off my lap.
7.	*window*	Did you shut the **window**?
8.	*Sunday*	I will go to the zoo on **Sunday**.
9.	*garden*	I grow flowers in my **garden**.
10.	*market*	We can buy jam at the **market**.
11.	*basket*	The cats sleep in this **basket**.
12.	*order*	Write the numbers in **order**.

Think and Write

Each word has two syllables. Each word also has the vowel-consonant-consonant-vowel (VCCV) pattern. Divide a word with the VCCV pattern between the two consonants to find the syllables. In each syllable look for spelling patterns you have learned.

VC	CV	VC	CV
Mon	**day**	**for**	**get**

Write the **twelve** Basic Words. Draw a line between the consonants to show the syllables.

Review
13. after 14. under

Challenge
15. expect 16. wisdom

Independent Practice

Spelling Strategy
To spell a word with the VCCV pattern, divide the word between the two consonants. Look for spelling patterns you have learned. Spell the word by syllables.

Phonics Use Basic Words in these exercises.
1. Write the word that has the |ō| sound.
2. Write the word that has the same first syllable as *under*.
3–4. Write the two words that begin with a capital letter.

5–7. Write the words that include these words.
  5. joy   **6.** get   **7.** nap

Vocabulary: Making Inferences Write the Basic Word that matches each clue.
8. Beans and carrots may grow here.
9. People can buy food in this place.
10. You do this when you send away for T-shirts.
11. You do this when you ask someone to a party.
12. You may use this to carry food to a picnic.

Challenge Words Write the Challenge Word that completes each sentence. Use your Spelling Dictionary.
13. He will _____ his friends at two o'clock.
14. Cally knows the _____ of saving money for a gift.

Dictionary

The Schwa Sound Say *useful*. The second syllable has a weak vowel sound called the **schwa** sound. The pronunciation key shows this sound as |ə|. The |ə| sound can be spelled with any vowel.

ə **a**bout, sil**e**nt, penc**i**l, lem**o**n, circ**u**s

Practice Look at each word and its pronunciation below. Write each word. Then underline the letter that spells the schwa sound.

1. second |sĕk′ ənd|
2. hopeful |hōp′ fəl|
3. teacher |tē′ chər|

4. stencil |stĕn′ səl|
5. alive |ə līv′|

Review: Spelling Spree

Classifying Write the Basic Word that names something that belongs in each group of pictures.

6.

7.

8.

9.

10.

How Are You Doing?
Write each spelling word in a sentence. Practice with a partner any words you spelled wrong.

Proofreading and Writing

Proofread for Spelling Proofread this journal entry. Find nine spelling mistakes. Write each word correctly.

April 22

    Last Munday a new boy came to my school. He was sad untill I decided to invit him to my party on Sanday. I also asked him to help me oder my cake at the market. He was happy aftr that. He also seemed to injoy the party. He left a note undr his present. "I will never forgat my good friend," it said.

Proofreading Marks

¶ Indent
∧ Add
⤺ Delete
≡ Capital letter
/ Small letter

Write a Paragraph

Pretend you were invited to visit a character in one of your favorite books. Write a paragraph describing your visit. What was it like? What did you do? Did you meet any other story characters? Try to use three spelling words. Read aloud your paragraph to a friend.

Proofreading Tip

Watch out for letters that have been left out of words.

Vocabulary Enrichment

Word Builder

Multiple Meanings Do you give orders? Are *1, 2,* and *3* in order? *Order* has many meanings.

> **or·der** |ôr′ dər| *n., pl.* **orders 1.** A grouping of things, one after another. **2.** A command or rule. **3.** A portion of food in a restaurant.

Which meaning of *order* is used in each sentence? For each sentence, write the correct meaning from above.

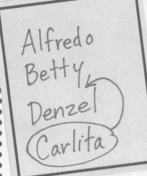

Tricia —
Pick up your room!
Please!
Mom

1. When Mom gives me an <u>order</u>, I follow it.

2. Nira asked the waiter for an <u>order</u> of rice.

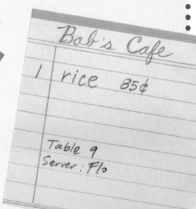

Bob's Cafe

1 rice   85¢

Table 9
Server: Flo

Alfredo
Betty
Denzel
Carlita

3. These words are in ABC <u>order</u>.

Work Together Work with two classmates. Each person takes a turn acting out one of the meanings of *order*, while the other two try to guess which meaning it is.

Language Arts

Invitations When you write an invitation, you need to include the date and the day of the week for the event. Look at the calendar page. Then write the correct day of the week for each date.

May

Sunday	Monday	Tuesday	Wednesday	Thursday	Friday	Saturday
1	2	3	4	5	6	7

____(1)____ , May 5   ____(4)____ , May 4

____(2)____ , May 7   ____(5)____ , May 6

____(3)____ , May 3

Try This
CHALLENGE

You Are Invited Write the words from the box to complete the invitation.

Thursday

You are invited to a picnic. It will take place day after tomorrow, on ___(6)___. If it rains, the picnic will be the next day, on ___(7)___. Please let me know by ___(8)___ (that's tomorrow) if you can come.

⭐⭐⭐ **Fact File**

You might see the letters R.S.V.P. on an invitation. These letters stand for *Répondez s'il vous plaît*, French words that mean "Please reply."

Double Consonants

Read and Say

READ the sentences. **SAY** each bold word.

rabbit

Basic

1.	rabbit	I have a pet **rabbit**.
2.	sudden	The car came to a **sudden** stop.
3.	follow	We will **follow** the trail.
4.	happen	What will **happen** next?
5.	butter	I put **butter** on my toast.
6.	lesson	I had my drum **lesson**.
7.	dollar	What can I buy with a **dollar**?
8.	button	I lost a **button** off my shirt.
9.	pretty	This pond looks so **pretty**!
10.	hello	The friendly clown said **hello**.
11.	letter	I got a **letter** from my friend.
12.	yellow	I like bright **yellow** flowers.

Think and Write

Each word has two syllables and the VCCV pattern. Divide between the consonants to find the syllables. Look for spelling patterns you have learned.

VC | CV	VC | CV
sud | den	**les | son**

Are the two consonants in the VCCV pattern the same or different?

Write the **twelve** Basic Words. Draw a line between the two consonants to show the syllables.

Review	Challenge
13. funny **14.** better	**15.** stubborn **16.** effort

Independent Practice

Spelling Strategy A VCCV word may have a double consonant. Divide between the consonants to find the syllables. Look for spelling patterns you know. Spell the word by syllables.

Phonics Use Basic Words in these exercises.

1–3. Write the three words that have the |ō| sound.

4–8. Write five words by adding a syllable to each syllable below.

    4. sud | ___   **7.** rab | ___

    5. ___ | pen   **8.** ___ | ty

    6. ___ | son

Vocabulary: Word Pairs Write Basic Words to complete each pair of sentences.

  9. You zip up your jacket to close it.
    You _____ your shirt to close it.

10. 6 is a number.
    A is a _____.

11. You put gravy on meat.
    You put _____ on toast.

12. Five nickels are worth one quarter.
    One hundred pennies are worth one _____.

Challenge Words Write the Challenge Word that completes each sentence. Use your Spelling Dictionary.

13. Lori made a special _____ to help her sister.

14. A mule is often a very _____ animal.

Review: Spelling Spree

Word Web 1–10. Find ten Basic or Review Words by matching the syllables. One word has been shown. Write the ten words.

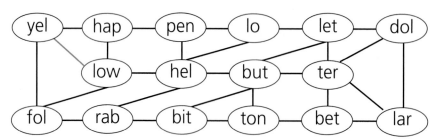

yel — hap — pen — lo — let — dol
low — hel — but — ter
fol — rab — bit — ton — bet — lar

Missing Letters Each missing letter fits in ABC order between the other two letters. Write the missing letters to spell a Basic or Review Word.

Example: r __ t   n __ p   e __ g   s __ u   *soft*

11. e __ g   t __ v   m __ o   m __ o   x __ z

12. r __ t   t __ v   c __ e   c __ e   d __ f   m __ o

13. k __ m   d __ f   r __ t   r __ t   n __ p   m __ o

14. o __ q   q __ s   d __ f   s __ u   s __ u   x __ z

pretty

How Are You Doing?
Write each spelling word as a partner reads it aloud. Did you spell any words wrong?

Proofreading and Writing

Proofread: Spelling and Commas Use a comma to separate the names of a city and a state and to separate the month and the day from the year.

Dallas, Texas

March 30, 1998

Proofread this diary entry. Find three spelling mistakes and two missing commas. Write the entry correctly.

May 8 1998

Dear Diary,

Gina sent me a funy letter and a book from Lima Ohio. The book cost just one doller! I read the story about a rabit.

Basic

1. rabbit
2. sudden
3. follow
4. happen
5. butter
6. lesson
7. dollar
8. button
9. pretty
10. hello
11. letter
12. yellow

Review
13. funny
14. better

Challenge
15. stubborn
16. effort

Proofreading Marks

¶   Indent
∧   Add
⌐   Delete
≡   Capital letter
/   Small letter

Write a Diary Entry

Remember the fable of the tortoise and the hare? Pretend you are the tortoise or the hare. Write a diary entry that tells about your big race. Try to use three spelling words.

Proofreading Tip   **Check that you used commas correctly.**

Phonics and Spelling

Word Builder

Spelling
Word Link
rabbit

The VCCV Pattern Send the tortoise and the hare to the FINISH line. Match the syllables on the path, and write the words you have formed. Hints: All the words have the VCCV pattern like the other spelling words. You form a new word every two steps.

1. _____?_____
2. _____?_____
3. _____?_____
4. _____?_____

5. _____?_____
6. _____?_____
7. _____?_____
8. _____?_____

START

pup mit

pet ten

wal lad

der

let muf fin

lit ter

gal low

lon pil

FINISH

Show What You Know! Write a sentence for each new word you wrote.

Language Arts

Fables All the words in the box have something to do with fables. Write those words to finish this page from a book about fables. Use your Spelling Dictionary.

Spelling Word Link

rabbit

tortoise
hare
brag
fable
finish

Ore well-known ___(1)___ tells about a furry ___(2)___ who liked to ___(3)___ about his speed. Then a slow ___(4)___ offered to race him. During the race the hare ran so far ahead that he took a nap. He awoke just as the tortoise crossed the ___(5)___ line!

Try This CHALLENGE

Yes or No? Is the underlined word used correctly? Write *yes* or *no*.

6. Always start a race at the *finish* line.
7. It is not nice to *brag* about winning.
8. Brush your *hare*, and then tie your shoe.

Fact File

In Aesop's fables, animals talk and act like people. Each story teaches a lesson about how to or how not to behave.

Spelling the |s| Sound in city

|s|
city

Read and Say

READ the sentences. **SAY** each bold word.

Basic

1.	place	I am moving to a new **place**.
2.	city	Many people live in that **city**.
3.	center	He sat in the **center** of the room.
4.	circle	Draw a **circle** on your paper.
5.	nice	Your teacher is **nice**.
6.	once	I caught a fish **once**.
7.	dance	Will you **dance** with me?
8.	circus	She is a clown in the **circus**.
9.	face	He had a smile on his **face**.
10.	certain	I am not **certain** who did it.
11.	pencil	Please write with a **pencil**.
12.	space	My bike can fit in that **space**.

Think and Write

Each word has the |s| sound spelled c.

|s| pla**c**e, **c**ircle

What vowel follows the c in *place*? What vowel follows the first c in *circle*?

A. Write the **eight** Basic Words in which the |s| sound is spelled c followed by e.

B. Write the **four** Basic Words in which the |s| sound is spelled c followed by i.

Review	Challenge
13. same **14.** house	**15.** concert **16.** entrance

Independent Practice

Spelling Strategy   The |s| sound may
be spelled c when the c is followed by i or e.

Phonics Use Basic Words in these exercises.
1. Write the word that starts with the sound you hear
   at the beginning of *one*.
2. Write the word that rhymes with *ice*.
3–4. Write the two words in which c spells the |k| sound.
5–7. Write *place*. Then write two other words that
   rhyme with *place*.

Vocabulary: Context Sentences
Write the Basic Word that completes
each sentence.
8. James likes the country,
   and I like the _____.
9. I want to draw that building,
   so I need a _____.
10. We saw some people sing
    and _____ in City Park.
11. She lives near here in the
    _____ of the city.
12. It is Friday, so I am _____
    the library is open.

Challenge Words Write the
Challenge Word that completes
each sentence. Use your Spelling Dictionary.
13. The town band has a _____ in the park every week.
14. This store has one _____ on Milk Street and another
    on Center Street.

Review: Spelling Spree

Hink Pinks Write a Basic or Review Word that fits each clue and rhymes with the given word.

Example: a wet light _____ **lamp** *damp*

1. a ribbon store **lace** _____
2. good seasoning _____ **spice**
3. something you play again _____ **game**
4. your turn to move to music _____ **chance**
5. a store in which masks are bought _____ **place**
6. the contest to reach Mars first _____ **race**
7. a small animal that stays inside _____ **mouse**

Name Game Write the Basic Word hidden in each name. Look for the c's to find the words. Use all small letters in your answers.

Example: Dr. Alf A. Celebrity *face*

8. Miss Pen Cilia
9. Mr. Mercir Cleats
10. Mrs. Perci R. Cusa
11. Mrs. Traci T. Yang
12. Mr. Onion C. Eddy
13. Mrs. Lancer Tainer
14. Miss Millicent Errs

Dr. Alf A. Celebrity

☑ **How Are You Doing?**
Write your spelling words in ABC order. Practice with a family member any words you spelled wrong.

Proofreading and Writing

Basic

1. place
2. city
3. center
4. circle
5. nice
6. once
7. dance
8. circus
9. face
10. certain
11. pencil
12. space
Review
13. same
14. house
Challenge
15. concert
16. entrance

Proofread: Spelling and Greetings and Closings
Begin the first word of a greeting or a closing with a capital letter. Put a comma after a greeting or a closing.

GREETING: Dear Juan,   CLOSING: Your cousin,

Proofread this letter. Find three spelling mistakes, a missing capital letter, and a missing comma. Write the letter correctly.

June 11, 1998

dear Ms. Rossi

I have moved to a new cite. I live

in a nice houes in the senter of Salem.

Sincerely yours,

Liza Tan

Proofreading Marks

¶ Indent
∧ Add
✌ Delete
≡ Capital letter
/ Small letter

Write a Letter

Pretend you live in a city on the moon. Write a letter to a friend or family member telling what the city is like. Try to use three spelling words.

Check that you began the first word of a greeting or a closing with a capital letter. Be sure to put a comma after a greeting or a closing.

Proofreading Tip

Vocabulary Enrichment

Word Builder

Spelling Word Link

nice

Using a Thesaurus "Be nice." "Have a nice day!"
Nice has many meanings, such as "kind" or "pleasant." Try to use exact words for *nice*. It makes your meaning clearer.

Find the word *nice* in each speech balloon. Write an exact word to replace it. Use your Thesaurus.

What a nice day!

1. ___?___

The police officer gave us nice directions.

2. ___?___

Aren't the people nice here?

3. ___?___

Show What You Know! Write three sentences about your favorite city. Use the three words you found for *nice*.

Social Studies

The City All the words in the box have something to do with the city. Write those words to finish this page from a personal narrative. Use your Spelling Dictionary.

Spelling Word Link

city

apartment
hotel
subway
taxi
skyscraper

> This was my family's first trip to the city. We made plans as we rode down the street and gazed out the __(1)__ window. First, we checked into our __(2)__. Next, we rode the __(3)__ under the city to visit Aunt Danice. She lives in an __(4)__ on the fiftieth floor of a __(5)__.

Try This
CHALLENGE

Write a Post Card Make a post card of a city you have visited or would like to visit. Draw a picture on the front. Then write a message for a friend on the back, telling about the city. Use words from the box.

Fact File

The Empire State Building in New York City has 102 floors. It was the tallest building in the world from 1931 to 1972.

30 Review: Units 25–29

Unit 25 The Prefixes re- and un- pp. 156–161

unfair	rewrite	unhappy
retell	unwrap	reuse

unhappy

Spelling Strategy   A **prefix** is a word part added to the beginning of a base word. **Re-** and **un-** are prefixes.

Write the word that means the opposite of each word below.

1. wrap   **2.** fair   **3.** happy

Write the word that completes each sentence.
4. Do not throw out that cup. You can _____ it.
5. I did not hear the story. Please _____ it.
6. Mom cannot read your note. Please _____ it.

Unit 26   The Suffixes -ful, -ly, -er   pp. 162–167

useful	teacher	friendly
quickly	hopeful	singer

teacher

Spelling Strategy   A **suffix** is a word part added to the end of a base word. Some words have the suffix **-ful**, **-ly**, or **-er**.

Write the words to complete the paragraph.
Our ___**(7)**___ invited a famous ___**(8)**___ to perform for our class today. She was very ___**(9)**___, and she taught us many ___**(10)**___ things about writing songs. After class, she had to leave ___**(11)**___, but we are ___**(12)**___ that she will visit us again.

win dow

Unit 27   The VCCV Pattern   pp. 168–173

napkin	enjoy	until
garden	basket	window

Spelling Strategy   Divide a word with the VCCV pattern between the two consonants to find the syllables.

Write the word that has the same first syllable as each word below.

13. winter   **14.** enter   **15.** garbage

Write the word that completes each sentence.

16. You may need a _____ when you eat that chicken.

17. Doug cannot play catch _____ this afternoon.

18. Nina uses a _____ to carry her groceries.

Unit 28   Double Consonants   pp. 174–179

sudden	lesson	follow
dollar	letter	hello

rabbit

Spelling Strategy   A VCCV word may have double consonants. Divide between the consonants to find the syllables.

Write the word with the same second syllable as each word below.

19. bitter   **20.** hidden   **21.** pillow

Write the word that belongs in each group.

22. penny, dime, _____   **24.** school, study, _____

23. hi, good morning, _____

|s|
city

circle	place	center
circus	pencil	dance

Spelling Strategy   The |s| sound may be spelled
c when the **c** is followed by an **i** or an **e**.

Write the word that completes each sentence.
25. Cory and I like to see the clowns at the _____.
26. Clowns often perform at the _____ of the ring.
27. Some clowns juggle, and some clowns _____.
28. That one jumps up and down in _____.
29. Cory brought a _____ to draw a clown.
30. We laughed when the clowns danced in a _____.

Challenge Words   Units 25–29   pp. 156–185

stubborn	listener	unimportant
expect	entrance	

**Write the word that has almost the same meaning as
each word below.**
31. await
32. opening

Write the word that completes each sentence.
33. If I have a problem, I talk to Julie because she is a
     good _____.
34. Mom cannot make Joshua eat his spinach because
     he is very _____.
35. Whether or not we wax the car today is _____.

Spelling-Meaning Strategy

Word Forms

A word may have a sound that is spelled in an unexpected way. Other words in its family usually spell that sound in the same way because they are related in meaning. Read this paragraph.

> I usually **place** my house key on a hook in the kitchen when I come home. I **misplaced** my key on Monday, and I still cannot find it.

Think How are *place* and *misplaced* alike in meaning? How are *place* and *misplaced* alike in spelling? Here are words in the *place* family.

place	placing	replace
misplaced	placed	placement

Apply and Extend

Complete these activities on another sheet of paper.

1. Look up the meaning of each word in the Word Box above in your Spelling Dictionary. Write six sentences, using one word in each sentence.

2. With a partner list words related to *ice*, *peace*, and *trace*. Then look in your Spelling-Meaning Index beginning on page 272. Add any other words in these families to your list.

Literature and Writing

based on

The Monster in the Mail Box

by Sheila Gordon

Julius ordered a monster from a mail order company in *The Monster in the Mail Box*. Julius might have written the letter below.

38 East Third Street
Tulsa, OK 74103
May 10, 1997

Dear Grammie,

Remember the monster I ordered? When it finally came, it was just a rubbery thing that popped right away. I made the company return my money. Then I bought a monster book. The stories and pictures are very scary.

Love,

Julius

Think and Discuss

1. To whom did Julius write the letter?

2. What information did Julius tell Grammie?

3. Why would this information interest her?

4. Name and explain the five parts of a letter. See the model on page 250.

The Writing Process

A Letter

Do you have a special message for a friend or a family member? You could write a letter! Just follow the Guidelines and use the Writing Process.

1 Prewriting
- Make a list of your friends or family members. Choose one person to write to.

2 Draft
- Write everything you want to say. Don't worry about mistakes now.

3 Revise
- Did you include interesting details?
- Is there anything you want to add?

4 Proofread
- Did you use commas correctly?
- Did you spell all names and addresses correctly?

5 Publish
- Mail a clean copy of your letter! Put it in an envelope. Add the address and a stamp.

· · · · · **Guidelines for Writing Letters**

✓ Include the five parts of a friendly letter: the heading, a greeting, the body, a closing, and your signature.
✓ Use details to make your letter interesting.

Composition Words

unlike
quickly
useful
Monday
order
happy
dollar
certain

Street
Town, State
Zip

Vowel Sounds in tooth and cook

Read and Say

READ the sentences. **SAY** each bold word.

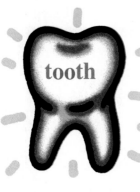

tooth

Basic

1.	tooth	I lost a baby **tooth**.
2.	chew	My dog will **chew** this bone.
3.	grew	The corn **grew** tall.
4.	cook	The **cook** needed a big pot.
5.	shoe	I have to tie my **shoe**.
6.	blue	The sky is very **blue**.
7.	boot	Some snow got inside my **boot**.
8.	flew	A plane **flew** over my house.
9.	shook	We **shook** hands when we met.
10.	balloon	I want a green **balloon**.
11.	drew	Who **drew** this picture?
12.	spoon	There is a **spoon** on the table.

Think and Write

Each word has the vowel sound in *tooth* or the vowel sound in *cook*. These sounds are shown as |o͞o| and |o͝o|.

|o͞o| t**oo**th, ch**ew** |o͝o| c**oo**k

How is the |o͞o| sound spelled in the Elephant Words?

A. Write **six** Basic Words that have |o͞o| or |o͝o| spelled *oo*.
B. Write **four** Basic Words that have |o͞o| spelled *ew*.
C. Write **two** Basic Words that have |o͞o| spelled other ways.

Review		Challenge	
13. good	**14.** soon	**15.** loose	**16.** crooked

Independent Practice

Spelling Strategy When you hear the |o͞o| sound, as in *tooth* or *chew*, remember that it may be spelled with the pattern *oo* or *ew*.

The |o͝o| sound, as in *cook*, may be spelled with the pattern *oo*.

Phonics Use Basic Words in this exercise.

1–5. Write the five words that have these consonants.

    1. gr _____   **4.** fl _____

    2. dr _____   **5.** sh _____ k

    3. ch _____

Vocabulary: Classifying Write the Basic Word that belongs in each group.

    6. fork, knife, _____

    7. firefighter, bus driver, _____

    8. kite, paper plane, _____

    9. umbrella, raincoat, _____

    10. toothbrush, toothpaste, _____

Elephant Words Write the Elephant Word that completes each sentence.

    11. Last week Dr. Valdez painted the walls of his office a light _____.

    12. Give Hiromi time to put on her other sock and _____, and then we will leave.

Challenge Words Write the Challenge Word that means the opposite of each word. Use your Spelling Dictionary.

    13. tight   **14.** straight

Review: Spelling Spree

Word Web 1–7. Find seven Basic and Review Words by matching the letters. Write the words. One word has been shown.

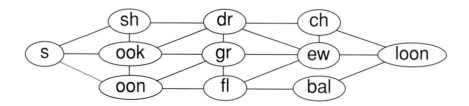

Hink Pinks Write the Basic or Review Word that fits each clue and rhymes with the given word.

Example: worried thief _____ **crook** *shook*

8. logs that will burn well _____ **wood**
9. paste that is the color of the sky _____ **glue**
10. silverware for an astronaut **moon** _____
11. footwear for boating **canoe** _____
12. a small place for fixing food _____ **nook**
13. footwear for an owl in the rain **hoot** _____
14. a place to clean your teeth _____ **booth**

How Are You Doing?

List the spelling words that are hard for you. Practice them with a family member.

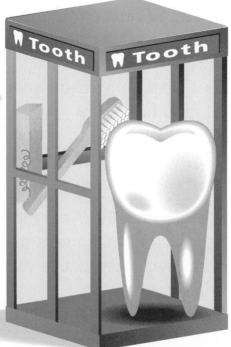

Proofreading and Writing

Proofread: Spelling and Abbreviations An **abbreviation** is the short form of a word. Begin an abbreviation of a person's title with a capital letter. End it with a period.

Dr. Rossi   **Mr.** Tobin   **Ms.** Yuan   **Mrs.** Ramos

Proofread this page from Ruby's story. Find three spelling mistakes, a missing capital letter, and a missing period. Write the page correctly.

I tripped over a shoo and broke a

tooth. When dr Cox checked it, he said he

would soone make it as gud as new.

Basic
1. tooth
2. chew
3. grew
4. cook
5. shoe
6. blue
7. boot
8. flew
9. shook
10. balloon
11. drew
12. spoon

Review
13. good
14. soon

Challenge
15. loose
16. crooked

Proofreading Marks

¶ Indent
∧ Add
⌐ Delete
≡ Capital letter
/ Small letter

Write a Description

Write about a time you went to the dentist. What happened during your visit? What was your doctor's name? Whom else did you meet? Try to use three spelling words and an abbreviation. Share your writing with a friend.

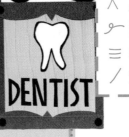

DENTIST

Proofreading Tip   **Check that you wrote abbreviations correctly.**

Rhyming Words

Words with $|\overline{oo}|$ **and** $|\breve{oo}|$ Match the words on the teeth with the sounds on the toothbrushes. Write the words under the correct sounds.

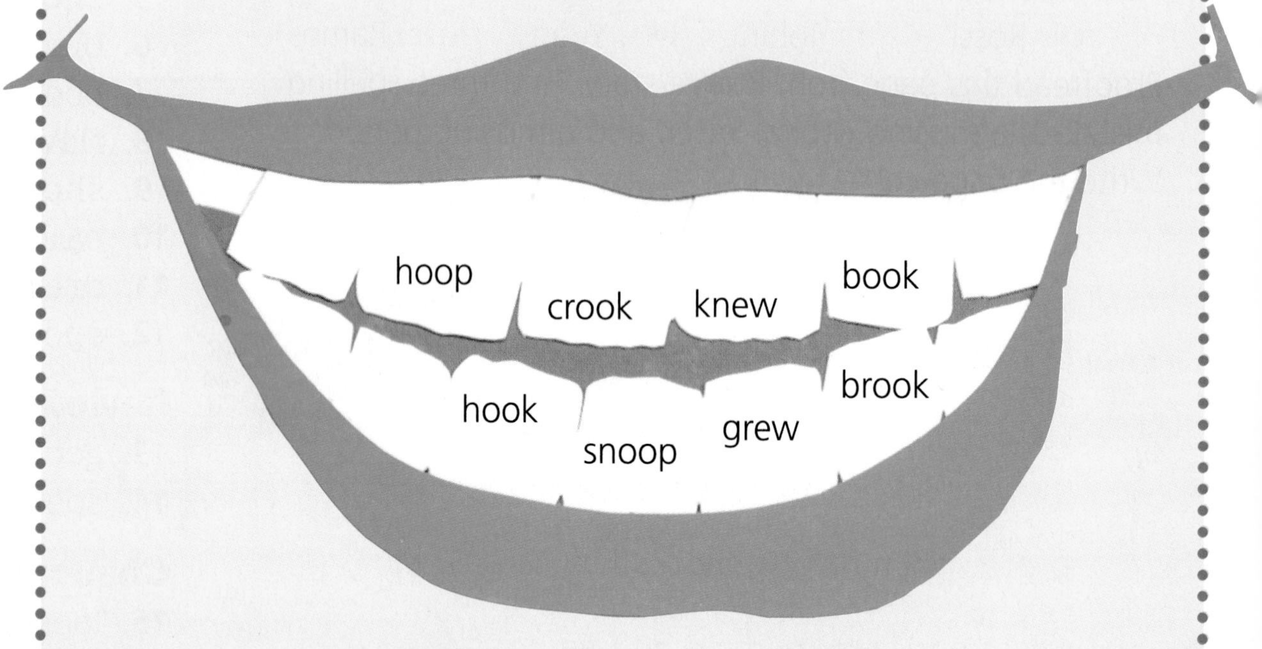

hoop

crook   knew   book

brook

hook   grew

snoop

$|\overline{oo}|$ $|\breve{oo}|$

1.	?
2.	?
3.	?
4.	?

5.	?
6.	?
7.	?
8.	?

Show What You Know! Write rhyming sentences, using at least four of the words.

Health

Visiting the Dentist All the words in the box have something to do with visiting the dentist. Write those words to complete this letter. Use your Spelling Dictionary.

Spelling Word Link

tooth

dentist
gums
floss
cavity
x-ray

June 11, 1998

Dear Grandma,

I had my teeth checked today. Dr. Lieu, my __(1)__, took pictures of them. One __(2)__ showed a dark spot on a back tooth. For me, having only one __(3)__ is very good. Cleaning between my teeth with dental __(4)__ has worked! When I brush my teeth now, my __(5)__ do not hurt. I'm sending you a picture so you can see my smile.

Love,
Rosa

Try This CHALLENGE

Make a Poster Make a poster about taking good care of your teeth. Draw pictures, or cut pictures out of magazines. Hang your poster at school or at home.

Fact File

Your baby teeth fall out because their roots dissolve. Then permanent teeth can push through the gums and fill empty spaces.

The Vowel Sound in bought

Read and Say

READ the sentences. SAY each bold word.

|ô|
bought

Basic

1.	caught	How many fish were **caught**?
2.	thought	I **thought** you were home.
3.	bought	Is that the cat you **bought**?
4.	laugh	The clowns make me **laugh**.
5.	through	We walked **through** the park.
6.	enough	Did you eat **enough** fish?
7.	fought	We **fought** to change the rules.
8.	daughter	Is that girl your **daughter**?
9.	taught	My dad **taught** me to swim.
10.	brought	We **brought** chairs to sit on.
11.	ought	You **ought** to go before dark.
12.	cough	The nurse heard him **cough**.

Think and Write

Most of the words have the vowel sound in *bought*. This sound is shown as |ô|.

|ô| b**ough**t, c**augh**t

What sounds are spelled with these patterns in the Elephant Words?

A. Write **five** Basic Words with the |ô| sound spelled *ough*.
B. Write **three** Basic Words with the |ô| sound spelled *augh*.
C. Write the **four** Basic Words in which *ough* or *augh* spell other sounds.

Review
13. teeth   14. was

Challenge
15. sought   16. naughty

Independent Practice

Spelling Strategy When you hear the |ô| sound, as in *bought* or *caught*, remember that it can be spelled with the pattern *ough* or *augh*.

Phonics Use Basic Words in this exercise.

1–4. Each word below is missing four letters that spell the |ô| sound. Write the four words correctly.

1. br __ __ __ __ t   **3.** b __ __ __ __ t

2. f __ __ __ __ t   **4.** t __ __ __ __ t

Vocabulary: Context Sentences Write the Basic Word that completes each sentence.

5. Mr. Pascal's _____ lost her cat Flint last week.

6. Kari said that she _____ to look for Flint.

7. I _____ that the Pascals should offer a reward.

8. Randy saw Flint sitting on a wall, and he _____ him.

Elephant Words Write the Elephant Word that completes each sentence.

9. My dog Blitz is so funny. He makes us _____.

10. There are _____ bones to last Blitz all week.

11. After I walked Blitz in the rain, I began to sneeze and _____.

12. I hope Blitz will not sneak _____ the fence again.

Challenge Words Write the Challenge Word that means the same as each clue below. Use your Spelling Dictionary.

13. bad   **14.** looked for

Dictionary

Spelling Table How can you look up *cough* if you do not know how to spell the |f| sound? Turn to the **spelling table**, which shows the different ways a sound can be spelled. Check each spelling for |f| until you find *cough*.

Sound	Spellings	Sample Words
|f|	**f, ff, gh**	**f**unny, o**ff**, enou**gh**

Practice Write the correct spelling for each word below. Use the spelling table above and your Spelling Dictionary.

1. ru + |f| + le
2. tou + |f|
3. scar + |f|
4. be + |f| + ore

Review: Spelling Spree

Code Breaker Some Basic and Review Words are written in the code below. Write the words.

⟨ = augh	☽ = e	∞ = n	↑ = t
● = c	□ = l	⊗ = ough	▱ = th

Example: ↑ ⊗   *tough*

5. ● ⊗
6. ↑ ⟨ ↑
7. ▱ ⊗ ↑
8. □ ⟨
9. ↑ ☽ ☽ ▱
10. ☽ ∞ ⊗
11. ⊗ ↑
12. ● ⟨ ↑

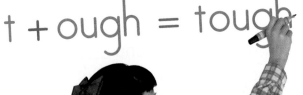

t + ough = tough

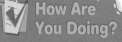

How Are You Doing?
Write each spelling word in a sentence. Practice with a partner any words you spelled wrong.

Proofreading and Writing

Basic

1. caught
2. thought
3. bought
4. laugh
5. through
6. enough
7. fought
8. daughter
9. taught
10. brought
11. ought
12. cough

Review

13. teeth
14. was

Challenge

15. sought
16. naughty

Proofread for Spelling Proofread this ad. Find six spelling mistakes. Write the words correctly.

> My dauter lost the new dog that she had bout. When she broght him home, he fot with a cat. He wuz last seen running throo the park. If you have caught him, please call 999-1100.
>
> PARK

Proofreading Marks

¶ Indent
∧ Add
⌐ Delete
≡ Capital letter
/ Small letter

Write a List

Write a list of things someone could do to find a lost pet. Try to use three spelling words. Put your list up on a bulletin board.

Proofreading Tip

Read what you have written aloud to a friend.

Word Builder

Spelling Word Link

laugh

roar
chuckle
giggle
snicker

Using a Thesaurus Exact words tell more about what you mean. Write the exact word for *laugh* that best fits each sentence. Use your Thesaurus.

1. I always blush and <u>laugh</u> when I'm nervous.
2. Do not <u>laugh in a mean way</u> at someone's mistake.
3. Dad will <u>laugh quietly</u> at a funny TV show.
4. My uncles <u>laugh very loudly</u> at funny jokes.

Ho Ho

Hee Hee

Ha

Ha

woof!

Show What You Know! Write two sentences about the picture. Use an exact word for *laugh* in each sentence.

Vocabulary Enrichment

Life Skills

A Lost Pet All the words in the box have something to do with a lost pet. Write those words from the box to complete this notice. Use your Spelling Dictionary.

Spelling Word Link

sought

notice
search
reward
worry
collar

Come Back, Little Fluffy, Come Back!

My little cat is gone. Will you help me __(1)__ for her? I am offering a twenty-dollar __(2)__ for finding her. Her name is Fluffy. It is printed on her __(3)__. I will __(4)__ about her until she is found. Please respond to this __(5)__ by calling 555-4838. Thank you!

Try This CHALLENGE

Yes or No? Is the underlined word used correctly? Write *yes* or *no*.

6. Jesse put a <u>notice</u> on the bulletin board.
7. Yellow is my favorite <u>collar</u>.
8. Amber got a <u>reward</u> when she didn't do her chores.

Fact File

An ID tag lists a pet's name and its owner's address and phone number. A lost pet that wears an ID tag may be found more quickly.

Words That End with er or le

Read and Say

READ the sentences. **SAY** each bold word.

|ər|
October

Basic

1.	summer	It is hot in the **summer.**
2.	winter	How cold is it in **winter**?
3.	little	My puppy is very **little**.
4.	October	We took a trip last **October**.
5.	travel	We will **travel** far.
6.	color	Blue is a **color** that I love.
7.	apple	He ate the **apple**.
8.	able	Who is **able** to carry the box?
9.	November	We will be busy in **November**.
10.	ever	How did you **ever** find me?
11.	later	I will have to do it **later** on.
12.	purple	We ran out of **purple** paint.

Think and Write

Each word ends with a schwa sound + *r* or a schwa sound + *l*. The schwa sound is shown as |ə|.

|ər| summ**er** |əl| litt**le**

How are these sounds spelled in the Elephant Words?

A. Write **seven** Basic Words that end with the |ər| sounds. Remember the Elephant Word.

B. Write **five** Basic Words that end with the |əl| sounds. Remember the Elephant Word.

Review	Challenge
13. flower **14.** people	**15.** thermometer **16.** icicle

Independent Practice

Spelling Strategy Remember that, in words with more than one syllable,

the final |ər| sounds are often spelled *er*

the final |əl| sounds can be spelled *le*.

Phonics Use Basic Words in these exercises.

1–2. Write the word that rhymes with each word below.

> **1.** never   **2.** stable

3–4. Write the two words with capital letters.

5–7. Write the three words with double consonants.

Vocabulary: Word Pairs Write the Basic Word that completes each pair of sentences.

> **8.** It is hot in summer. It is cold in _____.
>
> **9.** Yellow and blue make green. Red and blue make _____.

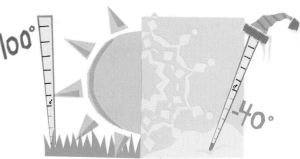

10. *Faster* is the opposite of *slower*. *Earlier* is the opposite of _____.

Elephant Words Write the Elephant Word that fits each clue.

11. red or blue   **12.** to go from city to city

Challenge Words Write the Challenge Word that completes each sentence. Use your Spelling Dictionary.

13. Look at the _____ to see how cold it is.

14. Jennifer used an _____ for her snowman's nose.

Dictionary

Stressed Syllables Say *apple*. Notice that the first syllable is said more strongly, or **stressed**. The dictionary pronunciation shows this syllable in dark print followed by an **accent mark** (′).

> **ap·ple** |ăp′ əl| *n., pl.* **apples** A red-skinned fruit.

Practice Write each word. Circle the stressed syllable. Use your Spelling Dictionary.

Example: later (lat)er

1. little   **3.** flower   **5.** happen
2. forget   **4.** able

Review: Spelling Spree

Puzzle Play Write a Basic or Review Word to fit each clue. Circle the letter that would appear in the box. Write those letters in order to spell two words that name something that stays green all year.

Example: a red fruit __ __ □ __ __ ap(p)le
   6. a rose □ __ __ __ __ __
   7. the same as *small* __ □ __ __ __ __
   8. a color __ __ □ __ __ __
   9. not *sooner* __ __ □ __ __
  10. the month after October __ __ __ __ __ __ __ __ □
  11. more than one person __ □ __ __ __ __
  12. a hot season __ __ __ __ □ __
Mystery Words: __ __ __ __ __ __ __

Proofreading and Writing

Proofread for Spelling Proofread this journal entry. Find seven spelling mistakes. Write the words correctly.

Sept. 18

I hope to be abel to go aple picking before wintr. It is aver so much fun! We could travle to a farm in Octber when the leaves change coler. November is too late!

Proofreading Marks

¶ Indent
∧ Add
⌐ Delete
≡ Capital letter
/ Small letter

Write a Fashion Guide

Write two paragraphs that tell how people in your town dress in summer and winter. Try to use three spelling words. Draw a picture for each paragraph. Share your guide with a friend.

Proofreading Tip

Check for letters that have been switched in words.

Word Builder

Spelling Word Link

purple

crimson
aqua
navy
beige

Using a Thesaurus A color can have different shades. These words name two shades of purple.

violet "bluish purple"   **lavender** "light purple"

When you write or speak, try to use exact words to describe colors. The words in the box are color words.

Write a color word from the box to replace each group of underlined words. Use your Thesaurus.

1. I like my <u>dark blue</u> pants.
2. Those apples are <u>bright red</u>.
3. The <u>light greenish-blue</u> water looked cool.
4. Reggie has a <u>light yellowish-brown</u> jacket.

Show What You Know! Write two sentences that describe this summer scene. Try to use at least one color word from the box in each sentence.

Science

Seasons All the words in the box have something to do with seasons. Write those words to finish this page from a magazine article. Use your Spelling Dictionary.

Spelling
Word Link

October

January
February
July
August
December

My Favorite Seasons

To me, each month is special. The first and last months of the year, __(1)__ and __(2)__, are cold and wintery. But by the end of __(3)__, I'm sick of winter. I like the summer months, __(4)__ and __(5)__, when we can go swimming!

Try This

CHALLENGE

Yes or No? Write *yes* or *no* to answer each question.

6. Is the first day of the year in July?
7. Is the last day of the year in December?
8. Is August in the winter in the United States?

⭐ **Fact File**

Early Native Americans believed that a warm fall was a gift from a kindly wind god. Warm fall weather is called Indian Summer.

Words That Begin with a or be

READ the sentences. **SAY** each bold word.

|bĭ|
behind

Basic

1.	*begin*	Class will **begin** soon.
2.	*again*	I will read this book **again**.
3.	*around*	We will run **around** the park.
4.	*before*	Please call **before** you come.
5.	*away*	The fox ran **away**.
6.	*about*	The book is **about** two friends.
7.	*alive*	The old tree was still **alive**.
8.	*because*	We cheered **because** we won.
9.	*ahead*	Who is in line **ahead** of me?
10.	*between*	Draw a line **between** the dots.
11.	*behind*	The dog hid **behind** the chair.
12.	*ago*	We ate an hour **ago**.

Think and Write

Each Basic Word has two syllables. The first syllable has the |ə| sound or the |bĭ| sounds.

|ə| **a**gain |bĭ| **be**fore

Is the first or the second syllable stressed in each Basic Word?

A. Write **seven** Basic Words that begin with the |ə| sound.

B. Write **five** Basic Words that begin with the |bĭ| sounds.

Review	Challenge
13. they **14.** want	**15.** among **16.** beyond

Independent Practice

Spelling Strategy In two-syllable words, the unstressed |ə| sound at the beginning of a word may be spelled *a*. The unstressed |bĭ| sounds may be spelled *be*.

Phonics Use Basic Words in these exercises.
1. Write the word with the |ō| sound.
2. Write the word with the |z| sound.
3–4. Write the two words with the |ou| sound, as in *found*.
5–6. Write the two words that have the |ī| sound.

Vocabulary: Context Sentences Write the Basic Word that completes each sentence.

7. My family went _____ on vacation last summer.
8. Just _____ we got to the beach, Dad got lost.
9. "Beach Road should _____ right here," he said.
10. "Go straight _____ for two blocks," a woman said.
11. Finally, we saw Beach Road _____ Plum Street and Marsh Lane.
12. Now we will know where to turn when we come back _____.

Challenge Words Write the Challenge Word that completes each sentence. Use your Spelling Dictionary.
13. Look left _____ the library to see the bus stop.
14. Look _____ the branches to find our tree house.

Review: Spelling Spree

Syllable Addition Write seven Basic Words by adding *a* or *be* to the words below.

Example: low   *below*

1. go

2. head

3. round

4. hind

5. cause

6. way

7. live

Word Maze 8–14. Begin at the arrow, and follow the Word Maze to find seven Basic or Review Words. Write the words in order.

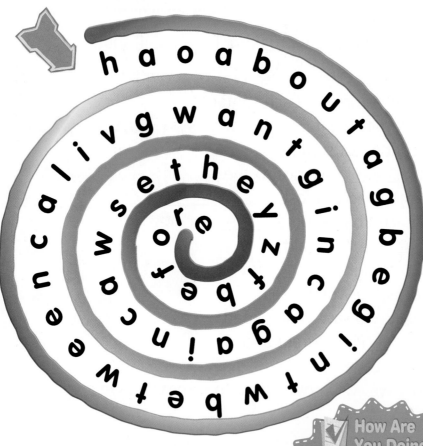

How Are You Doing?
Write your spelling words in ABC order. Practice with a family member any words you spelled wrong.

Proofreading and Writing

Proofread: Spelling and Abbreviations Each day of the week has an abbreviation. It begins with a capital letter and ends with a period. (See page 247 of the Student's Handbook for abbreviations of other days.)

Monday **Mon.** Tuesday **Tues.**

Proofread this list of things to do. Find three spelling mistakes, a missing capital letter, and a missing period. Write the list correctly.

1. begin
2. again
3. around
4. before
5. away
6. about
7. alive
8. because
9. ahead
10. between
11. behind
12. ago

Review
13. they
14. want

Challenge
15. among
16. beyond

Mon

Tell Tim to turn left befor Elm St., behind the store.

tues.

Ask the class if thay want to go to the museum agan.

Proofreading Marks

¶ Indent
∧ Add
ℛ Delete
≡ Capital letter
/ Small letter

Write a List of Things to Do

Things to do

Plan ahead. Write a list of things to do in the next few days. Use abbreviations for the days of the week. Try to use three spelling words.

Proofreading Tip

Check that you began abbreviations of each day of the week with a capital letter and ended them with a period.

Vocabulary Enrichment

Word Builder

The Syllables a and be Build more words that begin with the unstressed syllables *a* and *be*. Follow each path. Match the beginning syllables with the words to make new words.

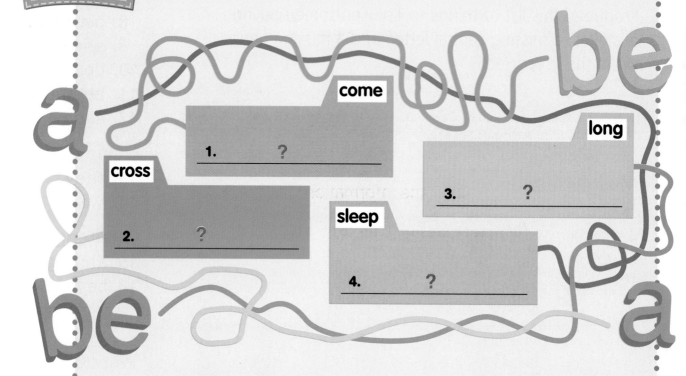

come

1. _____ ?

long

3. _____ ?

cross

2. _____ ?

sleep

4. _____ ?

Now write a sentence with each new word. Use your Spelling Dictionary to check the word's meaning.

Work Together Work with a friend to brainstorm some other words that begin with the unstressed syllables *a* or *be*. Check your words in a dictionary. How many words did you come up with?

Life Skills

Following Directions All the words in the box have something to do with following directions. Write those words to finish this advice column. Use your Spelling Dictionary.

Spelling Word Link

begin

copy
complete
repeat
directions
check

> Dear Lost in Amarillo,
>   If you do not know where a place is, ask for ___**(1)**___. Be sure they are ___**(2)**___. Then ___**(3)**___ your memory, and ___**(4)**___ them aloud. If you have a pencil and paper, ___**(5)**___ the information. I hope you get better at finding your way.
>   Aunt Annie

Try This CHALLENGE

Write a Note Imagine you are about to visit a place you have never been before. Write a note to yourself about what you should do to make sure you don't get lost. Use words from the box.

★★★ Fact File

A compass looks like a clock but tells direction, not time. The needle always points north. Knowing this, you can also tell where south, east, and wnest are.

Read and Say

READ the sentences. SAY each bold word.

she   is

she's

Basic

1.	*I'm*	I hope that **I'm** right.
2.	*he's*	Tell Scott that **he's** funny.
3.	*aren't*	We **aren't** saving these boxes.
4.	*couldn't*	The puppy **couldn't** jump high.
5.	*won't*	The knife **won't** cut the rope.
6.	*o'clock*	The show ends at one **o'clock**.
7.	*wouldn't*	I **wouldn't** walk up there.
8.	*weren't*	The trains **weren't** on time.
9.	*she's*	Ask Emma if **she's** warm.
10.	*wasn't*	I **wasn't** the last to leave.
11.	*I'd*	I think **I'd** like some help.
12.	*shouldn't*	The dog **shouldn't** be in here.

Think and Write

Each word is a contraction. A **contraction** is a short way of saying or writing two or more words. An apostrophe takes the place of letters that are dropped.

I am → **I'm**   are not → **aren't**

What are the contractions for *will not* and *of the clock*?

Write the **twelve** Basic Words.

Review
13. can't   14. isn't

Challenge
15. let's   16. who's

Independent Practice

Spelling Strategy   A **contraction** is a short way of saying or writing two or more words. An apostrophe takes the place of one or more letters.

Phonics   Use Basic Words in these exercises.

1–3. Write the three words that have a silent *l*.

4–5. Write the two words that begin with a capital letter.

Vocabulary: Context Sentences   Write the Basic Words that are contractions for the underlined words.

6. There <u>are not</u> many parts in the play.

7. Yoko likes machines, so <u>she is</u> doing the lighting.

8. Emily <u>was not</u> here for practice today.

9. The posters <u>were not</u> ready yesterday.

10. Marco is in the play, and <u>he is</u> sure his parents will come to it.

Elephant Words   Write the Elephant Word that completes each sentence.

11. The play will start at seven _____.

12. The tickets _____ go on sale until Tuesday.

Challenge Words   Write the Challenge Words that are contractions for the underlined words. Use your Spelling Dictionary.

13. When everyone is here, <u>let us</u> start practicing.

14. Do you know <u>who is</u> in charge of the music?

Review: Spelling Spree

Puzzle Play Write the Basic or Review Words that are the contractions for the words below. Circle the letters that would appear in the boxes. Write those letters in order. They will spell a mystery word.

Example: I am i ' ⬚m I'ⓜ

1. cannot c ⬚a n ' t
2. would not w o ⬚w l d n ' t
3. should not s h o u l ⬚d n ' t
4. is not ⬚i s n ' t
5. were not w ⬚e r e n ' t
6. will not w o ⬚n ' t
7. of the clock o ' c l o ⬚c k
8. are not a r ⬚e n ' t

Mystery Word: _ _ _ _ _ _ _ _

Ending Match Replace the second piece of each numbered puzzle with a new puzzle piece to make a Basic Word. Write the Basic Words.

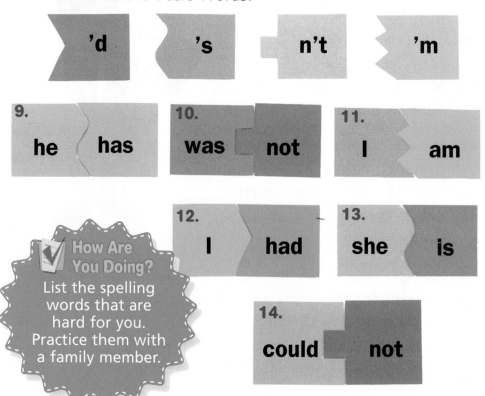

'd   's   n't   'm

9. he / has
10. was / not
11. I / am
12. I / had
13. she / is
14. could / not

How Are You Doing?
List the spelling words that are hard for you. Practice them with a family member.

Proofreading and Writing

Proofread: Spelling and Using I and me Use *I* as the subject of a sentence. Use *me* as the object of a verb. Name yourself last when you talk about another person and yourself.

<blockquote>

Al and **I** are late.
Mom saw **you** and **me**.

</blockquote>

Proofread this note. Find three spelling mistakes and two places where *I* or *me* is not used correctly. Write the note correctly.

> Sofia, Dad is'nt home yet. Me and you can't ride to the play with Becky. She will meet you and I there at two oclock. We wont be late.

Proofreading Marks

¶ Indent
∧ Add
ߊ Delete
≡ Capital letter
/ Small letter

Write a Skit

Choose a story, and rewrite an exciting part as a skit. Make sure the characters in the skit use the words *I* and *me*. Try to use three spelling words. Practice your play with friends.

I
M E

Proofreading Tip

Remember, a computer spell check won't tell you if you have used *I* and *me* correctly.

Vocabulary Enrichment

Word Builder

Homophones Some contractions are homophones. *You're* is a contraction for "you are." *Your* means "belonging to you."

You're sure that **your** aunt is coming today.

Write *you're* or *your* to finish what these friends are saying.

Here are ___(1)___ tickets for the play.

Thanks. Let me know when ___(2)___ going to be ready.

___(3)___ not sure what it's about?

No, ___(4)___ guess is as good as mine!

1. _____ ?

2. _____ ?

3. _____ ?

4. _____ ?

Show What You Know! Pretend that you are telling an audience about a play they will see. Write two sentences that use *you're* and *your*.

Performing Arts

Putting on a Play All the words in the box have something to do with putting on a play. Use those words to complete this notice about a class play. Use your Spelling Dictionary.

What: a play
Where: Carver Elementary
When: Saturday, June 6, two o'clock
Who: Ms. Nguyen's class

Ms. Nguyen's class is performing a short play, or ___(1)___, that Kevin Emerson wrote about a space trip. The play has one ___(2)___ that lasts ten minutes. It is about three astronauts, so the ___(3)___ is small. Each actor will wear a shiny silver ___(4)___ and put silver ___(5)___ on his or her face.

Spelling Word Link

o'clock

act
cast
skit
make-up
costume

Try This

CHALLENGE

Yes or No? Is the underlined word used correctly? Write *yes* or *no*.

6. We are painting the <u>skit</u> for the play.

7. The <u>cast</u> in our play worked very hard.

8. An <u>act</u> is the most important player.

Fact File

A funny play with a happy ending is a *comedy*. Some comedies are just for fun. Others make you think as well as laugh.

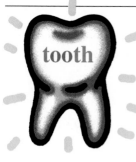

tooth

Unit 31 Vowel Sounds in tooth, cook pp. 192–197

tooth	shoe	blue
flew	balloon	shook

Spelling Strategy The vowel sound |ōō| may be spelled **oo** or **ew**. The vowel sound |ŏŏ| may be spelled **oo**.

Write the word that completes each sentence.

1. Mom _____ my shoulder until I woke up.
2. Molly likes sunny days and clear _____ skies.
3. I watched the flock of birds as they _____ by.
4. Your left _____ needs a little more polish.
5. Brian's loose front _____ fell out today.
6. The party _____ broke with a loud pop.

Unit 32 Vowel Sound in bought pp. 198–203

through	enough	laugh
brought	daughter	cough

|ô|
bought

Spelling Strategy The |ô| sound can have these patterns: **ough**, as in *bought*; **augh**, as in *caught*.

Write the word that completes each sentence.

7. Mrs. Levy _____ home a parrot last week.
8. She gave it to her _____ Emma.
9. The parrot was funny. It made Emma _____.
10. It acts as though it can sneeze and _____.
11. One day it tried to fly _____ an open window.
12. It wasn't quick _____. Emma caught it!

Unit 33 Words That End with er, le pp. 204–209

October	travel	color
purple	able	November

|er|
October

Spelling Strategy   In words with more than one syllable, the final |ər| sounds are often spelled *er,* and the final |əl| sounds are often spelled *le.*

Write the word that fits each clue.
13. This is the month before December.
14. You do this with paper and crayons.
15. This word means that you can do something.
16. This is the month after September.
17. Violets may be this color.
18. You do this when you go to a faraway place.

Unit 34 Words That Begin with a, be pp. 210–215

again	before	about
ahead	because	between

|bĭ|
behind

Spelling Strategy   In two-syllable words, the unstressed |ə| sound may be spelled *a.* The unstressed |bĭ| sounds may be spelled *be.*

Write the word that completes each sentence.
19. I learned all _____ ABC order in school today.
20. I like it _____ it can help me find words fast.
21. *Able* comes _____ *basket* in ABC order.
22. *Market* comes _____ *luck* and *napkin.*
23. *Summer* comes _____ of *travel.*
24. We will talk about ABC order _____ tomorrow.

| I'm | won't | o'clock |
| weren't | she's | shouldn't |

Spelling Strategy   A **contraction** is a short way of saying or writing two or more words. An apostrophe takes the place of one or more letters.

she is   *she's*

Write a contraction for each group of words.

25. were not   **26.** will not   **27.** of the clock

Write contractions for the underlined words.

28. We <u>should not</u> wait too long for Emily.

29. Susie says <u>she is</u> feeling well.

30. I like to eat a snack while <u>I am</u> reading.

| Challenge Words | Units 31–35 | pp. 192–221 |

| loose | naughty | |
| beyond | thermometer | let's |

Write the word that completes each sentence.

31. Dad looked at the _____ and said that it was too cold to go outside.

32. Ben's little brother can be very _____.

33. That toy truck is not working because one wheel is _____.

34. It's very hot today, so _____ go swimming.

35. Our new house is on Perkins Street, just _____ the bakery.

Spelling-Meaning Strategy

Word Forms

Words belong to families. The words in a family are spelled alike in some ways. They are also related in meaning. Read this paragraph.

> Mom's **laugh** floated out through the screen onto the porch where I was sitting. Then I heard Dad and Nina's **laughter**. I thought, "Uncle Carl is telling a story."

Think How are *laugh* and *laughter* alike in meaning? How are *laugh* and *laughter* alike in spelling?

Here are words in the *laugh* family.

laugh	laughing	laughed
laughter	laughingly	laughable

Apply and Extend

Complete these activities on another sheet of paper.

1. Look up the meaning of each word in the Word Box above in your Spelling Dictionary. Write six sentences, using one word in each sentence.

2. With a partner list words related to *thought*, *chew*, and *cook*. Then look in your Spelling-Meaning Index beginning on page 272. Add any other words in these families to your list.

Literature and Writing

from

When Winter Comes

by Russell Freedman

To stay alive through the cold winter months, some animals save lots of food. Other animals travel to warmer places. What do woodchucks and bears do?

The woodchuck sleeps so deeply that it almost seems dead. Its breathing slows down, and its body becomes cold and hard. If you touched the woodchuck, it wouldn't wake up. The woodchuck might seem dead, but it's really not. Its extra fat keeps it alive during its winter sleep. Its body uses the fat for food.

Bears also sleep in the winter, but not so deeply. They, too, get ready for their long winter sleep by eating a lot. They often sleep in caves. On warm winter days, they may wake up and go outside to look for something to eat. When it gets cold again, they go back to their caves and sleep some more.

Think and Discuss

1. What facts did you learn about how woodchucks and bears spend the winter?

2. What is the topic sentence of each paragraph?

The Writing Process
A Research Report

Is there a topic you would like to learn about? Write a research report! Follow the Guidelines and use the Writing Process.

1 Prewriting
- Make a web. Write your topic in the middle. Write three questions about your topic in the other circles.
- Find facts that answer your questions. Look in books and encyclopedias. Take notes.

2 Draft
- Turn your questions into topic sentences.

3 Revise
- Does your first sentence state the topic in an interesting way?
- Did you present all your facts in a clear and interesting way?

4 Proofread
- Did you use commas and end marks correctly?
- Is each word spelled correctly?

5 Publish
- Make a poster with your report, drawings, and other facts on it.

• • • Guidelines for Writing a Research Report

✓ Include a first sentence that introduces your topic.
✓ Include several paragraphs with topic sentences and supporting details.
✓ Finish with a last sentence that sums up your report.

Composition Words

chew
through
enough
later
able
because
about
shouldn't

Student's Handbook

Extra Practice and Review Cycle 1

mix	milk	smell
thick	send	stick

|ĭ|
mix

Spelling Strategy   In most words, the |ă| sound is spelled **a**, the |ĕ| sound is spelled **e**, and the |ĭ| sound is spelled **i**.

Write the word that belongs in each group.

1. stir, blend, _____   **3.** cream, butter, _____

2. see, taste, _____

Write the word that completes each sentence.

4. While you are away, please _____ me a letter.

5. I keep warm with a _____ blanket.

6. Andy stirred the paint with a _____.

lot	pond	rub
drum	hunt	crop

|ŏ|
pond

Spelling Strategy   In most words, the |ŏ| sound is spelled **o** and the |ŭ| sound is spelled **u**.

Write the word that matches each meaning.

7. a small body of water   **8.** a large amount

Write the word that completes each sentence.

9. Jason beat the _____ as we marched.

10. My cat likes to _____ its back on the fence.

11. A new _____ of tomatoes is ready to be picked.

12. Maria had a treasure _____ at her party.

|ō|
smoke

|ā|
paint

Unit 3   Vowel-Consonant-e Pattern   pp. 24–29

huge	life	wide
grade	note	mine

Spelling Strategy   A long vowel sound is often spelled vowel-consonant-**e**.

Write the word that belongs in each group.

13. big, large, _____
14. school, test, _____

Write the word that completes each sentence.

15. Daria wants to spend her _____ helping others.
16. My dentist says, "Open your mouth _____!"
17. Leave me a _____ if you decide to go out.
18. The workers found gold deep in the _____.

Unit 4   More Long Vowel Spellings   pp. 30–35

paint	feel	neighbor
lay	need	speak

Spelling Strategy   In many words, the |ā| sound is spelled **ai** or **ay**. The |ē| sound may be spelled **ea** or **ee**.

Write the word that rhymes with each word below.

19. seed   **20.** gray

Write the word that matches each clue.

21. You do this when you say something.
22. This is used to color something.
23. This person lives next door to you.
24. You do this when you touch something.

Unit 5 Spelling the Long o Sound pp. 36–41

float	blow	sold
hold	row	both

|ō|
coach

Spelling Strategy The |ō| sound can be spelled with the pattern **oa, ow,** or **o.**

Write the word that completes each sentence.

25. Betsy can _____ out ten birthday candles!

26. Can we _____ our boat across the lake?

27. Please _____ the tray with both hands.

28. Those toy ducks will _____ in the bathtub.

29. Zack and Pedro said they can _____ go out.

30. I was sad when we _____ our house and moved.

Challenge Words Units 1–5 pp. 12–41

explode	dodge	crisp
shallow	easel	

Write the word that matches each clue.

31. Artists use this while they work.

32. Balloons filled with too much air may do this.

Write the words to complete the paragraph.

The pond was too __(33)__ for swimming, but there were lots of frogs there. I tried to catch one, but it was able to __(34)__ me. It leaped from the water and hid among the __(35)__, dry leaves that lay by the shore of the pond.

Extra Practice and Review

throw

Unit 7	Three-Letter Clusters	pp. 48–53

strong	three	scream
spray	string	stream

Spelling Strategy   Some words begin with the consonant clusters **scr, spr, str,** and **thr.**

Write a word that means the same as each word.

1. brook
2. yell
3. cord

Write the word that completes each sentence.

4. Katie is _____ enough to carry those heavy suitcases.
5. After you wash the car, _____ it with the hose.
6. My _____ cats are named Bingo, Pixie, and Moe.

|ī| **wild** |ī| **tie**

Unit 8	Spelling the Long i Sound	pp. 54–59

sight	child	pie
tie	tight	might

Spelling Strategy   The |ī| sound can be spelled with the pattern **igh, i,** or **ie.**

Write the word that matches each clue.

7. This has a crust and filling.
8. This person is very young.
9. This word means the opposite of *loose.*
10. Without this, you cannot see.
11. This word rhymes with *sight* and *tight.*
12. You can wear this around your neck.

Unit 9   The Vowel Sound in clown   pp. 60–65

clown	round	bow
loud	cloud	mouth

|ou|
clown

Spelling Strategy   The |ou| sound, as in *clown* and *round*, is often spelled with the pattern **ow** or **ou**.

Write the word that rhymes with each word below.

13. south   **14.** gown

Write the word that completes each sentence.

15. After their song, all the singers will _____.
16. The _____ bowl was filled with fruit and nuts.
17. A fluffy white _____ floated past the sun.
18. The pot fell from the shelf with a _____ crash.

Unit 10   The Vowel Sound in lawn   pp. 66–71

lawn	raw	talk
wall	cost	also

|ô|
lawn

Spelling Strategy   These patterns can spell the |ô| sound:

  aw, as in *lawn*   **a** before **l**, as in *almost*
  o, as in *cloth*

Write a word that means the same as each word.

19. uncooked   **21.** speak
20. price   **22.** besides

Write the word that matches each clue.

23. Someone has to mow this.
24. This can divide one room into two.

write

Unit 11   Unexpected Patterns   pp. 72–77

knee	patch	wrap
match	knock	know

Spelling Strategy   Some words have unexpected consonant patterns.

|n| → **kn**ee |r| → **wr**ap |ch| → scra**tch**

Write the word that belongs in each group.

25. tap, bang, _____   **27.** ankle, hip, _____

26. fix, mend, _____

Write each word by adding the missing letters.

28. ma __ __ __

29. __ __ ow

30. __ __ ap

Challenge Words   Unit 7–11   pp. 48–77

sprout	lilac	struggle
knuckle	flaw	

Write the word that completes each rhyme.

31. Pencils are perfect for trying to draw,
But erasers are best for correcting a _____.

32. The blossoms will all come out,
After the plants begin to _____.

Write the word that fits each clue.

33. Your thumb has one of these.

34. You do this when something is hard to do.

35. This is both a flower and a color name.

Unit 13 Vowel + |r| Sounds pp. 84–89

storm	dark	star
art	smart	ear

|ôr|
storm

Spelling Strategy Remember these spelling patterns for the vowel + |r| sounds:

|är| → d**ar**k |îr| → cl**ear** |ôr| → st**or**m

Write the word that completes each sentence.
1. Sandy likes to paint in _____ class.
2. Carol has a good _____ for music.
3. Tino can act just like a movie _____.
4. Joyce always knows when a _____ is coming.
5. I wore a skirt of a _____ color.
6. When I grow up, I want to be as _____ as Dad.

Unit 14 Vowel + |r| Sounds in first pp. 90–95

girl	her	work
bird	hurt	dirt

|ûr|
girl

Spelling Strategy The |ûr| sounds can be spelled with the patterns **er, ir, ur,** and **or.**

Write the word that means the opposite of each word below.
7. play   8. boy   9. help

Write the word that completes each sentence.
10. Darrell helps his mother weed _____ garden.
11. Sometimes I wish I could fly like a _____.
12. Dave swept the _____ from the kitchen floor.

|oi|
coin

Unit 15   The Vowel Sound in coin   pp. 96–101

coin	oil	boil
boy	join	foil

Spelling Strategy   The |oi| sound, as in *coin* and *boy,* is spelled with the **oi** or **oy** pattern.

Write the word that matches each clue.
13. a child
14. something you spend

Write the words to complete the paragraph.
Would you like to ___(**15**)___ our cooking class? Today we will make chicken with broccoli. First, we cover the chicken with shiny ___(**16**)___. It cooks in the oven without butter or ___(**17**)___! Then we ___(**18**)___ the broccoli.

**large
jeans**

Unit 16   Spelling the |j| Sound   pp. 102–107

jump	stage	gym
jar	age	page

Spelling Strategy   The |j| sound can be spelled with **j** or with **g** followed by **e, i,** or **y**.

Write the word that matches each clue.
19. Actors perform a play on it.
20. This is part of a book.
21. Frogs and rabbits do this well.
22. You add a year to yours on every birthday.
23. You play indoor sports in this place.
24. You can use this to hold many things.

Unit 17   The |k| and |kw| Sounds   pp. 108–113

| park | queen | skin |
| quit | crack | quart |

|kw|
queen

Spelling Strategy   The |k| sound can be spelled with the **k, ck,** or **c** pattern. The |kw| sounds can be spelled with the **qu** pattern.

Write the word that rhymes with each word below.
25. pin   **26.** hit   **27.** mark

Write the word that completes each sentence.
28. Joe bought a _____ of milk at the store.
29. The United States is not ruled by a king or a _____.
30. The plate fell, but it did not _____.

Challenge Words   Units 13–17   pp. 84–113

| courage | freckles | destroy |
| argue | sturdy | |

Write the words to complete the paragraph.
  The girl with the red hair and __(31)__ on her nose is a fast runner. She has won many races. Her legs are not long, but they are very __(32)__. People like her because she is fair to other runners and does not __(33)__ with the coach. Losing a race does not __(34)__ her hopes. She does not win all the time, but she always has the __(35)__ to try again.

|âr|
bear

Unit 19   Vowel + |r| Sounds in hair   pp. 120–125

hair	care	pair
air	bare	share

Spelling Strategy   The |âr| sounds can have these patterns:

are, as in *care*   **air,** as in *hair*   **ear,** as in *bear*

Write the word that matches each clue.

1. This is two of something.
2. This grows on your head.
3. You breathe this.
4. The branches of winter trees may look like this.
5. Babies need lots of this.
6. Two people may do this with one sandwich.

our
**reading
hour**

Unit 20   Homophones   pp. 126–131

new	there	they're
knew	their	

Spelling Strategy   **Homophones** are words that sound the same but have different spellings and meanings.

Write the word that completes each sentence.

7. The twins want (there, their, they're) lunch.
8. Tina (new, knew) the answer to my question.
9. I will be (they're, there, their) at noon.
10. Pat and Jon are glad that (they're, their, there) best friends.
11. Cindy got a (new, knew) bike for her birthday.

Unit 21   Compound Words   pp. 132–137

| airplane | inside | sometimes |
| grandfather | something | herself |

air | plane

Spelling Strategy   A **compound word** is made up of two or more shorter words.

Write the words to complete the paragraph.

Last week Mom and I went to visit my __(12)__ . I flew in an __(13)__ for the first time! I could not believe how big the __(14)__ of it was! The ride was long, but there was always __(15)__ to do. I read, and __(16)__ I talked to people. One crew member told me about __(17)__ and her flying adventures.

Unit 22   Words with -ed or -ing   pp. 138–143

| chopped | saving | rubbed |
| dropped | grinning | patted |

chopped

Spelling Strategy   The spelling of some base words changes when **-ed** or **-ing** is added.

rub + b + ed = ru**bbed**   save − e + ing = sav**ing**

Write words by changing -ing to -ed.

18. rubbing   **20.** dropping
19. chopping   **21.** patting

Write the word that completes each sentence.

22. "Thanks for _____ my cat," I said to my neighbor.
23. After Stu told the joke we were all _____.

**pony + ies
= ponies**

| Unit 23 | Changing Final y to i | pp. 144–149 |

| babies | puppies | cried |
| flies | hurried | parties |

Spelling Strategy   When a base word ends with a consonant and **y,** change the **y** to **i** before adding **-es** or **-ed.**

Write the word that completes each sentence.
24. Sandra is going to two _____ this weekend.
25. Tony _____ when he scraped his knee.

Write words by adding -es or -ed to each base word below.
26. hurry   **27.** fly   **28.** baby   **29.** puppy

| Challenge Words | Units 19–23 | pp. 120–149 |

| canaries | suitcase |
| propped | flair |

Write the word that completes this rhyme.
30. When Mrs. Watson styles my hair,
       She does it with a certain _____.

Write the word that belongs in this group.
31. trunk, overnight bag, _____

Write the word that completes each sentence.
32. Those yellow _____ always sing sweetly in the morning.
33. Dad _____ the ladder against the wall.

Unit 25   The Prefixes re- and un-   pp. 156–161

unkind	remake	untie
unlike	unclear	unhurt

unhappy

Spelling Strategy   A **prefix** is a word part added to the beginning of a base word. **Re-** and **un-** are prefixes.

Write the word that means the opposite of each word below.

1. hurt   **2.** clear   **3.** kind   **4.** tie

Write the word that completes each sentence.

5. Aunt Ann was _____ anyone we had ever known.

6. My clay model looked all wrong, so I had to _____ it.

Unit 26   Suffixes -ful, -ly, -er   pp. 162–167

helper	careful	slowly
farmer	sadly	thankful

teacher

Spelling Strategy   A **suffix** is a word part added to the end of a base word. Some words have the suffix **-ful, -ly,** or **-er.**

Write the words to complete the paragraph.

   Uncle Neil raises cows and chickens. He is a __(7)__ .
I am his best __(8)__ . I do my chores well, but I do them
__(9)__ . I am always very __(10)__ when I gather the eggs.
Uncle Neil is always __(11)__ for my help. We both wave
__(12)__ when I have to leave.

win | dow

Unit 27   The VCCV Pattern   pp. 168–173

invite	Monday	forget
Sunday	market	order

Spelling Strategy   Divide a word with the VCCV pattern between the two consonants to find the syllables.

Write the word that has the same first syllable as each word below.

13. margin   **14.** forgive   **15.** inside

Write the word that completes each sentence.

16. My favorite day of the weekend is _____.

17. I go to school every _____.

18. I always _____ rice and beans with my tacos.

rabbit

Unit 28   Double Consonants   pp. 174–179

rabbit	happen	butter
yellow	button	pretty

Spelling Strategy   A VCCV word may have double consonants. Divide between the consonants to find the syllables.

Write the word that belongs in each group.

19. milk, cheese, _____   **21.** zipper, hook, _____

20. fox, deer, _____   **22.** red, blue, _____

Write the word that completes each sentence.

23. I wonder what will _____ at the game.

24. That quilt will look very _____ when it is finished.

Unit 29   The |s| Sound in city   pp. 180–185

city	nice	once
space	certain	face

|s|
city

Spelling Strategy   The |s| sound may be spelled **c** when the **c** is followed by **i** or **e**.

Write the word that matches each clue.

25. Stars and planets are found in this area.
26. You are this if you are sure about something.
27. You smile and frown with this.
28. This word rhymes with *rice*.
29. Many buildings are found in this place.
30. This word begins many fairy tales.

Challenge Words   Units 25–29   pp. 156–185

effort	concert	wisdom
review	calmly	

Write the word that has almost the same meaning as each word below.

31. knowledge   **32.** check

Write the word that completes each sentence.

33. Albert was very nervous about his piano _____.
34. He made a great _____ to practice every day so that he would not make mistakes.
35. When the big day came, Albert walked _____ on stage and played perfectly.

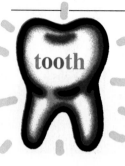

tooth

Unit 31 Vowel Sounds in tooth, cook pp. 192–197

grew	chew	cook
boot	spoon	drew

Spelling Strategy   Remember these spelling patterns:

|oo|, as in *tooth* or *chew* → **oo, ew**
|oŏ|, as in *cook* → **oo**

Write the word that rhymes with each word below.

1. shoot   **2.** book   **3.** soon

Write the word that completes each sentence.

4. Dan _____ a picture of his dog on the walk with chalk.

5. My dog likes to _____ on a bone.

6. Lily _____ another inch last year.

Unit 32   Vowel Sounds in bought   pp. 198–203

caught	bought	thought
fought	ought	taught

|ô|
bought

Spelling Strategy   The |ô| sound can have these patterns:

ough, as in *bought*   **augh**, as in *caught*

Write the word that means the opposite of each word below.

7. sold   **8.** threw   **9.** learned

Write the word that completes each sentence.

10. The lead runner _____ hard to stay in front.

11. Sam _____ he should do his homework before bed.

12. We _____ to leave soon, or we will be late.

Unit 33 Words That End with er, le   pp. 204–209

summer	winter	little
ever	later	apple

|ər|
October

Spelling Strategy   Remember that in words with more than one syllable, the final |ər| sounds are often spelled **er** and the final |əl| sounds are often spelled **le**.

Write the word that completes each sentence.

13. Buds turn into _____ green leaves in the spring.

14. The weather is often hot in _____.

15. I like to visit the _____ orchard in the fall.

16. This year we picked more fruit than _____!

17. Tomatoes ripen first, and corn ripens _____.

18. When it is _____, I can go sledding!

Unit 34 Words That Begin with a, be   pp. 210–215

begin	around	away
alive	ago	behind

|bĭ|
behind

Spelling Strategy   In two-syllable words, an unstressed first syllable may have one of these patterns:

|ə| → **a** |bĭ| → **be**

Write the word that completes each sentence.

19. Two weeks _____ I found a bird on the ground.

20. Its wing was hurt, but it was still _____.

21. I cupped my hands _____ it and picked it up.

22. I put my bag _____ a tree and ran to the vet.

23. She taped its wing so it could _____ to heal.

24. The bird flew _____ when it was better.

Unit 35   Contractions   pp. 216–221

he's	aren't	couldn't
I'd	wasn't	wouldn't

Spelling Strategy   A **contraction** is a short way of saying or writing two or more words. An apostrophe takes the place of one or more letters.

Write a contraction for each group of words.

25. are not   **26.** was not   **27.** he is

Write contractions for the underlined words.

28. I would like to have a sandwich for lunch.

29. Emily said she would not come over today.

30. Carlos could not find his hat this morning.

Challenge Words   Units 31–35   pp. 192–221

icicle	sought	
among	crooked	who's

Write the words to complete the paragraph.

Once upon a time, there lived a queen who loved winter. One day she said to her subjects, "Search ___(31)___ the trees on Frozen Mountain. From one branch hangs an ___(32)___ so cold it will never melt. I will reward anyone ___(33)___ clever enough to find it." The people ___(34)___ the treasure day and night. Finally, a young boy found the object hanging from the top of a ___(35)___ tree.

Writer's Resources

Capitalization and Punctuation Guide

Abbreviations

	An abbreviation is a short way to write a word. Most abbreviations begin with a capital letter and end with a period.
Titles	<u>Mr.</u> Juan Albano <u>Ms.</u> Leslie Clark <u>Mrs.</u> Janice Dodd <u>Dr.</u> Frances Wong Note: *Miss* is not an abbreviation and does not end with a period.
Days of the Week	Sun. *(Sunday)* Thurs. *(Thursday)* Mon. *(Monday)* Fri. *(Friday)* Tues. *(Tuesday)* Sat. *(Saturday)* Wed. *(Wednesday)*
Months of the Year	Jan. *(January)* Sept. *(September)* Feb. *(February)* Oct. *(October)* Mar. *(March)* Nov. *(November)* Apr. *(April)* Dec. *(December)* Aug. *(August)* Note: *May, June,* and *July* are not abbreviated.

Quotations

Quotation marks with commas and end marks	*Quotation marks* (" ") set off someone's exact words from the rest of the sentence. The first word of a quotation begins with a capital letter. Use a comma to separate the quotation from the rest of the sentence. Put the end mark before the last quotation mark. Linda said<u>,</u> <u>"</u>We don't know where Danny went.<u>"</u>

Capitalization

Rules for capitalization

Every sentence begins with a capital letter.

What a pretty color the roses are!

The pronoun _I_ is always a capital letter.

What should I do next?

Begin each important word in the names of particular persons, places, or things (proper nouns) with a capital letter.

George Herman Ruth   New Jersey   Liberty Bell

Titles or their abbreviations when used with a person's name begin with a capital letter.

Doctor Garcia   Mrs. Lin

Begin the names of days, months, and holidays with a capital letter.

Labor Day is on the first Monday in September.

The first and last words and all important words in the titles of books begin with a capital letter. Titles of books are underlined.

The Hill and the Rock   The Bashful Tiger

Punctuation

End marks

A _period (.)_ ends a statement or a command. A _question mark (?)_ follows a question. An _exclamation point (!)_ follows an exclamation.

The scissors are on my desk. _(statement)_
Look up the spelling of that word. _(command)_
How is the word spelled? _(question)_
This is your best poem so far! _(exclamation)_

Punctuation (continued)

Apostrophe	**Add an apostrophe (') and _s_ to a singular noun to make it show ownership.**
	doctor's father's grandmother's family's
	For a plural noun that ends in _s_, add just an apostrophe to show ownership.
	sisters' families' Smiths' hound dogs'
	Use an apostrophe in contractions in place of missing letters.
	can't _(cannot)_ we're _(we are)_ I'm _(I am)_
Comma	**Use commas to separate a series of three or more words.**
	Rob bought apples, peaches, and grapes.
	Use commas after _yes, no, well,_ and order words when they begin a sentence.
	First, set up the table. No, it is too early.
	Use a comma to separate the month and the day from the year.
	I was born on June 17, 1971.
	Use a comma between the names of a city and a state.
	Chicago, Illinois Miami, Florida
	Use a comma after the greeting and after the closing in a letter.
	Dear Uncle Rudolph, Your nephew,

Letter Model

Friendly Letter

Remember that a letter has **five** parts.

❶ The **heading** gives the writer's address and the date.

❷ The **greeting** says "hello."

❸ The **body** is the main part. It tells the message.

❹ The **closing** says "good-by."

❺ The **signature** tells who wrote the letter.

Use correct letter form when you write to someone. Use capital letters and commas correctly.

Study this letter model.

25 Mill Street
Santa Rosa, CA 95405 · · ◄ **Heading**
April 2, 1998

Dear Grandma, ◄ · · · · · · **Greeting**

I hope that you had a nice time in Florida. Did it rain much? I took your post card to school today. Everybody liked the picture of that big alligator!

Body

Closing · · · · · ► Love,

Lisa

Signature

Using the Thesaurus

How to Use This Thesaurus

This Thesaurus includes **main entries** for words you often use. The **main entry words** appear in blue. They are listed in ABC order. Each main entry includes

- the **part of speech**, a **definition**, and a **sample sentence** for the main entry word
- **subentry** words that could be used in place of the main entry word, with definitions and sample sentences
- **antonyms**, or opposites, for the main entry word.

For example Imagine you wanted to find a more exact word for *new* in this sentence:

*Our town is proud of our **new** hospital.*

❶ Find the main entry for *new* in your Thesaurus.

❷ Read the words, or subentries, that can be used in place of *new*: *fresh* and *modern*.

❸ Read the definition and the sample sentence for each subentry.

Now you can choose the best word for your sentence.

*Our town is proud of our **modern** hospital.*

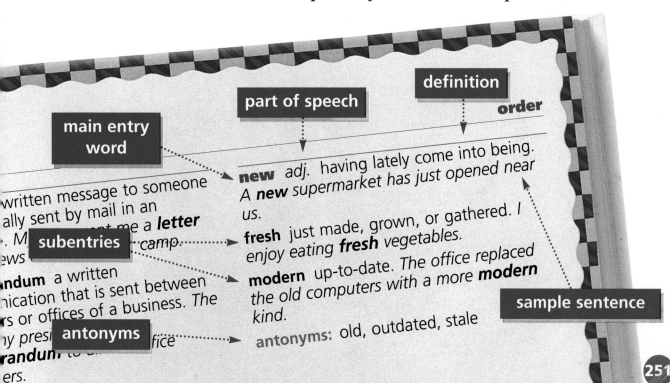

main entry word

part of speech

definition

order

written message to someone
ally sent by mail in an
...nt me a **letter**
...camp.

subentries

new *adj.* having lately come into being. A **new** supermarket has just opened near us.

fresh just made, grown, or gathered. I enjoy eating **fresh** vegetables.

ndum a written
...ication that is sent between
...s or offices of a business. The

modern up-to-date. The office replaced the old computers with a more **modern** kind.

sample sentence

antonyms

...fice

antonyms: old, outdated, stale

...y presi

...randum

ers.

Using the Thesaurus Index

The Thesaurus Index lists all the words in the Thesaurus in ABC order. The Thesaurus Index will help you find a word in this Thesaurus.

The Thesaurus Index lists all the main entry words, the subentries, and any antonyms included in the Thesaurus. The words in the Thesaurus Index are in alphabetical order.

When you look in the Thesaurus Index, you will see that words are shown in three ways.

Main entry words are shown in blue. For example, the word *strong* is a main entry word.

Subentries are shown in dark print. For example, *stunning* is a subentry of *pretty*.

Antonyms are shown in regular print. For example, *sturdy* is an antonym of *soft*.

> **strong** *adj.*
> **stunning pretty** *adj.*
> sturdy **soft** *adj.*
> **swell grow** *v.*

Practice Look up each word below in the Thesaurus Index. Write the main entry word for each word.

1. highway   **2.** grab   **3.** hammer   **4.** ugly   **5.** soggy

Use the Thesaurus to replace each underlined word. Rewrite each sentence, using the new word you chose.

6. Aunt Jessie is tall and has <u>thin</u> hands.
7. She is a <u>happy</u> person who is usually smiling.
8. Aunt Jessie sent me a <u>message</u> last week.
9. It said, "Come visit, and I will <u>cook</u> chicken."
10. I can already imagine the <u>smell</u> of this tasty treat.

Thesaurus Index

A

about **almost** adv.
accurate **wrong** adj.
actual real adj.
admire like v.
adorable pretty adj.
adult **child** n.
ailing ill adj.
alarm frighten v.
almost adv.
amend improve v.
answer talk v.
appreciate like v.
approximately
   almost adv.
aqua blue adj.
area n.
argue talk v.
arid **wet** adj.
aroma smell n.
arrangement
   order n.
assignment job n.
attempt try v.
attractive pretty adj.
authentic real adj.

B

baby child n.
bake cook v.
bang knock v.
barbecue cook v.
barely **very** adv.

bawl **laugh** v.
beautiful pretty adj.
becoming pretty adj.
begin **end** v.
beginning **last** adj.
beige brown adj.
bellow yell v.
better improve v.
big adj.
bind fasten v.
bird n.
blend mix v.
blue adj.
boil cook v.
bony thin adj.
boulevard road n.
broil cook v.
brown adj.
bulletin message n.
bumpy **even** adj.
business work n.
button fasten v.

C

calm **frighten** v.
canary bird n.
career work n.
carrot orange adj.
cheap **valuable** adj.
cheerful happy adj.
cheerful **sad** adj.
chestnut brown adj.
child n.
chop cut v.
chore job n.

chubby **thin** adj.
chuckle laugh v.
clasp hold v.
clean **dirty** adj.
clip cut v.
close fasten v.
close near adj.
clutch hold v.
common usual adj.
communication
   message n.
complete end v.
concluding last adj.
connect join v.
continue **end** v.
contract **grow** v.
convenient
   useful adj.
cook v.
correct **wrong** adj.
costly valuable adj.
cradle hold v.
criminal wrong adj.
crimson red adj.
crow bird n.
cry **laugh** v.
cut v.
cute pretty adj.

D

dainty pretty adj.
damp wet adj.
decrease **grow** v.
delicate soft adj.

highway road *n.*
hold *v.*
homely **pretty** *adj.*
hop jump *v.*
howl yell *v.*
hug hold *v.*
huge big *adj.*
hurdle jump *v.*
hurry *v.*
hurt **improve** *v.*

ill *adj.*
illegal wrong *adj.*
impractical useful *adj.*
improve *v.*
inaccurate
  wrong *adj.*
incorrect wrong *adj.*
inexact wrong *adj.*
inexpensive
  valuable *adj.*
infant child *n.*

job *n.*
join *v.*
jolly happy *adj.*
joyful happy *adj.*
jump *v.*
just **wrong** *adj.*

keep *v.*

knock *v.*
knot fasten *v.*

lane road *n.*
lanky thin *adj.*
large big *adj.*
last *adj.*
laugh *v.*
lavender purple *adj.*
lawful **wrong** *adj.*
lay put *v.*
lean thin *adj.*
leap jump *v.*
leisurely **quick** *adj.*
lemon yellow *adj.*
letter message *n.*
level even *adj.*
like *v.*
little **big** *adj.*
location area *n.*
loosen **fasten** *v.*
lose **save** *v.*
loud *adj.*
love like *v.*
lovely pretty *adj.*

magnificent
  pretty *adj.*
march walk *v.*
memorandum
  message *n.*
message *n.*

messy dirty *adj.*
mighty strong *adj.*
miserable **happy** *adj.*
mistaken wrong *adj.*
mix *v.*
modern new *adj.*
moist wet *adj.*
most very *adv.*
multiply grow *v.*

nasty **nice** *adj.*
naughty wrong *adj.*
navy blue *adj.*
near *adj.*
nearly almost *adv.*
neighboring
  near *adj.*
new *adj.*
nice *adj.*
noisy loud *adj.*
normal usual *adj.*
note message *n.*

occupation work *n.*
occur happen *v.*
odor smell *n.*
old **new** *adj.*
open **fasten** *v.*
orange *adj.*
order *v.*
ordinary usual *adj.*
outdated **new** *adj.*

outstanding **usual** adj.
overweight **thin** adj.
owl bird n.

P

parched **wet** adj.
patter knock v.
pattern order n.
peach orange adj.
peculiar **usual** adj.
phony **real** adj.
place put v.
plain **pretty** adj.
pleasant nice adj.
plump **thin** adj.
poach cook v.
pounce grab v.
pound knock v.
powerful strong adj.
practical useful adj.
precious
   valuable adj.
pretty adj.
priceless
   valuable adj.
profession work n.
purple adj.
put v.

Q

quick adj.
quiet **loud** adj.
quit end v.

rap knock v.
rare **usual** adj.
real adj.
recover save v.
red adj.
reduce **grow** v.
region area n.
release **grab** v.
rescue save v.
reserve keep v.
retain keep v.
right **wrong** adj.
road n.
roar laugh v.
roaring loud adj.
roast cook v.
robin bird n.
rough **even** adj.
roughly almost adv.
ruby red adj.
rush hurry v.

S

sad adj.
sad **happy** adj.
sample try v.
save v.
save keep v.
say v.
scamper hurry v.
scarcely **very** adv.
scare frighten v.

scent smell n.
scold talk v.
scrawny thin adj.
scream yell v.
screech yell v.
scribble draw v.
sea gull bird n.
seal fasten v.
seize grab v.
separate **join** v.
separate **mix** v.
sequence order n.
shriek yell v.
shrink **grow** v.
sick ill adj.
sickly ill adj.
silent **loud** adj.
simmer cook v.
simple **hard** adj.
sketch draw v.
skinny thin adj.
slender thin adj.
slice cut v.
slight thin adj.
slim thin adj.
slow **quick** adj.
small **big** adj.
smell n.
smooth even adj.
snatch grab v.
snicker laugh v.
snip cut v.
sob **laugh** v.
soft adj.
soft **loud** adj.
soggy wet adj.

soiled **dirty** *adj.*
solid **soft** *adj.*
soothe **frighten** *v.*
sopping **wet** *adj.*
space **area** *n.*
speedy **quick** *adj.*
spin **twist** *v.*
splendid **pretty** *adj.*
spotless **dirty** *adj.*
spread **grow** *v.*
spring **jump** *v.*
stale **new** *adj.*
start **end** *v.*
state **say** *v.*
steam **cook** *v.*
stew **cook** *v.*
stir **mix** *v.*
stop **end** *v.*
strange **usual** *adj.*
street **road** *n.*
stride **walk** *v.*
strong *adj.*
stunning **pretty** *adj.*
sturdy **soft** *adj.*
swell **grow** *v.*

T

take place **happen** *v.*
talk *v.*
tap **knock** *v.*
task **job** *n.*
tender **soft** *adj.*
terrify **frighten** *v.*
test **try** *v.*

thin *adj.*
thump **knock** *v.*
tie **fasten** *v.*
tiny **big** *adj.*
toast **cook** *v.*
toddler **child** *n.*
tot **child** *n.*
tough **hard** *adj.*
tough **soft** *adj.*
trace **draw** *v.*
trade **work** *n.*
tremendous **big** *adj.*
true **real** *adj.*
try *v.*
turn **twist** *v.*
turnpike **road** *n.*
twirl **twist** *v.*
twist *v.*

U

ugly **pretty** *adj.*
undertaking **job** *n.*
underweight
    thin *adj.*
unexpected **usual** *adj.*
unfair **wrong** *adj.*
unhappy **sad** *adj.*
unhealthy **ill** *adj.*
unite **join** *v.*
unjust **wrong** *adj.*
unlawful **wrong** *adj.*
unpleasant **nice** *adj.*
unwell **ill** *adj.*
upgrade **improve** *v.*

useful *adj.*
useless **useful** *adj.*
usual *adj.*

V

valuable *adj.*
very *adv.*
vicinity area *n.*
violet purple *adj.*

W

walk *v.*
weak **strong** *adj.*
weep **laugh** *v.*
well **ill** *adj.*
wet *adj.*
wicked **wrong** *adj.*
withhold **keep** *v.*
work *n.*
worsen **improve** *v.*
worthless **useful** *adj.*
worthless
    valuable *adj.*
wrong *adj.*

Y

yell *v.*
yellow *adj.*
youngster child *n.*

Z

zone area *n.*

Thesaurus

almost *adv.* just short of. *Loren is* ***almost*** *as old as Carrie.*

about nearly; almost. *It takes Ann* ***about*** *ten minutes to walk to school.*

approximately almost exactly. *That basket will hold* ***approximately*** *thirty apples.*

nearly almost but not quite. *Joey* ***nearly*** *caught the fish, but it got away.*

roughly about. *Both bedrooms are* ***roughly*** *the same size.*

---

area *n.* a surface. *Mom uses one* ***area*** *of the yard for her garden.*

location an area where something is placed or found. *The hardware store was moved to a new* ***location****.*

region usually a large area of the earth's surface. *The Antarctic is the* ***region*** *around the South Pole.*

space the open area between objects. *Will the sofa fit in this* ***space****, or will we have to put it somewhere else?*

vicinity a nearby or surrounding area. *This park is mainly used by people who live in the* ***vicinity****.*

zone an area set off from others by a special use. *The speed limit is fifteen miles per hour in a school* ***zone****.*

big *adj.* of great size. *It is easy to get lost in a* ***big*** *city.*

enormous very big. *Look at that* ***enormous*** *elephant!*

huge very big, giant-sized. *It took days to climb the* ***huge*** *mountain.*

large bigger than average. *The* ***large*** *yard gave us plenty of room to play in.*

tremendous great in size or amount. *The king lived in a* ***tremendous*** *castle that had five hundred rooms.*

antonyms: little, small, tiny

---

bird *n.* a warm-blooded animal that lays eggs. A bird has two wings and a body covered with feathers. *Did you ever wish you could fly like a* ***bird****?*

canary a songbird, often yellow in color, that can be kept as a pet in a cage. *My* ***canary*** *likes to perch on my finger.*

crow a large black bird with a harsh, hoarse call. *The* ***crow*** *sat on a branch and cawed loudly.*

owl a bird that has a large head, large eyes, and a short hooked bill. Owls usually fly and hunt at night. *An* ***owl*** *was sitting on the tree branch in the moonlight.*

robin a North American songbird with a rust-red breast and a dark gray back. *The cheerful chirping of a* ***robin*** *told us that spring was coming.*

sea gull a bird that lives on coasts and has long wings. It usually has gray and white feathers and webbed feet. *A **sea gull** circled high above the sailboat.*

blue *adj.* having the color of a clear sky. *On a sunny day, the **blue** boat matched the sky.*

aqua light greenish-blue. *The water near the shore has a lovely **aqua** color.*

navy dark blue. *The highway police wear **navy** uniforms.*

brown *adj.* of the color of wood or soil. *The leaves on the ground had all turned **brown.***

beige light yellowish-brown. *The **beige** rug will blend with the green and brown furniture in the living room.*

chestnut reddish-brown. *I stroked the pony's **chestnut** mane.*

child *n.* a young boy or girl. *Every man, woman, and **child** needs exercise to stay fit.*

baby a very young child; infant. *The **baby** crawled happily around the playpen and then began shaking its rattle.*

infant a child from the earliest period of life up to about two years of age. *She laid the **infant** in a crib.*

toddler a child who has learned to walk but is still unsteady on his or her feet. *The **toddler** walked a few steps and then fell down.*

tot a small child. *The clown leaned down and handed the **tot** a balloon.*

youngster a young person or child. *"When I was a **youngster**, there was no TV," Grandma said.*

antonyms: adult, grownup

Word Bank

cook *v.* to prepare food for eating by using heat.

bake	fry	steam
barbecue	poach	stew
boil	roast	toast
broil	simmer	

---

cut *v.* to form, separate, or divide by using a sharp instrument. *Please **cut** the rope into six pieces.*

chop to cut up into small pieces. *Dad **chopped** a carrot and some potatoes and put them in the soup.*

clip to cut the surface growth of. *Barb **clipped** the bushes to make them look neat.*

hack to cut with heavy blows. *Andy **hacked** his way through the thick jungle.*

slice to cut into thin, flat pieces. *I **sliced** two pieces of bread from the loaf.*

snip to cut with short, quick strokes. *Liza used scissors to **snip** the ribbons in half before she made the bows.*

D

dirty *adj.* full of or covered with dirt; not clean. *Don loaded the **dirty** laundry into the washing machine.*

filthy extremely dirty. *The walls were so **filthy** that you could not tell what color they were.*

grimy covered with heavy dirt. *He scrubbed the grease and soot from his **grimy** hands.*

grubby dirty and messy. *We fed the stray dog and washed his **grubby** coat.*

messy untidy. *I swept out the **messy** closet and put everything in order.*

soiled having become or been made dirty. *The tablecloth was **soiled** where someone had spilled gravy.*

antonyms: clean *adj.*, spotless

---

draw *v.* to make a picture with lines. *Mandy **drew** a picture of her apartment building.*

doodle to scribble while thinking about something else. *Molly **doodled** on a notepad while she listened to the story.*

scribble to draw carelessly. *I **scribbled** some lines with each crayon to try out the different colors.*

sketch to make a rough drawing. *Daniel quickly **sketched** the bird before it flew away.*

trace to copy by following lines seen through a sheet of transparent paper. *Louis carefully **traced** the sailboat picture in the magazine.*

E

end *v.* to bring to a close. *The president **ended** the meeting.*

complete to make or do entirely. *I **completed** the work in a day.*

finish to reach the end of. *He **finished** the book.*

quit to stop doing. *You will never win if you **quit** trying.*

stop to cut off an action. *The fence **stopped** me from going farther.*

antonyms: begin, continue, start

---

even *adj.* without bumps, gaps, or rough parts. *The table wiggled because the floor was not **even**.*

flat having a smooth, even surface. *I need something **flat** to write on.*

level having a flat, even surface. *It is easier to walk along **level** ground than to walk up and down hills.*

smooth having a surface that is not rough or uneven. *She likes to roller-skate where the sidewalk is **smooth**.*

antonyms: bumpy, rough

F

fasten *v.* to attach firmly. *She **fastened** the tag to her skirt.*

bind to hold together. *Birds **bind** their nests with mud.*

button to fasten or close a garment by slipping small disks through holes. ***Button** your coat, or you will be cold.*

close to shut. *The lid of the trunk would not **close**.*

knot to fasten by tying together one or more pieces of string, rope, or twine. *She **knotted** the two pieces of rope together.*

seal to close tightly with glue, wax, or other hardening material. *He **sealed** the letter shut so that no one would read it.*

tie to fasten with a cord or rope. *She **tied** the box shut with cord.*

antonyms: loosen, open *v.*

---

frighten *v.* to make or become afraid. *The thunder and lightning **frightened** us.*

alarm to make suddenly very worried. *News of the accident **alarmed** the family.*

scare to startle or shock. *A loud noise **scared** the sleeping cat.*

terrify to frighten greatly. *The spreading forest fire **terrified** the animals.*

antonyms: calm *v.*, soothe

---

grab *v.* to take hold of suddenly. *I **grabbed** the railing to stop myself from falling.*

grasp to take hold of firmly with the hand. *I **grasped** a branch and pulled myself up.*

pounce to seize by swooping. *The cat **pounced** on the rubber mouse.*

seize to take hold of suddenly and by force. *The thief **seized** the package and ran.*

snatch to grasp quickly. *Gabriel **snatched** the ball before his teammate could reach it.*

antonyms: drop *v.*, free *v.*, release

---

grow *v.* to become larger in size. *My little sister **grew** too big for me to pick up.*

expand to make or become large in size, volume, or amount. *The balloon **expanded** until it popped.*

extend to make longer; lengthen. *We plan to **extend** our visit from a week to ten days.*

multiply to make or become more in number. *The number of students in this school has **multiplied** in the past ten years.*

spread to stretch over a wider area. *As water continued dripping, the puddle **spread**.*

swell to become larger in size or volume as a result of pressure from the inside. *The sponge **swelled** as it soaked up water.*

antonyms: contract *v.*, decrease, reduce, shrink

---

happen *v.* to take place, occur. *When did the earthquake **happen**?*

occur to come to pass. *How did the accident **occur**?*

(continued)

happen (continued)

take place to come about. *The wedding will **take place** on board the ship.*

happy *adj.* very satisfied. *I was **happy** to hear the good news.*

cheerful merry, lively. *The **cheerful** song helps him forget his worries.*

glad pleased. *"I would be **glad** to help," said Victor.*

jolly full of fun. *The **jolly** waitress liked making us laugh.*

joyful showing, feeling or causing great joy or happiness. *The puppy galloped toward its owner with a **joyful** bark.*

antonyms: gloomy, miserable, sad

hard *adj.* difficult to solve, understand, or express. *This book is too **hard** for a first grader.*

difficult hard to make, do, or understand. *Denise practiced the **difficult** dance steps over and over.*

tough difficult to do. *Fixing the rusty old car was going to be a **tough** job.*

antonyms: easy, simple

hold *v.* to have or keep in the arms or hands. *Please **hold** this package for me so that I can unlock the door.*

clasp to hold or hug tightly. *The little girl **clasped** the wriggling puppy.*

clutch to hold tightly with the hands. *She **clutched** the handlebars of her bike as she rode down the street for the first time.*

cradle to hold as if in a small bed for a baby. *I **cradled** the kitten in my arms until it fell asleep.*

hug to put one's arms around and hold closely. *The two friends **hugged** each other when they said good-by.*

hurry *v.* to act or move quickly. *We will miss the bus unless we **hurry**.*

rush to act or move too quickly. *You are likely to make mistakes if you **rush** through your work.*

scamper to run or go hurriedly. *The squirrels **scampered** away when the cat suddenly appeared.*

ill *adj.* not healthy. *She stayed home from school because she was **ill**.*

ailing feeling ill or having pain. *My **ailing** uncle will stay with us until he is better.*

sick suffering from an illness. *The vet gave us medicine for our **sick** cat.*

sickly tending to become sick. *My **sickly** brother usually has the flu at least five times every winter.*

unhealthy harmful to one's health. *They often eat **unhealthy** foods, such as candy.*

unwell not well; sick. *"I am sorry to hear that you have been **unwell**," he said.*

antonyms: fit *adj.*, healthy, well *adj.*

improve *v.* to make or become more excellent. *Bonita can **improve** her grades by studying harder.*

amend to change so as to improve. *The law was **amended** to make it more fair.*

better to improve. *The new library will better the lives of those who use it.*

help to aid the progress of. *Hard practice has helped her piano playing.*

upgrade to raise to a higher rank or level of excellence. *The factory upgraded its products by using better materials.*

antonyms: harm, hurt, worsen

job *n.* a piece of work. *Building a house is a big job.*

assignment a job that has been given to someone. *Katie's assignment was to sweep the floors and halls.*

chore a small job, usually done on a regular schedule. *His least favorite chore was to put out the garbage every Monday.*

task a piece of work to be done. *Moving that dresser is a task for two people.*

undertaking a task that one accepts or attempts. *Fixing a roof can be a dangerous undertaking.*

join *v.* to bring or come together. *Let's join hands in a circle.*

connect to serve as a way of joining things. *A wire connects the lamp with the plug.*

unite to join in action for a certain purpose. *Neighbors from near and far united to repair the flood damage.*

antonyms: divide, separate *v.*

jump *v.* to rise up or move through the air by using the leg muscles. *Tom jumped as he threw the basketball.*

hop to move with light, quick leaps. *A robin hopped along the ground looking for worms.*

hurdle to jump over. *Debby hurdled a low stone wall and kept running.*

leap to jump quickly or suddenly. *I leaped to the left when I saw the bicycle coming.*

spring to move upward or forward in one quick motion. *The deer easily sprang across the brook.*

keep *v.* to have and not give up. *Did Rob give you that watch to keep?*

reserve to set aside for a special purpose. *I reserve my warmest and most comfortable boots for winter hiking.*

retain to continue to have. *The company moved, but it retained most of its long-time employees.*

(continued)

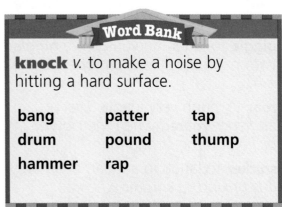

Word Bank

knock *v.* to make a noise by hitting a hard surface.

bang	patter	tap
drum	pound	thump
hammer	rap	

keep (continued)

save to keep from wasting or spending. *She will save her money this week.*

withhold to refuse to give. *The boss withheld their paychecks until the job was completely finished.*

last *adj.* coming, being, or placed after all others. *The last person to leave must remember to lock the door.*

concluding bringing or coming to an end; finishing. *The teacher said a few concluding words and then let the class go.*

final coming at the end. *After the final act, all the actors came out to take a bow.*

antonyms: beginning, first

laugh *v.* to smile and make sounds to show amusement or scorn. *That funny TV program always makes me laugh.*

chuckle to laugh quietly. *She chuckled to herself as she read the comic strip.*

giggle to laugh nervously. *We giggled with excitement as Mom opened the gift.*

roar to laugh very loudly. *The audience roared when the clown picked up the strong man.*

snicker to laugh in a mean or sly way. *It is unkind to snicker when a classmate gives the wrong answer.*

antonyms: bawl, cry *v.*, sob *v.*, weep

like *v.* to be fond of. *He likes to hike in the mountains.*

admire to look at with great pleasure. *Everyone admired her beautiful hair.*

appreciate to know the worth or quality of. *She appreciated the careful drawings.*

enjoy to get pleasure from. *We enjoyed the cool weather.*

love to have strong, warm feelings for. *Eddy loves his new puppy.*

antonyms: dislike *v.*, hate *v.*

loud *adj.* having a large amount of sound. *The window slammed shut with a loud bang.*

noisy making or filled with loud or unpleasant sound. *They had to shout to be heard in the noisy factory.*

roaring making a loud, deep sound. *The roaring engine drowned out the radio.*

antonyms: quiet *adj.*, silent, soft

message *n.* words that are sent from one person or group to another. *He wrote a brief message on the post card.*

bulletin a short announcement on a matter of public interest. *The TV program was interrupted by a special news bulletin.*

communication a message sent by speech, signals, or writing. *The ship sent a communication to shore by radio.*

letter a written message to someone that is usually sent by mail in an envelope. *My sister sent me a **letter** full of news about summer camp.*

memorandum a written communication that is sent between members or offices of a business. *The company president sent a **memorandum** to all the office managers.*

note a short letter or message. *I wrote my uncle a **note** to thank him for the gift.*

---

mix *v.* to combine or blend. ***Mix** the peanuts and raisins in a bowl.*

blend to combine completely. *To make the color orange, **blend** red and yellow.*

stir to mix by using repeated circular motions. ***Stir** the soup as you heat it.*

antonyms: divide *v.*, separate *v.*

---

near *adj.* close in distance or time. *We will choose a winner in the **near** future.*

close near in space, time, or relationship. *Yoko is a **close** friend of mine.*

neighboring living near or located close by; bordering. *People from all the **neighboring** towns came to Greenville for the circus.*

antonyms: distant, far

new *adj.* having lately come into being. *A **new** supermarket has just opened near us.*

fresh just made, grown, or gathered. *I enjoy eating **fresh** vegetables.*

modern up-to-date. *The office replaced the old computers with a more **modern** kind.*

antonyms: old, outdated, stale

---

nice *adj.* kind, pleasant, agreeable. *The boy in the picture has a **nice** smile.*

friendly showing friendship. *Some **friendly** children asked her to join their game.*

helpful providing aid. *The police officer was **helpful** when we got lost.*

pleasant giving pleasure; agreeable. *We enjoyed the **pleasant** scent of the pine trees.*

antonyms: disagreeable, nasty, unpleasant

---

orange *adj.* of a reddish-yellow color. *The **orange** curtains made the room look like a bright sunset.*

carrot of a bright orange color named for the vegetable. *He has **carrot**-red hair.*

peach of a yellowish-pink color named for the fruit. *Her **peach** dress matched the glow in her cheeks.*

---

order *n.* a group of things one after another. *The students' names were called in ABC **order**.*

(continued)

order (continued)

arrangement the way things are placed in relation to each other. *We planned the seating* **arrangement** *for the dinner party.*

formation a particular arrangement. *Wild geese fly in a V-shaped* **formation**.

pattern a group of things or events that forms a regular arrangement. *He did not like to change the* **pattern** *of his daily duties.*

sequence the following of one thing after another in a regular, fixed way. *The seasons always follow each other in the same* **sequence**.

Word Bank

pretty *adj.* pleasing to the eye or ear.

adorable	enchanting	handsome
attractive	fair	lovely
beautiful	good-looking	magnificent
cute	gorgeous	splendid
dainty	graceful	stunning

antonyms: homely, plain, ugly

purple *adj.* of a color between blue and red. *The king wore a robe of* **purple** *velvet.*

lavender light purple. *The flower had pale* **lavender** *blossoms.*

violet bluish-purple. **Violet** *clouds streaked the sky at sunset.*

put *v.* to cause to be in a certain place. **Put** *the spoons in the drawer.*

lay to put or set down. *He* **lays** *his coat on the bed.*

place to put in a particular place or order. *She* **placed** *a bowl of fruit in the center of the table.*

quick *adj.* very fast; rapid. *The frog disappeared into the pond with one* **quick** *leap.*

hasty done too quickly to be correct or wise; rash. *Manuel is careful and never makes a* **hasty** *decision.*

speedy moving or happening quickly. *The* **speedy** *horse soon galloped out of sight.*

antonyms: leisurely, slow

real *adj.* not artificial or made up. *Those silk flowers look just like* **real** *ones.*

actual really existing or happening. *I have seen pictures of rainbows, but I have never seen an* **actual** *rainbow.*

authentic worthy of belief; true. *The book gave an* **authentic** *picture of life in the Wild West.*

genuine not false; real or pure. *He examined the pearls carefully to make sure that they were* **genuine**.

true being in agreement with fact or reality. *Is it **true** that bees make honey?*

antonyms: fake, false, phony

---

red *adj.* having the color of strawberries. *Stop signs are usually **red**.*

crimson bright red. *The American flag has **crimson** and white stripes.*

ruby deep red. *The **ruby**-colored flowers were beautiful in the sunlight.*

---

road *n.* an open way for vehicles, persons, or animals to pass along or through. *This **road** will take you to the next town.*

boulevard a broad street, often with trees and grass planted in the center or along the sides. *Shoppers enjoyed strolling along the shady **boulevard**.*

highway a main public road. *Which **highway** is the fastest route between St. Paul and Minneapolis?*

lane a narrow path or road between fences, hedges, or walls. *We walked along the **lane** between the corn field and the wheat field.*

street a road in a city or town. *The post office and the town hall are on this **street**.*

turnpike a wide highway that drivers pay a toll to use. *Cars on the **turnpike** slowed as they neared the toll booths.*

sad *adj.* feeling or causing sorrow. *The teacher's illness was **sad** news for the class.*

gloomy sad and discouraged. *The losing team felt **gloomy**.*

unhappy without joy or pleasure. *She tried to forget the **unhappy** summer.*

antonyms: *cheerful, glad, happy*

---

save *v.* to keep from danger or harm. *She grabbed the railing and **saved** herself from falling on the ice.*

recover to get something back; to regain. *The police **recovered** the lost truck.*

rescue to remove from a dangerous place. *I **rescued** my cat from the tree.*

antonyms: endanger, lose

---

say *v.* to make known or put across in words. *What did your brother **say** in the letter?*

exclaim to cry out or say suddenly. *"That's mine!" **exclaimed** the child.*

state to say in a very clear, exact way. *The rule **states** that the pool closes at 5:00 P.M.*

---

smell *n.* what the nose senses. *The **smell** of smoke warns us of fire.*

aroma a pleasant smell. *The **aroma** of Aunt Carrie's cooking made us all hungry.*

(continued)

smell (continued)

odor a strong smell. *The **odor** of mothballs clung to the coat.*

scent a light smell. *The woman had left, but the **scent** of her perfume remained.*

soft *adj.* not hard or firm. *The **soft** cheese spread smoothly.*

delicate very easily broken or torn. *A slight tug will snap the **delicate** chain.*

fluffy having hair, feathers, or material that stands up in a soft pile. *I want a warm **fluffy** bathrobe for winter.*

tender easily bruised or hurt. *Her **tender** hands were sore from pulling weeds.*

antonyms: solid, sturdy, tough

strong *adj.* having much power, energy, or strength. *A **strong** wind made the treetops sway.*

mighty having or showing great power, strength, or force. *All the animals in the forest feared the **mighty** mountain lion.*

powerful having power, authority, or influence. *The **powerful** king ruled over every city, town, and village in the land.*

antonyms: feeble, weak

talk *v.* to say words. *Carmen and I **talked** on the phone last night.*

answer to say, write, or do something in reply or in reply to. *"Yes, I would enjoy going to your party," Terry **answered**.*

argue to disagree. *Jane and Michael **argued** about which movie to see.*

gossip to repeat talk that is often not true. *That silly boy likes to **gossip** about people he does not even know.*

scold to speak angrily to for doing something bad. *I **scolded** my cat for scratching the chair.*

Shades of Meaning

How thin is thin?

thin *adj.* having little fat on the body.

1. thin:

   lanky   slender

   lean   slim

2. thinner:

   slight   underweight

3. very thin:

   bony   scrawny   skinny

antonyms: chubby, fat, overweight, plump

try *v.* to put to use for the purpose of judging. *If you like apples, **try** these.*

attempt to make an effort. *The student pilot **attempted** his first solo landing today.*

experiment to do a number of tests to learn or prove something. *She **experimented** to find out which colors looked best in her design.*

sample to test by trying a small part. ***Sample** a dish before you serve it to guests.*

test to use in order to discover any problems. ***Test** the brakes and the horn to be sure that they work.*

---

twist *v.* to move in a winding path. *The road **twisted** through the mountains.*

spin to move very quickly and continuously around a center. *The ice skater **spun** on one foot like a top.*

turn to move or cause to move around a center, rotate. ***Turn** the cap to the right to open the jar.*

twirl to cause to move quickly around a center. *The cowhand **twirled** the lasso and then threw it.*

---

useful *adj.* being of use or service; helpful. *The car and the telephone have turned out to be very **useful** inventions.*

convenient suited to one's needs or purpose. *It is **convenient** to have a supermarket nearby.*

handy useful, convenient, serving many purposes. *The rope that I took on the camping trip turned out to be very **handy**.*

helpful providing what is needed or useful. *A map can be very **helpful** when you are lost.*

practical having or serving a useful purpose. *Would you rather receive a **practical** gift or one that is just for fun?*

antonyms: impractical, useless, worthless

---

usual *adj.* happening regularly or all of the time. *Her **usual** breakfast is toast and orange juice.*

common found or occurring often. *Squirrels are **common** in many parts of the United States.*

familiar well-known. *Jason played several **familiar** songs, and everyone sang along.*

normal of the usual or regular kind. *We had the **normal** amount of rain this spring.*

ordinary not unusual in any way. *A visit from my aunt turns an **ordinary** day into a special event.*

antonyms: extraordinary, outstanding, peculiar, rare, strange, unexpected

valuable *adj.* worth a lot of money. *Land that contains oil is very **valuable**.*

costly of high price or value. *The queen wore a **costly** diamond necklace and earrings.*

expensive having a high price. *Nina has been saving her money for a year to buy an **expensive** bike.*

precious having very great value. *The crown contained diamonds, rubies, and other **precious** gems.*

priceless too valuable to be given a price. *A museum guard watched over the **priceless** paintings.*

antonyms: cheap, inexpensive, worthless

---

very *adv.* to a high degree. *We were **very** tired after a hard day's work.*

especially more than usually. *All my friends are nice, but Ginny is **especially** kind.*

extra unusually; especially. *Last week the weather was **extra** hot, even for summer.*

extremely to a very high degree. *Dinosaurs were **extremely** large animals.*

greatly very much; to a large degree. *That artist's work has been **greatly** admired for centuries.*

most to a high degree. *"This has been a **most** delightful evening," said the guest.*

antonyms: barely, hardly, scarcely

walk *v.* to move on foot at an easy and steady pace. *I had to **walk** home when my bike broke.*

march to walk to an even beat. *The soldiers **marched** in the parade.*

stride to walk with long steps. *John **strode** to the chalkboard, sure of his answer.*

---

wet *adj.* being covered or soaked with water. *I wiped the table with a **wet** cloth.*

damp slightly wet. *His feet left footprints in the **damp** sand.*

drenched wet through and through. *Take this umbrella, or you will get **drenched**!*

dripping being so wet that drops fall. *I wiped my **dripping** forehead after running in the hot sun.*

moist slightly wet. *In the morning the grass is **moist** with dew.*

soggy soaked with moisture. *Her sneakers were **soggy** from walking in the rain.*

sopping thoroughly soaked. *He pulled his **sopping** hat from the puddle and squeezed out the water.*

antonyms: arid, dry, parched

---

work *n.* a way by which a person earns money. *Michael is looking for gardening **work**.*

business a person's occupation, trade, or work. *Mrs. Roth is in the **business** of selling houses.*

(continued)

work (continued)

career a profession that a person follows as a life's work. *My father began his **career** as a firefighter when he was twenty.*

occupation a profession, business, or job. *Working as an airline pilot is an interesting **occupation**.*

profession a job that requires training and special study. *Her college courses will prepare her for the teaching **profession**.*

trade an occupation, especially one requiring special skill with the hands. *My aunt chose carpentry as her **trade** because she likes working with wood.*

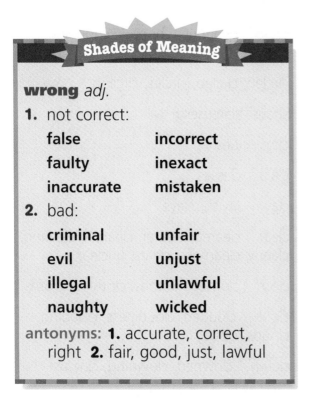

Shades of Meaning

wrong *adj.*

1. not correct:

false	incorrect
faulty	inexact
inaccurate	mistaken

2. bad:

criminal	unfair
evil	unjust
illegal	unlawful
naughty	wicked

antonyms: **1.** accurate, correct, right **2.** fair, good, just, lawful

yell *v.* to cry out loudly. ***Yell** for help.*

bellow to shout in a deep, loud voice. *"Who goes there?" the giant **bellowed**.*

howl to make a long, wailing cry. *He **howled** with pain when he stubbed his toe.*

scream to make a long, loud, piercing cry or sound. *The child **screamed** when the dog ran away with his ball.*

screech to make a high, harsh cry or sound. *"Pretty Polly," the parrot **screeched**.*

shriek to make a loud, shrill sound. *She **shrieked** in fright when the window suddenly slammed shut.*

yellow *adj.* having the color of the sun. ***Yellow** tulips lined the sidewalk in front of the apartment building.*

gold having a deep yellow color. *Wheat turns a **gold** color when it is ripe.*

lemon having the color of ripe lemons. *The **lemon**-yellow walls seemed to fill the room with sunshine.*

Spelling-Meaning Index

able ability, abler, ablest, ably, disable, unable

age aged, ageless, ages, aging

air aired, airing, airless, airplane, airplanes

apple apples

art artful, artist, artistic, artists, arts

---

baby babied, babies, babyhood, babying, babyish

balloon ballooned, ballooning, balloons

bare bareback, bared, barefoot, barehanded, bareheaded, barely, bareness, barer, bares, barest, baring

baseball baseballs

basket basketful, basketry, baskets

bear bear hug, bearish, bearishly, bears, bearskin, grizzly bear, polar bear

begin beginner, beginning, begins

bird birds

birthday birthdays

blow blower, blowing, blown, blows

blue blueness, bluer, blues, bluest

boil boiled, boiler, boiling, boils

boot booted, bootie, boots

bow¹ bows

bow² bowed, bowing, bows

boy boyhood, boyish, boys

bright brighten, brightener, brighter, brightest, brightly, brightness

butter buttered, buttering, butters, buttery, unbuttered

button buttoned, buttoning, buttons, unbutton

---

care cared, careful, carefully, careless, carelessly, cares, caring

carry carriage, carried, carrier, carries, carrying

center centered, centering, centers, central

certain certainly, certainty

chair chairs

chew chewable, chewed, chewing, chews, chewy

child childhood, childish, childishly, childishness, childless, childlessness, childlike, children

chop chopped, chopper, chopping, chops

circle circled, circles, circling

circus circuses

city cities

class classes

clay clayish, clays

clear cleared, clearer, clearest, clearing, clearly, clearness, clears, unclear

cloth clothed, clothes, clothing, cloths

cloud clouded, cloudiness, clouding, clouds, cloudy

clown clowned, clowning, clowns

coach coached, coaches, coaching

coin coins

color colored, colorful, colorfully, coloring, colorless, colors

come become, comes, coming, incoming

cook cooked, cooker, cookery, cookie, cooking, cooks, overcooked, precooked, uncooked, undercooked

cost costing, costly, costs

cough coughed, coughing, coughs

count account, countable, counted, counter, counting, countless, counts, miscount, recount, uncounted

crack cracked, cracker, cracking, cracks

crop crops

crowd crowded, crowding, crowds

crown crowned, crowning, crowns

cry cried, cries, crying

cube cubes, cubic

dance danceable, danced, dancer, dances, dancing

dark darken, darker, darkest, darkly, darkness

daughter daughters

die died, dies, dying

dirt dirtily, dirtiness, dirty

do doer, does, doing, redo, undo

dollar dollars

door doors

drop dropped, dropper, dropping, droplet, drops

drum drummed, drummer, drumming, drums

dry dried, drier, driest, dryer, drying, dryness

ear earful, ears

eight eighteen, eighth, eightieth, eights, eighty

face faced, faceless, faces, facing

fair[1] fairer, fairest, fairly, fairness, unfair, unfairly, unfairness

fair[2] fairs

farm farmed, farmer, farming, farms

feel feeler, feeling, feels, unfeeling

fight fighter, fighting, fights

fix fixable, fixed, fixer, fixes, fixing

float floatable, floated, floating, floats

fly[1] flier, flies, flying

fly[2] flies

foil[1] foiled, foiler, foiling, foils

foil[2] foils

follow followed, follower, following, follows

forget forgetful, forgetfully, forgetfulness, forgets, forgettable, forgetting, unforgettable

four fours, fourteen, fourth

friend befriend, friendless, friendliness, friendly, friends, unfriendly

front front, frontier, fronting, fronts

garden gardened, gardener, gardening, gardens

giraffe giraffes

Spelling-Meaning Index

girl girlhood, girlish, girlishly, girls

grade graded, grader, grades, grading

grandfather grandfatherly, grandfathers

grandmother grandmotherly, grandmothers

grin grinned, grinning, grins

ground grounded, grounding, grounds

hair hairless, hairs, hairy

happen happened, happening, happens

happy happier, happiest, happily, happiness, unhappy

head headed, heading, headless, heads

hear heard, hearer, hearing, hears

hello helloed, helloes, helloing

help helped, helper, helpful, helpfully, helpfulness, helping, helpless, helplessly, helplessness

her hers, herself

him himself

hold holder, holding, holds

hope hoped, hopeful, hopefully, hopefulness, hopeless, hopelessly, hopelessness, hopes, hoping

hour hourly, hours

huge hugely, hugeness, huger, hugest

hunt hunted, hunter, hunting, hunts

hurry hurried, hurriedly, hurriedness, hurries, hurrying, unhurried

hurt hurtful, hurting, hurts, unhurt

ice iced, ices, icier, iciest, iciness, icing, icy

inside insider, insides

invite invitation, invited, invites, inviting

it its

jar jarful, jars

join joined, joiner, joining, joins, joint, rejoin

joke joked, joker, jokes, joking, jokingly

joy enjoy, enjoyable, enjoyably, enjoyment, joyful, joyfully, joyfulness, joyless, joylessly, joylessness, joyous, joyously, joyousness, joys

judge judged, judges, judgeship, judging, judgment

jump jumped, jumper, jumping, jumps, jumpy

kind kinder, kindest, kindliness, kindly, kindness, unkind

knee kneel, knees

knife knives

knock knocked, knocker, knocking, knocks

knot knots, knotted, knotting, knotty

know knowable, knowing, knowingly, knowledge, known, knows, unknown

large enlarge, enlargement, largely, largeness, larger, largest

last lastly

late lately, lateness, later, latest

laugh laughable, laughably, laughed, laughing, laughingly, laughs, laughter

law lawful, lawfully, lawfulness, lawless, lawlessly, lawlessness, laws, lawyer, outlaw, outlawed, unlawful, unlawfully

lawn lawns

lay layer, layered, layering, lays

leave leaves, leaving

lesson lessons

letter lettered, letterer, lettering, letters

lie lies, lying

life lifeless, lifelike, lives

like liken, likeness, likewise, unlike

little littler, littlest

loud aloud, louder, loudest, loudly, loudness

love lovable, lovableness, lovably, loved, loveless, loveliness, lovely, lover, loves, loving, lovingly

luck luckily, luckiness, luckless, lucky, unlucky

make maker, makes, making, remake

market marketed, marketing, markets

match¹ matchable, matched, matcher, matches, matching, matchless

match² matches

milk milked, milker, milkiness, milking, milks, milky

mind mindful, mindfully, mindfulness, mindless, mindlessly, mindlessness, minds, remind, reminder, unmindful

mine mined, miner, mines, mining

mix mixable, mixed, mixer, mixes, mixing, mixture, unmixed

most mostly

mouth mouthed, mouthful, mouthing, mouths

napkin napkins

near neared, nearer, nearest, nearing, nearly, nearness, nears

need needed, needful, needing, needless, needs, needy

neighbor neighbored, neighborhood, neighboring, neighborly, neighbors

new anew, newer, newest, newly, newness, renew

nice nicely, niceness, nicer, nicest

noise noiseless, noises, noisily, noisiness, noisy

north northerly, northern, northerner

note noted, notes, noting

nothing nothingness

oil oiled, oiliness, oiling, oils, oily

orange orangeade, oranges

order disorder, ordered, ordering, orderly, orders, reorder

our ours, ourselves

outside outsider

own owned, owner, ownership, owning, owns

page paged, pages, paging

Spelling-Meaning Index

paint   painted, painter, painting, paints, repaint

pair   paired, pairing, pairs

park   parked, parking, parks

party   partied, parties, partying

pat   pats, patted, patting

patch   patchable, patched, patches, patching, patchy

pay   payable, payer, paying, payment, pays, repay, repayment

peace   peaceable, peaceably, peaceful, peacefully, peacefulness

pear   pears

pencil   penciled, penciling, pencils

penny   pennies, penniless, pennilessness

picnic   picnicked, picnicker, picnicking, picnics

pie   pies

place   displace, misplace, misplaced, placed, placement, places, placing, replace

point   pointed, pointer, pointing, points, pointy

pond   ponds

pony   ponies

pretty   prettier, prettiest, prettily, prettiness

puppy   puppies

purple   purpled, purples, purpling, purplish

quart   quarter, quartered, quartering, quarterly, quartet, quarts

queen   queenlike, queenly, queens

quick   quicken, quicker, quickest, quickly, quickness

quit   quits, quitter, quitting

rabbit   rabbits

raw   rawer, rawest, rawness

read   readable, reading, reads

round   around, rounded, rounder, roundest, rounding, roundness, rounds

row   rowed, rower, rowing, rows

rub   rubbed, rubbing, rubs

sad   sadden, sadder, saddest, sadly, sadness

save   saved, saver, saves, saving, savings

scare   scared, scares, scaring, scary

school   preschool, preschooler, schooled, schooling, schools, unschooled

scratch   scratched, scratches, scratching, scratchy

scream   screamed, screaming, screams

screen   screened, screening, screens

second[1]   seconds

second[2]   secondary, seconded, seconding, secondly, seconds

seem   seemed, seeming, seemingly, seems

send   sender, sending, sends, sent

serve   servant, served, server, serves, service, serving

sew   sewed, sewing, sewn, sews

share   shared, sharer, shares, sharing

shoe   shoeing, shoeless, shoes

shut   shuts, shutter, shutting

sight   sighted, sighting, sightless, sights

sing   singable, singer, singing, sings

skin   skinned, skinning, skinny, skins.

slow   slowed, slower, slowest, slowing, slowly, slowness, slows

smart   smarten, smarter, smartest, smartly, smartness

smell   smelled, smelling, smells, smelly

smile   smiled, smiles, smiling

smoke   smoked, smokeless, smokes, smokiness, smoking, smoky

soap   soaped, soaping, soaps, soapy

sock   socks

soft   soften, softer, softest, softly, softness

soil   soils

sold   resold, unsold

son   grandson, son-in-law, sons, stepson

sound   sounded, sounding, soundless, soundlessly, soundproof, sounds

space   spaced, spaces, spacing

speak   speakable, speaker, speaking, speaks

spoil   spoiled, spoiling, spoils, unspoiled

spoon   spooned, spoonful, spooning, spoons

spray   sprayed, sprayer, spraying, sprays

spread   spreadable, spreading, spreads

spring   springlike, springs

squeeze   squeezable, squeezed, squeezer, squeezes, squeezing

stage   staged, stages, staging

star   starless, starlet, starred, starring, starry, stars

stick   sticker, stickers, stickier, stickiest, stickily, stickiness, sticking, sticks, sticky, unstick

storm   stormed, storming, storms, stormy

story   stories

straight   straighten, straightener, straighter, straightest

straw   straws

stream   streams

street   streets

string   restring, stringing, strings, stringy

strong   stronger, strongest, strongly

sudden   suddenly, suddenness

summer   summers, summery

sun   sunbeam, sunburn, sunburst, sundial, sundown, sunflower, sunglasses, sunless, sunlight, sunnier, sunniest, sunny, sunrise, sunset, sunshine, suntan

talk   talkative, talked, talker, talking, talks

tap   tapped, tapper, tapping, taps

Spelling-Meaning Index

teach   reteach, teacher, teaches, teaching

tell   retell, teller, telling, tells

thank   thanked, thankful, thankfully, thankfulness, thanking, thankless, thanks

their   theirs

thick   thicken, thickener, thickening, thicker, thickest, thicket, thickly, thickness

thin   thinly, thinned, thinner, thinness, thinnest, thinning, thins

third   thirdly, thirds

thought   rethought, thoughtful, thoughtfully, thoughtfulness, thoughtless, thoughtlessly, thoughtlessness

three   threefold, threes, threesome

throw   thrower, throwing, thrown, throws

tie   retie, tied, ties, tying, untie

tight   tighten, tighter, tightest, tightly, tightness

tooth   toothed, toothing, toothless, toothy

toy   toys

trace   retrace, traceable, traced, traceless, tracer, traces, tracing

travel   traveled, traveler, traveling, travelogue, travels

try   trial, tried, tries, trying, untried

turn   turned, turning, turns, unturned

use   misuse, reuse, reusable, usable, usage, used, useful, usefully, usefulness, useless, uselessly, uselessness, user, uses, using

walk   walked, walker, walking, walks

wall   walled, walling, walls

watch   watched, watcher, watches, watchful, watchfulness, watching

weak   weaken, weaker, weakest, weakling, weakly, weakness

week   biweekly, weekday, weekend, weekender, weekly, weeknight, weeks

weigh   weighed, weigher, weighing, weighs, weight, weights

wide   widely, widen, wideness, wider, widest, width

wild   wilder, wildest, wildness

window   windows

winter   winters, wintry

word   reword, worded, wordiness, wording, wordless, words, wordy

work   rework, workable, worked, worker, working, works

wrap   wrapped, wrapper, wrapping, wraps, unwrap

write   rewrite, writer, writes, writing, written

wrong   wronged, wrongful, wronging, wrongs

yellow   yellowed, yellowing, yellowish, yellows, yellowy

Spelling Dictionary

Spelling Table

This Spelling Table shows many of the letter combinations that spell the same sounds in different words. Use this table for help in looking up words that you do not know how to spell.

Sounds	Spellings	Sample	Sounds	Spellings	Sample
|ă|	a, ave, au	bat, have, laugh	|h|	h, wh	hat, who
			|hw|	wh	when
|ā|	a, ai, ay, ea, eigh, ey	tale, later, rain, pay, great, eight, they	|ĭ|	e, ee, i, ui, y	before, been, mix, give, build, gym
|âr|	air, are, ear, eir, ere	fair, care, bear, their, where	|ī|	i, ie, igh, uy, y	time, mind, pie, fight, buy, try
|ä|	a, al	father, calm	|îr|	ear, ere	near, here
|är|	ar	art	|j|	dge, g, ge, j	judge, gym, age, jet
|b|	b, bb	bus, rabbit	|k|	c, ch, ck, k	picnic, school, stick, keep
|ch|	ch, tch	chin, match			
|d|	d, dd	dark, sudden	|kw|	qu	quick
|ĕ|	a, ai, e, ea, ie	any, said, went, head, friend	|l|	l, ll	last, all
			|m|	m, mm	mop, summer
|ē|	e, ea, ee, ey, y	these, we, beast, tree, honey, lady	|n|	kn, n, nn	knee, nine, penny
|f|	f, ff, gh	funny, off, enough	|ng|	n, ng	think, ring
|g|	g, gg	get, egg	|ŏ|	a, o	was, pond

279

Spelling Dictionary

Sounds	Spellings	Sample	Sounds	Spellings	Sample
|ō|	ew, o, oa, oe, ough, ow	sew, most, hope, float, toe, though, row	|t|	ed, t, tt	fixed, tall, kitten
			|*th*|	th	they
			|th|	th	thin, teeth
|ô|	a, al, aw, o, ough	wall, talk, lawn, soft, brought	|ŭ|	o, oe, u	front, come, does, sun
|ôr|	oor, or, ore	door, storm, store	|yo͞o|	u	use
|oi|	oi, oy	join, toy	|ûr|	ear, er, ir, or, ur	learn, herd, girl, word, turn
|ou|	ou, ow	loud, now	|v|	f, v	of, very
|o͝o|	oo, ou	good, could	|w|	o, w	one, way
|o͞o|	ew, o, oe, oo, ou, ough, ue	flew, do, shoe, spoon, you, through, blue	|y|	y	yes
			|z|	s, z	please, zoo
|p|	p, pp	paint, happen	|zh|	s	usual
|r|	r, wr	rub, write	|ə|	a, e, i, o, u	about, silent, pencil, lemon, circus
|s|	c, s, ss	city, same, grass			
|sh|	s, sh	sure, sheep			

How to Use a Dictionary

Finding an Entry Word

Guide Words

The word you want to find in a dictionary is listed in ABC order. To find it quickly, turn to the part of the dictionary that has words with the same first letter. Use the guide words at the top of each page for help. Guide words name the first entry word and the last entry word on each page.

Base Words

To find a word ending in **-ed** or **-ing**, you usually must look up its base word. To find **chewed** or **chewing**, for example, look up the base word **chew**.

Reading an Entry

Read the dictionary entry below. Look carefully at each part of the entry.

The **entry word** is shown, separated into syllables.

The **part of speech** (verb) is identified by an abbreviation (*v.*).

The **-ed** and **-ing** forms of a verb are often shown.

The **pronunciation** shows you how to say the entry word.

easel–fable

en·joy |ĕn joi′| *v.* **enjoyed, enjoying** To get pleasure from: *We enjoy living on a rocky seacoast.*

The **definition** tells you what the word means.

en·joy·a·ble |ĕn joi′ ə bəl| *adj.* Giving joy or happiness: *We had an* ̶ e *trip to the zoo.*

A **sample sentence** or phrase helps to make the meaning clear.

en·joy·ment |ĕn joi′ mənt| *n., pl.* **enjoyments** The act or condition of ̶ something: *Luis gets great*

281

Spelling Dictionary

a·ble |ā′ bəl| *adj.* **abler, ablest**
Having what is needed to do
something: *I will be able to see you
tomorrow.*

a·bout |ə bout′| *prep.* Concerned
with: *That book is about pets.*

ac·ro·bat |ăk′ rə băt′| *n., pl.*
acrobats A person who can do stunts
such as swinging from a trapeze or
walking on a tightrope: *An acrobat
rode a little bicycle across the
tightrope.*

acrobat

a·cross |ə krôs′| *prep.* To the other
side of: *They rode bicycles across the
park.*

act |ăkt| *n., pl.* **acts** One of the main
parts of a play: *The first act takes
place in a factory.*

a·dult |ə dŭlt′| *or* |ăd′ ŭlt′| *n., pl.*
adults A person who is fully grown;
grown-up: *Tickets for adults cost
$3.00.*

af·ter |ăf′ tər| *prep.* Behind in place
or order: *The clowns came after the
elephants in the parade.*
conj. Following the time that: *We can
eat after we get home.*

a·gain |ə gĕn′| *adv.* Once more: *If
you don't win this time, try again.*

age |āj| *n., pl.* **ages** The length of
time someone or something has been
alive: *Pablo's age is eight.*

a·go |ə gō′| *adj.* and *adv.* Before the
present time: *They moved to Chicago
five years ago.*

a·head |ə hĕd′| *adj.* and *adv.* In, at,
or toward the front: *We moved ahead
in line.*

air |âr| *n., pl.* **airs** **1.** The colorless,
odorless, tasteless mixture of gases
that surrounds the earth: *We breathe
air.* **2.** The open space above the
earth: *The batter hit the ball high into
the air.*

air·plane |âr′ plān′| *n., pl.*
airplanes A vehicle with wings that
can fly through the air.
Airplanes are driven by propellers or jet
engines.

a·live |ə līv′| *adj.* Living: *My
grandfather is dead, but my
grandmother is still alive.*

al·most |ôl′ mōst′| *adv.* Nearly;
just short of: *The muffins are almost
done.*

al·so |ôl′ sō| *adv.* Besides; too: *My
watch tells time and gives the date
also.*

a·mong |ə mŭng′| *prep.* In or
through the middle of: *A tall
apartment building stood among the
low houses.*

an·gry |ăng′ grē| *adj.* **angrier, angriest** Feeling or showing that one is strongly displeased: *You say that you aren't angry, but your frown looks angry.*

an·i·mal |ăn′ ə məl| *n., pl.* **animals** A living being that is not a plant. Most animals move around and eat food: *People, horses, fish, and ants are all animals.*

an·y |ĕn′ ē| *adj.* One or some out of three or more: *Take any books that you want to read.*

a·part·ment |ə pärt′ mənt| *n., pl.* **apartments** One or more rooms used as a place to live: *Bill and his parents live in a two-bedroom apartment.*

ap·ple |ăp′ əl| *n., pl.* **apples** A red-skinned fruit.

A·pril |ā′ prəl| *n.* The fourth month of the year. April has 30 days.

a·pron |ā′ prən| *n., pl.* **aprons** A piece of clothing worn over the front of the body to protect the clothes underneath: *Meg wore an apron to keep her dress clean.*

are |är| *v.* **1.** Second person singular present tense of **be**: *You are my friend.* **2.** First, second, and third person plural present tense of **be**: *They are my grandparents.*

aren't |ärnt| Contraction of "are not": *They aren't here yet.*

ar·gue |är′ gyo͞o| *v.* **argued, arguing** To discuss something with someone who has different ideas; disagree: *They argued about what color to paint the room.*

a·round |ə round′| *prep.* In a circle surrounding: *I wore a belt around my waist.*

art |ärt| *n., pl.* **arts** An activity, such as painting, in which something beautiful is made.

a·sleep |ə slēp′| *adj.* Not awake: *The baby is asleep in her crib.*

Au·gust |ô′ gəst| *n.* The eighth month of the year. August has 31 days.

aunt |ănt| *or* |änt| *n., pl.* **aunts** The sister of one's father or mother.

au·tumn |ô′ təm| *n., pl.* **autumns** The season of the year between summer and winter when many crops are harvested; fall.

a·way |ə wā′| *adv.* At or to a distance: *The lake is two miles away.*

ba·by |bā′ bē| *n., pl.* **babies** A very young child; infant. A baby grows up to be an adult.

bait |bāt| *n.* Food placed on a hook or in a trap to attract and catch fish, birds, or other animals: *We used worms as bait to catch fish.*

bal·loon |bə loon′| *n., pl.* **balloons** A small, bright-colored rubber bag that floats when filled with air or another gas.

band·age |băn′ dĭj| *n., pl.* **bandages** A strip of cloth used to cover and protect a cut or an injury: *We put a bandage on the puppy's scraped leg.*

bare |bâr| *adj.* **barer, barest** Without clothing or covering; naked: *The sand tickled my bare feet.*
♦ These sound alike **bare, bear.**

base |bās| *n., pl.* **bases** One of the four corners of a baseball diamond that a runner must touch to score a run: *She hit the baseball and ran to first base.*

base·ball |bās′ bôl′| *n., pl.* **baseballs** A game played with a bat and ball by two teams of nine players each. Baseball is played on a field with four bases. *A run is scored when a player is able to touch all the bases while his or her team is at bat.*

bas·ket |băs′ kĭt| *n., pl.* **baskets** A container made of woven grasses or strips of wood often used to carry things.

basket

bath·robe |băth′ rōb′| *or* |bäth′ rōb′| *n., pl.* **bathrobes** A loose piece of clothing worn as a covering: *John put on his bathrobe and slippers.*

batter |băt′ ər| *n., pl.* **batters** A beaten mixture of flour, eggs, and milk or water that becomes solid when cooked. Batter is used to make pancakes and breads: *Let's mix the batter for pancakes.*

be |bē| *v.* To have a quality: *Jake and Pablo are always truthful.*

bear |bâr| *n., pl.* **bears** A large animal with a shaggy coat and a very short tail. Bears eat mainly fruit and insects.
♦ These sound alike **bear, bare.**

be·cause |bĭ kôz′| *conj.* For the reason that: *I left because I was sick.*

be·come |bĭ kŭm′| *v.* **became, become, becoming** To grow or come to be: *It became cold when the sun set.*

been |bĭn| *v.* Past participle of **be:** *Anthony and I had already been at the bus station for an hour before Dad arrived.*

be·fore |bĭ fôr′| *adv.* Earlier: *Class ends at noon, not before. prep.* Ahead of; earlier than: *The dog got home before me.*

be·gin |bĭ gĭn′| *v.* **began, begun, beginning** **1.** To start to do: *I began taking piano lessons last year.* **2.** To have as a starting point: *Proper nouns begin with capital letters.*

be·hind |bĭ hīnd′| *prep.* To or at the back of: *The apple trees are behind the barn. adv.* In the place or situation being left: *My friends stayed behind.*

be·long |bĭ lông′| *v.* **belonged, belonging** To be owned by: *That sweater belongs to Maria.*

bet·ter |bĕt′ ər| *adj.* Comparative of good: *This car is better than that one. adv.* Comparative of *well: My dog behaves better than Carla's does.*

be·tween |bĭ twēn′| *prep.* In the space separating: *A few trees stand between the house and the road.*

be·ware |bĭ wâr′| *v.* To be careful; look out: *Beware of the ice. It is slippery.*

be·yond |bĭ yŏnd′| *prep.* On or to the far side of: *The forest is beyond the lake.*

bird |bûrd| *n., pl.* **birds** A warm-blooded animal that lays eggs. A bird has two wings and a body covered with feathers.

birth·day |bûrth′ dā′| *n., pl.* **birthdays** The day of a person's birth.

bi·week·ly |bī wēk′ lē| *adv.* Once every two weeks: *I have a music lesson biweekly.*

black |blăk| *adj.* Of the darkest of all colors; the opposite of white.

blaze |blāz| *n., pl.* **blazes** A brightly burning fire: *The blaze destroyed two stores.*

bleach·ers |blē′ chərz| *pl. n.* Seats in rows placed one above another for people watching a sports event: *Three hundred fans sat in the bleachers watching the baseball game.*

blew |bloo| *v.* Past tense of **blow**: *A breeze blew the leaves all over the yard.*
♦ *These sound alike* **blew, blue.**

blood |blŭd| *n.* The liquid that the heart moves through the body. Blood carries oxygen to all parts of the body and carries away waste materials.

Pronunciation Key

ă	pat	ō	go	th	thin	
ā	pay	ô	paw, for	hw	which	
â	care	oi	oil	zh	usual	
ä	father	oo	book	ə	ago,	
ĕ	pet	oo	boot		item,	
ē	be	yoo	cute		pencil,	
ĭ	pit	ou	out		atom,	
ī	ice	ŭ	cut		circus	
î	near	û	fur	ər	butter	
ŏ	pot	th	the			

blow |blō| *v.* **blew, blown, blowing** To shape by pushing air into: *Can you blow a bubble?*

blue |bloo| *adj.* Having the color of a clear sky.
♦ *These sound alike* **blue, blew.**

board |bôrd| *n., pl.* **boards** A piece of sawed lumber; plank: *We nailed boards together to make a bookcase.*

boil |boil| *v.* **boiled, boiling** To cook in a very hot liquid: *Mom boiled the potatoes for twenty minutes.*

boot |boot| *n., pl.* **boots** A covering for the foot or shoe. A boot usually covers the ankle and often part of the leg: *Wear your boots when it's raining.*

both |bōth| *pron.* The one as well as the other; the two alike: *I talked to both of them. adj.* The two; the one as well as the other: *Both sides of the valley are steep.*

bought |bôt| *v.* Past tense and past participle of **buy**: *My little sister sold her tricycle and bought a bicycle.*

bounce |bouns| *v.* **bounced, bouncing 1.** To spring back after hitting a surface: *The ball bounced off the wall.* **2.** To cause to hit a surface and spring back: *I bounced a ball on the sidewalk.*

bow[1] |bō| *n., pl.* **bows** A weapon for shooting arrows.

bow[2] |bou| *v.* **bowed, bowing** To bend the body, head, or knee to show agreement or respect: *He bowed when he met the king. n., pl.* **bows** A bending of the body or head to show respect or thanks: *The jugglers took a bow at the end of the act.*

bow[3] |bou| *n., pl.* **bows** The front part of a ship or a boat.

boy |boi| *n., pl.* **boys** A young male person: *The boy helped his father carry a large box.*

brag |brăg| *v.* **bragged, bragging** To speak with too much pride about oneself: *She bragged about her grades until no one would listen anymore.*

branch |brănch| *n., pl.* **branches** A part that grows out from a trunk or stem of a plant: *The lowest branch of the tree is covered with buds.*

bread |brĕd| *n., pl.* **breads** A food made from flour that is mixed with water or milk, kneaded, and baked: *Use two slices of bread to make a sandwich.*

breathe |brēth| *v.* **breathed, breathing** To take air into the lungs and force it out: *Runners need to breathe deeply.*

bright |brīt| *adj.* **brighter, brightest** Giving off or filled with a lot of light; shining: *The bright sun lit up the meadow.*

bright·en |brīt′n| *v.* **brightened, brightening** To give off or fill with light; to make brighter: *Sunlight brightened the room.*

bright·ly |brīt′ lē| *adv.* In a shining way: *The sun shone brightly on the water.*

bright·ness |brīt′ nĭs| *n.* The quality of being bright: *The brightness of the headlights shone through the night.*

bring |brĭng| *v.* **brought, bringing** To take with oneself: *Bring the books home.*

broth·er |brŭth′ ər| *n., pl.* **brothers** A boy or man having the same mother and father as another person.

brought |brôt| *v.* Past tense and past participle of **bring**: *She brought her homework with her.*

brush |brŭsh| *n., pl.* **brushes** A tool for taking care of the hair. A brush is made of bristles or wire fastened to a hard back or a short handle.

build |bĭld| *v.* **built, building** To make by putting together parts; construct: *Carpenters build houses and stores.*

bum·ble·bee |bŭm′ bəl bē′| *n., pl.* **bumblebees** A large, black and yellow bee that flies with a humming sound.

bumblebee

bump·y |bŭm′ pē| *adj.* **bumpier, bumpiest** Causing jerks and jolts: *He tripped on the bumpy sidewalk.*

burn |bûrn| *v.* **burned** *or* **burnt, burning** 1. To be or set on fire: *The logs burned in the fireplace.* 2. To be or cause to be hurt by heat or fire: *I burned my fingers with a match.*

burnt |bûrnt| *v.* A past tense and past participle of **burn**: *The pizza was burnt, so we couldn't eat it.*

but·ter |bŭt′ ər| *n., pl.* **butters** A soft, yellowish fatty food that is made from milk or cream.

but·ton |bŭt′ n| *n., pl.* **buttons** 1. A disk used to fasten together parts of a piece of clothing. 2. A part that looks like a button: *I pushed the button to turn on the light. v.* **buttoned, buttoning** To fasten or close with buttons: *Don't forget to button your coat.*

buy |bī| *v.* **bought, buying** To get by paying for: *We bought the car that Mickey was selling. n., pl.* **buys** Something bought at a lower price than usual; bargain: *The coat was a good buy.*

buzz |bŭz| *v.* **buzzed, buzzing** To make a low, humming sound like that of a bee: *The alarm clock buzzed.*

cack·le |kăk′ əl| *v.* **cackled, cackling** To make a shrill sound, such as a hen makes.

calf |kăf| *n., pl.* **calves** A young cow or bull.

calm·ly |käm′ lē| *adv.* Not excitedly; without being nervous.

can |kăn| *helping v.* 1. Have the knowledge or skill to: *You can skate well.* 2. Be able to: *I can lift those books.*

ca·nar·y |kə nâr′ ē| *n., pl.* **canaries** A songbird, often yellow in color, that can be kept as a pet in a cage.

canary

can·not |kăn′ ŏt| *or* |kă nŏt′| *v.* Can not: *Sue has lost her money and cannot find it.*

can't |kănt| Contraction of "can not": *I can't untie this knot.*

care |kâr| *n., pl.* **cares** The responsibility of keeping well and safe: *Are you in the doctor's care? v.* **cared, caring** To keep well and safe: *I know how to care for a puppy.*

287

care·ful |kâr′ fəl| *adj.* Taking the necessary care; not careless: *She is careful when she crosses the street.*

car·ry |kăr′ ē| *v.* **carried, carrying** **1.** To take from one place to another: *Dad carried the groceries into the house.* **2.** To hold up the weight of; support: *These posts carry the weight of the porch roof.*

cast |kăst| *n., pl.* **casts** The actors in a play or a movie: *The cast took a bow at the end of the play.*

catch |kăch| *v.* **caught, catching** **1.** To get hold of or grasp something that is moving: *I'll throw the ball, and you catch it.* **2.** To come upon suddenly; surprise: *The wolf caught the deer in a small meadow.*

caught |kôt| *v.* Past tense and past participle of **catch**: *She caught the ball that he threw.*

cav·i·ty |kăv′ ĭ tē| *n., pl.* **cavities** A hole: *The dentist filled the cavity in my tooth.*

cen·ter |sĕn′ tər| *n., pl.* **centers** The middle position, part, or place: *Put the vase of flowers in the center of the table.*

cer·tain |sûr′ tn| *adj.* Having no doubt; sure: *Are you certain that you left the book on the bus?*

chair |châr| *n., pl.* **chairs** A piece of furniture made for sitting on. A chair has a seat, a back, and usually four legs. Some chairs have arms.

char·coal |chär′ kōl′| *n., pl.* **charcoals** A black material made of carbon. Charcoal is made by heating wood or other plant or animal material. Charcoal is often used for cooking outdoors.

check |chĕk| *v.* **checked, checking** To test, to make sure something is correct; review: *Check your answers after doing the arithmetic problems.*

chew |chōō| *v.* **chewed, chewing** To crush or wear away with the teeth: *Always chew your food well.*

chick |chĭk| *n., pl.* **chicks** A young chicken or bird.

child |chīld| *n., pl.* **children** A young boy or girl: *I'm a child now, but I will grow up to be an adult.*

chirp |chûrp| *n., pl.* **chirps** The short, high sound made by some small birds and insects: *The finch let out a little chirp.* *v.* **chirped, chirping** To make a chirp: *Canaries chirp, and ducks quack.*

chop |chŏp| *v.* **chopped, chopping** To cut by hitting with a heavy, sharp tool, such as an ax: *I chopped the wood into pieces.*

cir·cle |sûr′ kəl| *n., pl.* **circles** Something that is more or less round: *There is a circle of children around the clown.*

cir·cus |sûr′ kəs| *n., pl.* **circuses** A colorful traveling show with acrobats, clowns, and trained animals.

cit·y |sĭt′ ē| *n., pl.* **cities** A place where many people live close to one another. Cities are larger than towns.

city

class |klăs| *n., pl.* **classes 1.** A group of students who learn together at the same time: *Mr. Raymond teaches my class.* **2.** The time that such a class meets: *No talking is allowed during the class.*

clay |klā| *n., pl.* **clays** A firm kind of earth made up of small pieces. Clay is soft when wet, and it can be formed into shapes: *We used clay to make pots in art class.*

clear |klîr| *adj.* **clearer, clearest 1.** Free from clouds, mist, or dust: *Today the sky was clear.* **2.** Free from anything that makes it hard to see through: *We could see fish in the clear water.*

cloth |klôth| *n., pl.* **cloths 1.** Material made by weaving together threads of cotton, wool, silk, linen, or manmade fibers. **2.** A piece of cloth used for a special purpose, such as a tablecloth or a washcloth.

cloud |kloud| *n., pl.* **clouds** A white or gray object in the sky made up of tiny drops of water or ice floating high in the air: *A rain cloud drifted toward us.*

clown |kloun| *n., pl.* **clowns** A performer in a circus who does tricks or funny stunts.

coach |kōch| *n., pl.* **coaches** A person who trains or teaches athletes, teams, or performers: *The baseball coach showed Tammy how to hold the bat.*

coat |kōt| *n., pl.* **coats** A piece of clothing with sleeves, usually worn outdoors. It is worn over other clothing.

Pronunciation Key

ă	pat	ō	go	th	thin
ā	pay	ô	paw, for	hw	which
â	care	oi	oil	zh	usual
ä	father	ŏŏ	book	ə	ago,
ĕ	pet	ōō	boot		item,
ē	be	yōō	cute		pencil,
ĭ	pit	ou	out		atom,
ī	ice	ŭ	cut		circus
î	near	û	fur	ər	butter
ŏ	pot	th	the		

---

cob·web |kŏb′ wĕb′| *n., pl.* **cobwebs** The web spun by a spider: *Charlotte the spider made a beautiful cobweb.*

coin |koin| *n., pl.* **coins** A piece of metal used as money, such as a penny or a dime.

cold |kōld| *adj.* **colder, coldest 1.** Being at a low temperature: *The water was cold.* **2.** Chilly: *I was cold without my coat.*

col·lar |kŏl′ ər| *n., pl.* **collars 1.** The part of a piece of clothing that fits around the neck. **2.** A leather or metal band for the neck of an animal: *Attach the dog's leash to its collar.*

col·or |kŭl′ ər| *n., pl.* **colors** A tint other than black or white: *This picture includes all the colors of the rainbow.* *v.* **colored, coloring** To give color to: *Color the truck red with a crayon.*

come |kŭm| *v.* **came, come, coming 1.** To move toward the speaker or toward a place: *The children came home quickly when they were called for dinner.* **2.** To reach a particular condition: *The plants came to life after we watered them.*

com·pare |kəm pâr′| *v.* **compared, comparing** To study in order to see how things are the same or different: *We compared bees and spiders.*

com·plete |kəm **plēt′**| *adj.* Having all that is necessary: *A complete chess set has 32 pieces and a board.*

con·cert |**kŏn′** sûrt| *n., pl.* **concerts** A musical performance given by one or more musicians.

con·test |**kŏn′** tĕst′| *n., pl.* **contests** A struggle between two or more people to win, usually for a prize: *Jan won the spelling contest and received a blue ribbon.*

cook |kŏŏk| *n., pl.* **cooks** A person who prepares food: *The cook put the meat in the oven.*

cool |kōōl| *adj.* **cooler, coolest** Somewhat cold: *It was a cool fall day.*

cop·y |kŏp′ ē| *v.* **copied, copying** To make something that is exactly like something else: *I copied the address so I would not forget it.*

cost |kôst| *n., pl.* **costs** The amount paid for something; price: *The cost of the tickets was $15.00.* *v.* **cost, costing** To have as a price: *The tickets cost $15.00 each.*

cos·tume |kôs′ tōōm′| *or* |kôs′ tyōōm′| *n., pl.* **costumes** Clothes worn by a person playing a part in a play or movie: *We wore dog costumes in the school play.*

cough |kôf| *v.* **coughed, coughing** To force air from the lungs with a sudden sharp noise: *The smoky campfire made Jan cough.*

could |kŏŏd| *or* |kəd| *v.* Past tense of **can:** *He could watch the baseball game on television if he wanted to.*

could·n't |kŏŏd′ nt| Contraction of "could not": *They couldn't find their boots.*

count |kount| *v.* **counted, counting 1.** To find the total of; add up: *Count your change.* **2.** To name numbers in order: *We counted from 1 to 10.*

cour·age |kûr′ ĭj| *n.* Bravery: *The firefighter showed courage when she saved a child from the burning house.*

crack |krăk| *v.* **cracked, cracking 1.** To break with a sudden sharp sound: *We cracked the ice.* **2.** To break without splitting into parts: *The mirror cracked.*

cray·on |krā′ ŏn′| *or* |krā′ ən| *n., pl.* **crayons** A coloring stick: *She drew a bird with her blue crayon.*

crisp |krĭsp| *adj.* **crisper, crispest** Firm but breaks easily; not soggy: *The crisp celery made a crunching sound when we ate it.*

crook·ed |krŏŏk′ ĭd| *adj.* Not straight.

crop |krŏp| *n., pl.* **crops** A plant that is grown and harvested: *Corn and wheat are important farm crops.*

crowd |kroud| *n., pl.* **crowds** A large number of people gathered together: *A crowd waited for the train.*

crown |kroun| *n., pl.* **crowns 1.** A head covering, often made of gold and jewels. A crown is worn by a king or queen. **2.** The top part: *We climbed toward the crown of the hill.*

crumb |krŭm| *n., pl.* **crumbs** A tiny piece of food, especially of bread or cake.

cry |krī| *v.* **cried, crying 1.** To shed tears; weep: *We cried at the end of the sad story.* **2.** To make a special sound or call, as an animal does.

cub |kŭb| *n., pl.* **cubs** A young bear, wolf, or lion.

cube |kyōōb| *n., pl.* **cubes** **1.** A solid shape that has six square faces of equal size. **2.** Something having this shape: *Put the ice cubes in your water.*

cup |kŭp| *n., pl.* **cups** A measurement equal to sixteen tablespoons or half a pint.

dai·sy |dā′ zē| *n., pl.* **daisies** A plant that has flowers with narrow white, yellow, or pink petals around a yellow center: *We picked a bunch of daisies.*

daisy

damp |dămp| *adj.* **damper, dampest** Slightly wet; moist: *The clothes were not quite dry; they were still damp.*

dance |dăns| *v.* **danced, dancing** To move in time to music. *n., pl.* **dances** A set of steps and motions, usually performed to music: *I learned a new square dance.*

	Pronunciation Key			
ă	pat	ō	go	th	thin
ā	pay	ô	paw, for	hw	which
â	care	oi	oil	zh	usual
ä	father	ŏŏ	book	ə	ago,
ĕ	pet	ōō	boot		item,
ē	be	yōō	cute		pencil,
ĭ	pit	ou	out		atom,
ī	ice	ŭ	cut		circus
î	near	û	fur	ər	butter
ŏ	pot	*th*	the		

dark |därk| *adj.* **darker, darkest** Of a deep shade close to black or brown: *Your eyes are a dark color. n.* Lack of light: *Cats' eyes adjust quickly to the dark.*

daugh·ter |dô′ tər| *n., pl.* **daughters** A female child: *Mrs. Harris has two daughters and one son.*

day |dā| *n., pl.* **days** The time of light between sunrise and sunset.

day·time |dā′ tīm′| *n.,* The time between dawn and dark.

De·cem·ber |dĭ sĕm′ bər| *n.* The twelfth month of the year. *December has 31 days.*

de·light |dĭ līt′| *n., pl.* **delights** **1.** Great pleasure: *The baby laughed with delight.* **2.** Something that gives pleasure: *The birthday party was a delight.*

den·tist |dĕn′ tĭst| *n., pl.* **dentists** A person who takes care of teeth: *The dentist showed me how to floss my teeth.*

de·stroy |dĭ stroi′| *v.* **destroyed, destroying** To ruin completely: *The fire destroyed several homes.*

die |dī| *v.* **died, dying** To stop living; become dead: *The flowers died in the spring snowstorm.*

di·rec·tion |dĭ rĕk' shən| *n., pl.*
directions An instruction or order:
Follow the directions on the package.

dirt |dûrt| *n.* **1.** Earth or soil.
2. Something filthy, such as mud.

dish |dĭsh| *n., pl.* **dishes 1.** A flat or
shallow container for holding food.
2. Food prepared in a certain way:
Soup is my favorite dish in the winter.

do |do͞o| *v.* **did, done, doing, does**
1. To carry out an action: *I don't
know what to do.* **2.** To act or
behave: *Do as I say.*

dodge |dŏj| *v.* **dodged,
dodging 1.** To move quickly to the
side: *The quarterback dodged
and ran for a touchdown.* **2.** To keep
away from someone or
something by moving quickly:
I dodged the snowballs thrown at me.

does |dŭz| *v.* Third person
singular present tense of **do**: *How
does Chris do his homework so
quickly?*

dol·lar |dŏl' ər| *n., pl.* **dollars** A unit
of money equal to 100 cents.

door |dôr| *n., pl.* **doors** A movable
panel at the entrance to a room,
building, or vehicle: *Who is at the
back door?*

draw |drô| *v.* **drew, drawn,
drawing** To make a picture with lines;
sketch.

drew |dro͞o| *v.* Past tense of **draw**:
She drew a picture of her family.

drop |drŏp| *n., pl.* **drops**
A small bit of liquid in a round mass:
A drop of sweat ran down my face. v.
dropped, dropping 1. To fall or let
fall in drops. **2.** To fall or let fall: *I
dropped a dish on the floor.*

drum |drŭm| *n., pl.* **drums**
A musical instrument that is hollow
and has a thin layer of material
stretched across one or both ends:
*She plays the drum in our marching
band.*

drum

dry |drī| *v.* **dried, drying**
To make or become free from water or
moisture: *Jill dried the wet puppy with
a towel.*

dry·er |drī' ər| *n., pl.* **dryers**
A device that removes moisture:
*Use a hair dryer and brush to style
your hair.*

duck·ling |dŭk' lĭng| *n., pl.*
ducklings A young duck.

ear |îr| *n., pl.* **ears 1.** The part of the
body with which people and animals
hear. **2.** The sense of hearing: *The
sound of music is pleasant to the ear.*

ear·ly |ûr' lē| *adv.* **earlier, earliest**
Before the usual or expected time: *The
plane landed earlier than planned.*

ea·sel |ē′ zəl| *n., pl.* **easels** A stand for holding a painting: *The artist placed her picture on an easel.*

ef·fort |ĕf′ ərt| *n., pl.* **efforts** A sincere attempt; try: *Please make an effort to arrive on time.*

eight |āt| *n., pl.* **eights** A number, written 8, that is equal to the sum of 7 + 1. *adj.* Being one more than seven.

el·e·phant |ĕl′ ə fənt| *n., pl.* **elephants** A very large land animal with a long, bendable trunk and long, curved tusks: *Elephants are the biggest land animals.*

emp·ty |ĕmp′ tē| *adj.* Having nothing inside: *Fill the empty jar with orange juice.*

en·joy |ĕn joi′| *v.* **enjoyed, enjoying** To get pleasure from: *We enjoy living on a rocky seacoast.*

en·joy·a·ble |ĕn joi′ ə bəl| *adj.* Giving joy or happiness: *We had an enjoyable trip to the zoo.*

en·joy·ment |ĕn joi′ mənt| *n., pl.* **enjoyments** The act or condition of enjoying something: *Luis gets great enjoyment from his stamp collection.*

e·nough |ĭ nŭf′| *adj.* Being as much or as many as needed: *There is enough food for everybody. adv.* To or in the amount needed: *You know them well enough to believe what they say.*

en·trance |ĕn′ trəns| *n., pl.* **entrances** A door or opening: *We used the back entrance to the theater.*

-er A suffix that forms nouns. The suffix "-er" means "a person who": *teacher.*

Pronunciation Key

ă	pat	ō	go	th	**th**in
ā	pay	ô	paw, **for**	hw	**wh**ich
â	care	oi	**oi**l	zh	usual
ä	father	o͝o	book	ə	ago,
ĕ	pet	o͞o	boot		item,
ē	be	yo͞o	cute		pencil,
ĭ	pit	ou	**ou**t		atom,
ī	ice	ŭ	cut		circus
î	near	û	fur	ər	butter
ŏ	pot	*th*	**the**		

es·cape |ĭ skāp′| *v.* **escaped, escaping** To get free; to get away from: *The dogs escaped by jumping over the fence.*

ev·er |ĕv′ ər| *adv.* In any way: *How could I ever forget that day?*

eve·ry·bod·y |ĕv′ rē bŏd′ ē| *pron.* Every person; everyone: *Everybody makes a mistake sometime.*

ex·pect |ĭk spĕkt′| *v.* **expected, expecting** To look for as likely to happen or appear; await: *The farmers expect an early frost this year.*

ex·plode |ĭk splōd′| *v.* **exploded, exploding** To burst with a loud noise; blow up: *Suddenly the gas tank exploded.*

eye |ī| *n., pl.* **eyes** The organ of sight in people and animals: *I wear glasses because my left eye is weak.*
♦ *These sound alike* **eye, I.**

fa·ble |fā′ bəl| *n., pl.* **fables** A story that is meant to teach a lesson. A fable often has animal characters that speak and act like human beings.

face |fās| *n., pl.* **faces** The front part of the head from the forehead to the chin.

fair |fâr| *n., pl.* **fairs** A showing of farm and home products, often together with entertainment, such as a Ferris wheel.
♦ *These sound alike* **fair, fare.**

fare |fâr| *n., pl.* **fares** The money a person must pay to travel on a plane, train, or bus.
♦ *These sound alike* **fare, fair.**

farm·er |fär′ mər| *n., pl.* **farmers** A person who raises crops or animals on a farm: *The farmer fed his chickens, cows, pigs, and ducks.*

fawn |fôn| *n., pl.* **fawns** A young deer.

fawn

Feb·ru·ar·y |fĕb′ r$\overline{oo}$ ĕr′ ē| *or* |fĕb′ y$\overline{oo}$ ĕr′ ē| *n.* The second month of the year. February has 28 days except in leap year when it has 29.

feel |fēl| *v.* **felt, feeling 1.** To notice by using the sense of touch: *I feel leaves brushing against my cheek.* **2.** To notice being in a certain condition: *I feel sleepy.*

field |fēld| *n., pl.* **fields 1.** A broad area of open or cleared land. **2.** An area of land where a crop is grown or a special activity is done: *They practiced kicking on the football field.*

fight |fīt| *n., pl.* **fights 1.** A meeting between animals, persons, or groups in which each side, using bodies or weapons, tries to hurt the other: *One dog bit the other during the fight.* **2.** An angry disagreement; argument: *They had a fight about whose turn it was. v.* **fought, fighting** To struggle or make an effort: *I was so tired that I had to fight to stay awake.*

find |fīnd| *v.* **found, finding** To look for and discover: *Please help me find my pen.*

fin·ish |fĭn′ ĭsh| *n., pl.* **finishes** The end: *The finish of the race was exciting.*

first |fîrst| *adj.* Coming before all others: *The first house on the block is nicer than the last one. adv.* Before all others: *I'll go first, and you follow.*

fish·ing rod |fĭsh′ ĭng rŏd| *n., pl.* **fishing rods** A long, slender rod or stick with a hook, a line, and often a reel, used for catching fish: *I caught two fish with my fishing rod.*

fix |fĭks| *v.* **fixed, fixing** To repair.

flag·pole |flăg′ pōl′| *n., pl.* **flagpoles** A pole for flying a flag: *On July 4 we hang our flag on the flagpole.*

flair |flâr| *n., pl.* **flairs** A natural talent: *She has a flair for painting with bright colors.*

flaw |flô| *n., pl.* **flaws** A mistake: *There was a flaw in the beautiful vase, so Mom returned it.*

flew |fl$\overline{oo}$| *v.* Past tense of **fly**[1]: *The plane flew over the ocean.*

float |flōt| *v.* **floated, floating** To be held up in or at the top of water or air: *Balloons floated in the air.*

floss |flôs| *n., pl.* **flosses** A strong thread used to clean between the teeth: *She uses a toothbrush, toothpaste, and floss to clean her teeth.*

flour |flour| *n., pl.* **flours** A fine powder made by grinding wheat or another grain. Flour is used for making bread and muffins: *You need eggs, milk, and flour to make pancakes.*

flow·er |flou′ ər| *n., pl.* **flowers** A plant that usually has colorful petals: *Roses and daisies are flowers.*

fly[1] |flī| *v.* **flew, flown, flying** To move through the air with wings.

fly[2] |flī| *n., pl.* **flies** An insect, such as the common housefly, that has a single pair of thin, clear wings.

fog |fôg| *n., pl.* **fogs** A cloud of water droplets floating near the ground: *There was so much fog that we could hardly see the road.*

foil[1] |foil| *v.* **foiled, foiling** To keep from success: *The alarm foiled the thief.*

foil[2] |foil| *n., pl.* **foils** A thin sheet of metal: *Wrap the meat in foil.*

fold |fōld| *v.* **folded, folding** To bend or double over so that one part lies over another: *I have to fold the clothes in the dryer and put them away.*

fol·low |fŏl′ ō| *v.* **followed, following** **1.** To go or come after: *The ducklings followed their mother to the pond.* **2.** To take the same path as: *I followed the trail for a mile.* **3.** To come after in order or time: *Night follows day.*

Pronunciation Key

ă	pat	ō	go	th	thin
ā	pay	ô	paw, for	hw	which
â	care	oi	oil	zh	usual
ä	father	ŏŏ	book	ə	ago,
ĕ	pet	ōō	boot		item,
ē	be	yōō	cute		pencil,
ĭ	pit	ou	out		atom,
ī	ice	ŭ	cut		circus
î	near	û	fur	ər	butter
ŏ	pot	*th*	the		

foot |fŏŏt| *n., pl.* **feet** The part of the leg of a person or an animal on which it stands or walks.

foot·print |fŏŏt′ prĭnt′| *n.* A mark left by a foot: *Al left lots of footprints where he stepped.*

for·est |fôr′ ĭst| *n., pl.* **forests** A large growth of trees: *Many wild animals live in the forest.*

for·get |fər gĕt′| *v.* **forgot, forgotten** or **forgot, forgetting** To be unable to remember: *I forgot my friend's new address.*

fought |fôt| *v.* Past tense and past participle of fight: *My dog was hurt when it fought with another dog.*

fourth |fôrth| *adj.* Coming after the third: *Tuesday is the third day of the week, and Wednesday is the fourth day.*

frame |frām| *v.* **framed, framing** To enclose in or as if in a frame: *A border of tulips framed the garden.*

freck·le |frĕk′ əl| *n., pl.* **freckles** A small brown spot on the skin: *Antonio has freckles on his arms.*

freeze |frēz| *v.* **froze, frozen, freezing** To hurt or to kill by cold: *This snow will freeze the flowers.*

Fri·day |frī′ dē| or |frī′ dā| *n., pl.* **Fridays** The sixth day of the week.

friend |frĕnd| *n., pl.* **friends** A person one knows, likes, and enjoys being with.

friend·ly |frĕnd' lē| *adj.* **friendlier, friendliest 1.** Showing friendship; not unfriendly: *My new neighbor gave me a friendly smile.* **2.** Liking to meet and to talk with others: *A friendly guide asked us if we needed more directions.*

front |frŭnt| *n., pl.* **fronts** The area directly ahead of the forward part: *The front of the theater is on Main Street. adj.* In or facing the forward part: *The front door is locked.*

frown |froun| *v.* **frowned, frowning** To wrinkle the forehead to show that one is unhappy or puzzled: *Mom frowned at the mess.*

-ful A suffix that forms adjectives. The suffix "-ful" means "full of" or "having": *beautiful.*

full |fo͝ol| *adj.* **fuller, fullest** Holding as much as possible; filled: *Water ran down the side of the full bucket.*

fun·ny |fŭn' ē| *adj.* **funnier, funniest 1.** Causing amusement or laughter. **2.** Strange; odd: *I heard a funny noise.*

gal·lon |găl' ən| *n., pl.* **gallons** A measurement equal to four quarts: *Tina bought a gallon of milk at the store.*

gar·den |gär' dn| *n., pl.* **gardens** A piece of land where flowers, vegetables, or fruit are grown.

garden

gib·bon |gĭb' ən| *n., pl.* **gibbons** A small ape of southeastern Asia. Gibbons live in trees and swing from branch to branch with their long arms.

gi·raffe |jĭ răf'| *n., pl.* **giraffes** A tall African animal with short horns, very long neck and legs, and a tan coat with brown spots.

girl |gûrl| *n., pl.* **girls** A young female person: *The girl greeted her friends.*

give |gĭv| *v.* **gave, given, giving 1.** To make a gift of: *My sister gave me a new watch.* **2.** To pay: *Sid will give me fifteen dollars for my old bike.*

glad |glăd| *adj.* **gladder, gladdest 1.** Bringing joy or pleasure: *The letter brought glad news.* **2.** Pleased; happy: *We were glad to be home again.*

go |gō| *v.* **went, gone, going, goes** To move away from a place; leave.

gog·gles |gŏg′ əlz| *pl. n.* A pair of glasses worn to protect the eyes against water, dust, wind, or sparks: *The welder wore goggles when he used a blowtorch.*

good |gŏod| *adj.* **better, best**
1. Suitable for a particular use: *Crayons are good for drawing.* **2.** Not weakened or damaged: *The old dog's hearing is still good.*

grade |grād| *n., pl.* **grades 1.** A class or year in a school: *The twins will enter the fourth grade next fall.* **2.** A mark showing what kind of work a student does: *I got a good grade in science.*

grand·fa·ther |grănd′ fä′ thər| *n., pl.* **grandfathers** The father of one's father or mother.

grand·moth·er |grănd′ mŭ*th*′ ər| *n., pl.* **grandmothers** The mother of one's father or mother.

green |grēn| *n., pl.* **greens** The color of most plant leaves and growing grass. *adj.* **greener, greenest** Of the color green.

grew |grōo| *v.* Past tense of **grow**: *The puppies grew into large dogs.*

grill |grĭl| *n., pl.* **grills** A cooking device on which food, such as meat or fish, may be broiled: *We cooked hamburgers on the grill.*

grin |grĭn| *v.* **grinned, grinning** To smile: *The child grinned with delight at the birthday present.*

ground |ground| *n., pl.* **grounds** The solid surface of the earth; land: *We sat on a blanket on the ground.*

grow |grō| *v.* **grew, grown, growing** To become larger in size: *Our class studied how plants grow.*

Pronunciation Key

ă	pat	ō	go	th	thin
ā	pay	ô	paw, for	hw	which
â	care	oi	oil	zh	usual
ä	father	ŏŏ	book	ə	ago,
ĕ	pet	ōō	boot		item,
ē	be	yōō	cute		pencil,
ĭ	pit	ou	out		atom,
ī	ice	ŭ	cut		circus
î	near	û	fur	ər	butter
ŏ	pot	*th*	the		

gum |gŭm| *n., pl.* **gums** The firm flesh that is around the teeth: *Using dental floss will help keep your gums healthy.*

gym |jĭm| *n., pl.* **gyms** A room for indoor sports and exercise: *Sharon, Louise, Lee, and I sometimes play basketball or volleyball in the gym after school.*

hair |hâr| *n., pl.* **hairs** A covering of fine, thin strands that grow from the skin: *Lou has curly red hair.*
♦ *These sound alike* **hair, hare.**

ham·bur·ger |hăm′ bûr′ gər| *n., pl.* **hamburgers** A patty of fried or broiled ground beef, usually served in a roll or bun: *Dad cooked hamburgers for dinner.*

hap·pen |hăp′ ən| *v.* **happened, happening** To take place; occur: *Tell me everything that happened today.*

hard |härd| *adj.* and *adv.* **harder, hardest 1.** Not bending when pushed; firm: *The steel blade is hard.* **2.** Having much force: *I suddenly felt a hard wind on my back, and it almost knocked me over.*

Spelling Dictionary

hare |hâr| *n., pl.* **hares** An animal that looks like a rabbit, but has longer ears and larger back feet.
♦ *These sound alike* **hare, hair.**

have |hăv| *v.* **had, having, has**
1. To own: *I have a bicycle.* **2.** To contain: *A year has 365 days.* **3.** To hold in one's mind: *I have my doubts.*
4. To go through; to experience: *I have a cold.*

head |hĕd| *n., pl.* **heads** The top part of the body, containing the brain, eyes, ears, nose, mouth, and jaws.

hear |hîr| *v.* **heard, hearing** To take in sounds through the ear: *We heard a dog barking.*
♦ *These sound alike* **hear, here.**

heat |hēt| *n., pl.* **heats** The condition of being hot; warmth: *I could feel the heat of the sun on my back.*

hel·lo |hĕ lō′| *or* |hə lō′| *or* |hĕl′ ō| *interj.* A word used as a greeting.

help |hĕlp| *v.* **helped, helping 1.** To give or do what is needed or useful: *I helped my parents with the dishes.* **2.** To give relief from: *This medicine will help your cold.*

help·er |hĕlp′ ər| *n., pl.* **helpers** Someone or something that helps: *My dad needs a helper at the gas station.*

help·ful |hĕlp′ fəl′| *adj.* Providing help: *The librarian was very helpful.*
adv. **helpfully** In a helpful way: *Clara helpfully gave me a push up into the tree.*

her |hûr| *pron.* The objective case of **she:** *Do you see her? adj.* Relating or belonging to **her**: *Where did she put her hat?*

here |hîr| *adv.* At or in this place: *Put the package here.*
♦ *These sound alike* **here, hear.**

her·self |hər sĕlf′| *pron.* Her own self: *She blamed herself.*

he's |hēz| Contraction of "he is" or "he has": *He's my best friend.*

him·self |hĭm sĕlf′| *pron.* His own self: *He found himself in a strange place.*

hiss |hĭs| *v.* **hissed, hissing** A sound like a long *s,* such as a snake makes.

hive |hīv| *n., pl.* **hives** A home for honeybees: *The beekeeper has dozens of hives filled with honeybees.*

hive

hold |hōld| *v.* **held, holding** To have or keep in the arms or hands without dropping: *The baby is learning to hold a cup.*

home run |hōm′ rŭn′| *n., pl.* **home runs** A hit in baseball that allows the batter to touch all bases and score a run: *The fans cheered when he hit a home run.*

hon·ey |hŭn′ ē| *n., pl.* **honeys** A sweet thick liquid that bees make from flowers and use as food: *Mom usually uses honey instead of sugar to sweeten foods.*

hook |ho͝ok| *n., pl.* **hooks** A bent object, often made of metal, that is used to catch, hold, or pull something: *A fish bit the hook at the end of my fishing line.*

hope |hōp| *v.* **hoped, hoping** To wish and at the same time expect that the wish will come true: *He hopes that he will do well on the test.*

hope·ful |hōp′ fəl| *adj.* Feeling or showing hope.

ho·tel |hō tĕl′| *n., pl.* **hotels** A house or building where travelers pay to live and eat: *Dad stays in a hotel when he goes away on business.*

hour |our| *n., pl.* **hours** A unit of time that is equal to 60 minutes: *There are 24 hours in a day.*
♦ *These sound alike* **hour, our.**

house |hous| *n., pl.* **houses** A building people live in: *We moved into our new house.*

huge |hyo͞oj| *adj.* **huger, hugest** Very big; enormous.

hunt |hŭnt| *v.* **hunted, hunting** To make a careful search: *Help me hunt for my glasses. n., pl.* **hunts** A careful search: *The hunt for my lost keys was a success.*

hur·ry |hûr′ ē| *v.* **hurried, hurrying** **1.** To act or move quickly; rush: *Do not hurry through your work.* **2.** To take, send, or move quickly: *The doctor hurried the patient to the hospital.*

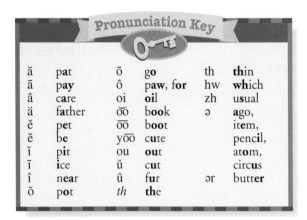

Pronunciation Key					
ă	pat	ō	go	th	thin
ā	pay	ô	paw, for	hw	which
â	care	oi	oil	zh	usual
ä	father	o͝o	book	ə	ago,
ĕ	pet	o͞o	boot		item,
ē	be	yo͞o	cute		pencil,
ĭ	pit	ou	out		atom,
ī	ice	ŭ	cut		circus
î	near	û	fur	ər	butter
ŏ	pot	th	the		

hurt |hûrt| *v.* **hurt, hurting** **1.** To cause pain or injury to: *I fell and hurt my wrist.* **2.** To have a bad effect on: *The dogs can't hurt that old couch.*

I |ī| *pron.* The person who is the speaker or writer: *I like cats a lot, but cats don't seem to like me.*
♦ *These sound alike* **I, eye.**

i·ci·cle |ī′ sĭ kəl| *n., pl.* **icicles** A thin, pointed, hanging piece of ice.

icicle

I'd |īd| Contraction of "I had," "I would," or "I should": *I'd rather leave now, not later.*

I'm |īm| Contraction of "I am": *I'm ready to go.*

insect

in·sect |ĭn' sĕct'| *n., pl.* **insects** An animal that has six legs, a body with three main parts, and usually wings. Flies, bees, grasshoppers, and butterflies are insects.

in·side |ĭn' sīd'| *or* |ĭn sīd'| *adj.* Inner or interior: *This jacket has an inside pocket. adv.* **1.** Into; within: *I'm staying inside because of my cold.* **2.** On the inner side: *I scrubbed the tub inside and out until it was clean.*

in·vite |ĭn vīt'| *v.* **invited, inviting** To ask someone to come somewhere to do something: *How many guests did you invite to the party?*

is·n't |ĭz' ənt| Contraction of "is not": *That isn't my dog.*

its |ĭts| *adj.* Belonging to **it:** *Everything was in its place.*
◆ *These sound alike* **its, it's.**

it's |ĭts| Contraction of "it is" or "it has": *It's raining.*
◆ *These sound alike* **it's, its.**

Jan·u·ar·y |jăn' yo͞o ĕr' ē| *n.* The first month of the year. January has 31 days.

jar |jär| *n., pl.* **jars** A container with a wide opening. Jars are usually made of glass, pottery, or plastic.

jeans |jēnz| *pl. n.* Pants usually made of a strong blue cloth.

job |jŏb| *n., pl.* **jobs** A piece of work; task: *Who gets the job of sweeping the floor?*

join |join| *v.* **joined, joining** **1.** To enter into the company of: *Please join us for lunch.* **2.** To become a member of: *I would like to join the club.*

joke |jōk| *v.* **joked, joking** To say or do something funny: *I was only joking when I said that.*

joy |joi| *n., pl.* **joys** **1.** A feeling of great happiness or delight: *We felt joy at being with our family again.* **2.** A cause of joy: *It was a joy to see Mom feeling better.*

joy·ful |joi' fəl| *adj.* Feeling, showing, or causing joy: *Grandpa's birthday was a joyful family event.*

joy·ous |joi' əs| *adj.* Joyful.

judge |jŭj| *n., pl.* **judges** **1.** A person who listens to and decides about cases in a court of law. **2.** A person who decides the winner of a contest or race. *v.* **judged, judging** To decide; to settle a contest or a problem: *Craig will judge the art contest.*

jug·gler |jŭg' lər| *n., pl.* **jugglers** A person who tosses things into the air and catches them to entertain people: *The juggler tossed four balls and a plate into the air.*

Ju·ly |jo͞o lī'| *n.* The seventh month of the year. July has 31 days.

jump |jŭmp| *v.* **jumped, jumping** To rise up or move through the air by using the legs; leap: *Grasshoppers can jump very high.*

June |jo͞on| *n.* The sixth month of the year. Summer begins in June.

knee |nē| *n., pl.* **knees** The place where the thigh bone and lower leg bone come together: *The dancer bent his knee and then straightened his leg.*

knew |no͞o| *or* |nyo͞o| *v.* Past tense of **know**: *I knew how to solve the problem.*
♦ These sound alike **knew, new.**

knife |nīf| *n., pl.* **knives** A sharp blade attached to a handle. A knife is used for cutting or carving.

knock |nŏk| *v.* **knocked, knocking** To make a loud noise by hitting a hard surface; rap: *I knocked and knocked, but nobody came to the door.*

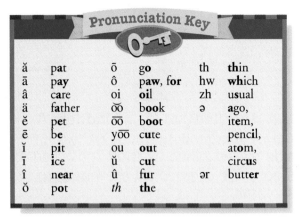

ă	pat	ō	go	th	thin
ā	pay	ô	paw, for	hw	which
â	care	oi	oil	zh	usual
ä	father	o͝o	book	ə	ago,
ĕ	pet	o͞o	boot		item,
ē	be	yo͞o	cute		pencil,
ĭ	pit	ou	out		atom,
ī	ice	ŭ	cut		circus
î	near	û	fur	ər	butter
ŏ	pot	*th*	the		

knot |nŏt| *n., pl.* **knots** **1.** A fastening made by tying together pieces of string, rope, or twine. **2.** A tightly twisted clump; tangle: *The dog's fur is full of knots. v.* **knotted, knotting** To tie or fasten in a knot: *I knotted my shoelaces together.*

know |nō| *v.* **knew, known, knowing** **1.** To understand or have the facts about: *Do you know what causes thunder?* **2.** To be sure: *I know that I am right.*
♦ These sound alike **know, no.**

knuck·le |nŭk' əl| *n., pl.* **knuckles** The place where the bones of the finger or thumb come together.

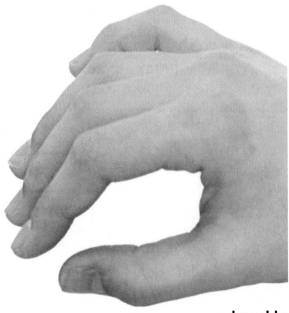

knuckle

L

lad·der |lăd′ ər| *n., pl.* **ladders** A device for climbing, made of two long side pieces joined by short rods used as steps: *We climbed up the ladder to the attic.*

la·dy |lā′ dē| *n., pl.* **ladies** A woman: *A lady on the bus gave us directions.*

lane |lān| *n., pl.* **lanes** A set route through water or air for swimmers, ships, or planes: *The swimmer in the third lane of the pool won the race.*

large |lärj| *adj.* **larger, largest** Bigger than average: *The zoo has large animals, such as hippos and giraffes.*

last |lăst| *adj.* Coming, being, or placed after all others; final: *We won the last game of the season. We had won a game at last.*

late |lāt| *adj.* **later, latest** Coming after the proper time: *We were late for school. adv.* **later, latest** After the proper time: *The train arrived later than expected.*

laugh |lăf| *v.* **laughed, laughing** To smile and make sounds to show amusement or scorn. *n., pl.* **laughs** The act or sound of laughing.

laugh·a·ble |lăf′ ə bəl| *adj.* Likely to cause laughter or amusement: *The sack race was a laughable event.*

laugh·ing·ly |lăf′ ĭng lē′| *adv.* Jokingly: *Paula laughingly said that I swim like a stone fish.*

laugh·ter |lăf′ tər| *n.* The act or sound of laughing: *The baby's laughter told us that he was happy.*

laun·dro·mat |lôn′ drə măt′| *n.* A laundry where people can clean and dry their own clothes: *Sandy washed his shirts at the laundromat.*

laun·dry |lôn′ drē| *n., pl.* **laundries** Clothing that must be washed or that has just been washed.

law |lô| *n., pl.* **laws** A rule that tells people what they must or must not do: *It is against the law to drive without a license.*

lawn |lôn| *n., pl.* **lawns** A piece of ground, often near a house or in a park, planted with grass.

lay |lā| *v.* **laid, laying 1.** To put or set down: *You can lay your books on my desk.* **2.** To put in place: *We helped lay new tiles in the bathroom.*

learn |lûrn| *v.* **learned** *or* **learnt, learning** To get knowledge of something by studying or being taught it: *The third graders are learning Spanish.*

least |lēst| *adv.* In the smallest or lowest degree: *I like tennis best and baseball least. n.* The smallest amount or degree: *The least you can do is offer to help.*

leave |lēv| *v.* **left, leaving 1.** To go away from; go: *Are you leaving this afternoon?* **2.** To let stay behind: *I will leave your book on the desk.* **3.** To have remaining: *Four from seven leaves three.*

left[1] |lĕft| *n.* The side from which a person begins to read a line of English; the side or direction opposite the right: *The number 9 is on the left of a clock's face.*

left[2] |lĕft| *v.* Past tense and past participle of **leave:** *After dinner some dishes were left on the table.*

lem·ming |lĕm′ ĭng| *n., pl.*
lemmings A short-tailed animal that
lives in northern regions. The lemming
is related to the mouse.

les·son |lĕs′ ən| *n., pl.* **lessons**
Something to be learned or taught:
*Janet goes to her skating lesson every
Saturday.*

let's |lĕts| Contraction of "let us":
Let's play this game.

let·ter |lĕt′ ər| *n., pl.* **letters 1.** A
written mark that stands for a sound
and is used to spell words. There are
26 letters in the English alphabet.
2. A written message to someone that
is usually sent by mail in an envelope.

li·brar·y |lī′ brĕr′ ē| *n., pl.* **libraries**
A place where books, magazines,
records, and other reference materials
are kept for reading and borrowing.

lie¹ |lī| *v.* **lay, lain, lying** To be in a
flat or resting position: *I lay down
under an elm tree.*

lie² |lī| *n., pl.* **lies** A statement that is
not the truth; fib.

life |līf| *n., pl.* **lives 1.** The fact of
being alive or staying alive: *I risked my
life to save the drowning child.* **2.** The
time between birth and death; lifetime:
*Uncle Louis spent his life helping other
people.*

li·lac |lī′ lək| *n., pl.* **lilacs** A shrub
that has purple or white flowers.

lilac

lis·ten |lĭs′ ən| *v.* **listened,
listening 1.** To try to hear something:
If you listen, you can hear the ocean.
2. To pay attention: *Now listen to me!*

lis·ten·er |lĭs′ ən ər| *n., pl.* **listeners**
Someone who listens.

lit·tle |lĭt′ l| *adj.* **littler** or **less,
littlest** or **least** Small: *Dolls look like
little people.*

load |lōd| *n., pl.* **loads** An amount of
work to be done: *We have a load of
dry cleaning to do.*

loose |lōōs| *adj.* **looser, loosest** Not
tight: *I put on a loose sweater.*

lot |lŏt| *n., pl.* **lots** A large number or
amount: *I have a lot of work to do.*

loud |loud| *adj.* and *adv.*
louder, loudest Having a large
amount of sound; noisy: *We heard a
loud radio. adv.* In a loud manner:
Speak louder.

love |lŭv| *v.* **loved, loving** To have
warm feelings for; lacking hate: *The
mother loved her baby.*

luck |lŭk| *n.* The chance happening
of good or bad events; fortune: *We
had good luck selling our books at the
yard sale.*

-ly A suffix that forms adverbs. The
suffix "-ly" means "in a way that is":
quickly.

main |mān| *adj.* Most important: *Look for the main idea in each paragraph.*

♦ *These sound alike* **main, mane.**

make |māk| *v.* **made, making** To form, shape, or put together: *I made a shirt.*

make-up *or* **make·up** |māk′ ŭp′| *n., pl.* **make-ups** *or* **makeups** Materials put on the face or body for a play: *The make-up made the boy look like an old man.*

mane |mān| *n., pl.* **manes** The long heavy hair growing from the neck and the head of an animal, such as a horse.

♦ *These sound alike* **mane, main.**

mane

March |märch| *n.* The third month of the year. March has 31 days.

mark·er |mär′ kər| *n., pl.* **markers** Something used to draw marks or to color: *I used markers to make signs for the fair.*

mar·ket |mär′ kĭt| *n., pl.* **markets** A store that sells food: *I bought lamb chops at the meat market.*

match[1] |măch| *v.* **matched, matching** To be alike: *The two colors match exactly.*

match[2] |măch| *n., pl.* **matches** A strip of wood or cardboard covered at one end with something that catches fire when it is rubbed on a rough surface.

may |mā| *helping v., past tense* **might** Used to show or express a request for permission: *May I take a swim?*

May |mā| *n.* The fifth month of the year. May has 31 days.

med·al |měd′l| *n., pl.* **medals** A small, flat piece of metal with a design. A medal may be given for an action or an accomplishment: *Frank won the jumping medal.*

meet |mēt| *n., pl.* **meets** A gathering for sports contests: *The school held a track meet.*

might |mīt| *v.* Past tense of **may**: *We might have gone swimming, but it rained.*

milk |mĭlk| *n.* A whitish liquid from cows that is used as food by human beings.

mind |mĭnd| *n., pl.* **minds** The part of a human being that thinks, feels, understands, and remembers: *You use your mind to do arithmetic.*

mine[1] |mīn| *n., pl.* **mines** An underground tunnel from which minerals such as iron or gold can be taken: *He needed a shovel and a helmet to work in the coal mine.*

mine[2] |mīn| *pron.* The one or ones that belong to me: *The red scarf on the chair is mine.*

mis·place |mĭs **plās'**| v. **misplaced, misplacing** **1.** To put in the wrong place: *I misplaced my math book this morning.* **2.** To lose: *I misplaced my keys.*

mis·take |mĭ **stāk'**| n., pl. **mistakes** Something that is done incorrectly: *I fixed the mistake that I made in math.*

mitt |mĭt| n., pl. **mitts** A large, padded leather glove that is worn to protect the hand when catching a baseball: *Sid jumped and caught the baseball in his mitt.*

mix |mĭks| v. **mixed, mixing** To combine or blend: *Mix the flour, water, and eggs to make batter.*

moist |moist| adj. **moister, moistest** Slightly wet; damp: *That plant grows best in moist soil.*

Mon·day |mŭn' dē| or |mŭn' dā| n., pl. **Mondays** The second day of the week.

mos·qui·to |mə skē' tō| n., pl. **mosquitoes** or **mosquitos** A small flying bug that sucks blood from animals and people.

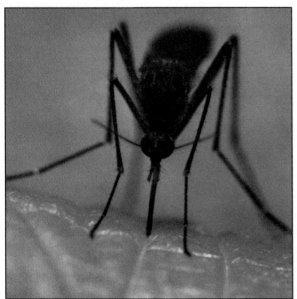

mosquito

most |mōst| adj. **1.** Greatest, as in number or size: *The player with the most points won the game.* **2.** The majority of: *Most birds can fly.* n. The greatest number or quantity: *Most of the houses in our neighborhood are old.* adv. In the greatest degree or size: *The roller coaster is the most exciting ride.*

mouth |mouth| n., pl. **mouths** The opening through which an animal takes in food. The human mouth is part of the face and contains the teeth and tongue.

move·ment |mōōv' mənt| n., pl. **movements** The act or process of moving or changing position: *The player snatched up the ball in a quick movement.*

much |mŭch| adj. **more, most** Great in quantity, degree, or extent; a lot of: *We put much work into this project.* adv. **more, most** To a great degree or extent: *The test was much harder than I thought.*

mu·sic |myōō' zĭk| n. Sounds that have rhythm, melody, and harmony: *Dad and Mom danced to the music on the radio.*

nap·kin |năp′ kǐn| *n., pl.* **napkins** A piece of cloth or soft paper used while eating to protect the clothes or to wipe the mouth and fingers.

naugh·ty |nô′ tē| *adj.* **naughtier, naughtiest** Behaving in a disobedient way; bad: *Brian was naughty because he stayed at the park too long.*

near |nîr| *adv.* To, at, or within a short distance or time: *The deer ran off as we came near.* *prep.* Close to: *Stay near me when we cross the street.*

need |nēd| *n., pl.* **needs** A lack of something that is necessary or wanted: *Their crops are in need of water.* *v.* **needed, needing 1.** To have to: *I need to return the book today.* **2.** To have need of: *This toaster needs repair.*

neigh·bor |nā′ bər| *n., pl.* **neighbors** A person who lives next door to or near another.

new |nōō| *or* |nyōō| *adj.* **newer, newest** Having lately come into being; not old: *The new supermarket just opened.*
♦ *These sound alike* **new, knew.**

nib·ble |nǐb′ əl| *v.* **nibbled, nibbling 1.** To eat with small, quick bites. **2.** To bite at gently: *The puppy nibbled my toes.*

nice |nīs| *adj.* **nicer, nicest** Kind; pleasant; agreeable: *What a nice thing to say!*

night |nīt| *n., pl.* **nights** The time between sunset and sunrise, especially the hours of darkness.

no |nō| *adv.* Not so: *No, I'm not going.* *adj.* Not any.
♦ *These sound alike* **no, know.**

noise |noiz| *n., pl.* **noises 1.** A loud or unpleasant sound. **2.** Sound of any kind: *The only noise was the wind in the pines.*

no one |nō′ wŭn′| *pron.* Nobody; not anyone: *I thought someone was at the door, but no one was.*

north |nôrth| *n.* The direction to the right of a person who faces the sunset: *Polar bears live in the north, where ice and snow cover the ground most of the year.*

note |nōt| *n., pl.* **notes** A short letter: *My parents sent a note to my teacher, explaining why I had been absent.*

noth·ing |nŭth′ ĭng| *pron.* **1.** Not anything: *I bought nothing, but Tim bought something for two dollars.* **2.** Someone or something of little or no importance or interest: *There's nothing on television tonight.*

no·tice |nō′ tǐs| *n., pl.* **notices** A printed announcement: *The notice said that the game was on Saturday.*

No·vem·ber |nō věm′ bər| *n.* The eleventh month of the year. November has 30 days.

o'clock |ə klŏk′| *adv.* Of or according to the clock: *When the bell rings, it will be 11 o'clock.*

Oc·to·ber |ŏk tō′ bər| *n.* The tenth month of the year. October has 31 days. Halloween is in October.

oc·to·pus |ŏk′ tə pəs| *n., pl.*
octopuses A sea animal that has a
large head, a soft, rounded body, and
eight long arms. The undersides of the
arms have sucking disks used for
holding.

of |ŭv| *or* |ŏv| *prep.* **1.** Belonging to
or connected with: *The walls of the
room are white.* **2.** From the group
making up: *Four of the students are
here.* **3.** Made from: *We built the
house of wood.*

oil |oil| *n., pl.* **oils** A greasy, usually
liquid substance that burns easily and
does not mix with water.
Oils are used as fuel and food. They
help parts of machines move easily:
*Mom added a quart of oil to the truck
engine.*

once |wŭns| *adv.* **1.** One time only:
We feed our dog once a day. **2.** At a
time in the past: *Once upon a time, a
boy lived in a forest.*

o·pos·sum |ə pŏs′ əm| *n., pl.*
opossums A furry animal that lives
mostly in trees and carries its young in
its pouch. The opossum can hang by
its tail.

opossum

or·ange |ôr′ ĭnj| *n., pl.* **oranges**
1. A round, juicy fruit with a reddish-
yellow skin. Oranges grow in warm
places. **2.** A reddish-yellow color.

Pronunciation Key					
ă	pat	ō	go	th	thin
ā	pay	ô	paw, for	hw	which
â	care	oi	oil	zh	usual
ä	father	ŏŏ	book	ə	ago,
ĕ	pet	ōō	boot		item,
ē	be	yōō	cute		pencil,
ĭ	pit	ou	out		atom,
ī	ice	ŭ	cut		circus
î	near	û	fur	ər	butter
ŏ	pot	*th*	the		

or·der |ôr′ dər| *n., pl.* **orders**
1. A grouping of things, one after
another. **2.** A command or rule.
3. A portion of food in a restaurant.
4. A request for items to be sent: *The
teacher placed an order for 20
arithmetic books. v.* **ordered,
ordering** To place an order for: *We
ordered a new washing machine.*

ot·ter |ŏt′ ər| *n., pl.* **otters** An
animal with webbed feet that
lives in or near water. Otters have
thick dark-brown fur and are good
swimmers.

ought |ôt| *helping v.* Used to show:
1. Duty: *We ought to try to help
them.* **2.** What is likely: *Dinner ought
to be ready by this time.*

our |our| *adj.* Belonging to us: *Our
car is being repaired.*
◆ *These sound alike* **our, hour.**

out |out| *adv.* **1.** Away from the
inside or center: *I went out for fresh
air.* **2.** Away from work, home, or the
usual place: *My parents went out for
the evening.*

out·side |out sīd′| *or* |out′ sīd′| *adj.*
Of, relating to, or located on the outer
surface: *We came in through the
outside door. adv.* Away from the
inside: *The children went outside to
play.*

ov·en |ŭv′ ən| *n., pl.* **ovens** An enclosed space, as in a stove, used for baking, heating, or drying: *We bake muffins in the oven.*

o·ver·sleep |ō′ vər slēp′| *v.* **overslept, oversleeping** To sleep longer than planned: *I missed the bus this morning because I overslept.*

own |ōn| *adj.* Of or belonging to oneself or itself: *The typewriter came with its own carrying case. v.* **owned, owning** To have or possess: *Do your parents own a compact car or a truck?*

page |pāj| *n., pl.* **pages** One side of a printed or written sheet of paper, as in a book or newspaper: *Turn to page 24 in your spelling book.*

paid |pād| *v.* Past tense and past participle of **pay**: *Dad paid all the bills.*

pail |pāl| *n., pl.* **pails** A bucket.

♦ *These sound alike* **pail, pale.**

paint |pānt| *n., pl.* **paints** Coloring matter put on surfaces to protect or decorate them. *v.* **painted, painting** To cover or decorate with color: *We painted the porch brown and white.*

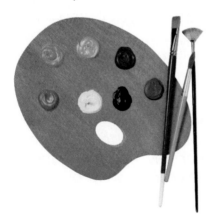

paint

pair |pâr| *n., pl.* **pairs** Two matched things that are usually used together: *I lost a pair of running shoes.*

♦ *These sound alike* **pair, pear.**

pa·ja·mas |pə jä′ məz| *or* |pə jăm′ əz| *pl. n.* A loose jacket and pants for sleeping: *Please put on your pajamas, and get ready for bed.*

pale |pāl| *adj.* **paler, palest** Having skin that is a lighter color than usual.

♦ *These sound alike* **pale, pail.**

park |pärk| *n., pl.* **parks** An area of land used for recreation: *We play in the park. v.* **parked, parking** To stop and leave a car for a time: *Where did you park the car?*

part·ner |pärt′ nər| *n., pl.* **partners** Either of a pair of persons dancing together: *The partners danced quickly across the floor.*

par·ty |pär′ tē| *n., pl.* **parties** A gathering of people for fun: *We went to a birthday party.*

paste |pāst| *n., pl.* **pastes** A material, such as a mixture of flour and water, used to stick things together. *v.* **pasted, pasting** To stick with glue: *He pasted pictures in his scrapbook.*

pat |păt| *v.* **patted, patting** To touch gently with an open hand: *Don't pat the dog.*

patch |păch| *n., pl.* **patches** **1.** A piece of material used to mend a hole, a rip, or a worn place.
2. A small area that is different from what is around it: *There is a patch of snow on the ground. v.* **patched, patching** To mend with a patch.

pay |pā| *v.* **paid, paying** To give or spend money for things bought or for work done: *I paid for my ticket.*

pear |pâr| *n., pl.* **pears** A yellow or brown fruit that has a round bottom and is narrow at the top. Pears grow on trees.
♦ *These sound alike* **pear, pair.**

pen·cil |pĕn′ səl| *n., pl.* **pencils** A thin stick of black or colored material used for writing or drawing.

pen·ny |pĕn′ ē| *n., pl.* **pennies** A coin used in the United States and Canada; cent. One hundred pennies equal one dollar.

peo·ple |pē′ pəl| *n., pl.* **people** Human beings; persons: *Many people came to the football game.*

per·fect |pûr′ fĭkt| *adj.* Without any mistakes: *My drawing is a perfect copy of yours.*

pic·nic |pĭk′ nĭk′| *n., pl.* **picnics** A party in which people carry their food with them and then eat it outdoors.

pic·ture |pĭk′ chər| *n., pl.* **pictures** A painting, drawing, or photograph of a person or thing: *Leo painted a picture of me.*

pie |pī| *n., pl.* **pies** A food made of a filling, such as of fruit or meat, baked in a crust.

pint |pīnt| *n., pl.* **pints** A measurement equal to two cups or half a quart.

pitch |pĭch| *n., pl.* **pitches** A throw of the baseball by a pitcher to a batter: *The third pitch was a curve, and the batter could not hit the ball.*

place |plās| *n., pl.* **places** **1.** A particular location, as a city: *In what place were you born?* **2.** A space for one person to sit or stand: *Save a place for me at the movies. v.* **placed, placing** To put in a particular place or order: *I placed cups and spoons on the table.*

Pronunciation Key

ă	pat	ō	go	th	thin
ā	pay	ô	paw, for	hw	which
â	care	oi	oil	zh	usual
ä	father	o͞o	book	ə	ago,
ĕ	pet	o͞o	boot		item,
ē	be	yo͞o	cute		pencil,
ĭ	pit	ou	out		atom,
ī	ice	ŭ	cut		circus
î	near	û	fur	ər	butter
ŏ	pot	*th*	the		

place·ment |plās′ mənt| *n., pl.* **placements** The act of putting things in a special arrangement or order: *He will be in charge of the placement of the pictures on the wall.*

plan |plăn| *n., pl.* **plans** **1.** A way of doing something that has been thought out ahead of time: *What are your plans for the evening?* **2.** A drawing showing how the parts of something are put together: *We followed the plans to make the model car.*

play |plā| *v.* **played, playing** **1.** To amuse oneself: *We went out to play, and Dad went back to work.* **2.** To take part in a game of: *We will play baseball after school.*

play·ful |plā′ fəl′| *adj.* **1.** Full of high spirits; lively: *Edgar was in a silly, playful mood.* **2.** Said or done in fun; humorous: *Tommy was just being playful with his jokes. adv.* **playfully** In a playful way: *I playfully tickled the dog's tummy.*

plunge |plŭnj| *v.* **plunged, plunging** To throw oneself suddenly into water: *We plunged into the waves.*

point |point| *n., pl.* **points** A sharp end, as of a pencil. *v.* **pointed, pointing** To call attention to something with the finger: *The librarian pointed to the sign that said "Quiet."*

pond |pŏnd| *n., pl.* **ponds** A small body of water: *Frogs and fish live in the pond.*

pond

po·ny |pō′ nē| *n., pl.* **ponies** A kind of horse that remains small when grown.

po·ster |pō′ stər| *n., pl.* **posters** A large sheet of paper with a picture or printing on it that is put up as an ad, a notice, or a decoration: *The poster showed that the circus was coming to town.*

pret·ty |prĭt′ ē| *adj.* **prettier, prettiest** Pleasing to the eye or ear.

prize |prīz| *n., pl.* **prizes** Something won in a game or a contest: *The first prize in the bike race is a new helmet.*

pro·gram |prō′ grăm| *n., pl.* **programs** A list of events and names: *The program showed the names of the actors in the play.*

prop |prŏp| *v.* **propped, propping** To keep from falling; support: *I propped myself up on the bed with pillows.*

pup·py |pŭp′ ē| *n., pl.* **puppies** A young dog.

pur·ple |pûr′ pəl| *n., pl.* **purples** A color between blue and red. *adj.* Of the color purple: *Grape juice is purple.*

quack |kwăk| *n.,pl.* **quacks** The sound made by a duck. *v.* **quacked, quacking** To make a quack.

quar·rel |kwôr′ əl| *v.* **quarreled, quarreling** To argue: *The children quarreled over which book to read.*

quart |kwôrt| *n., pl.* **quarts** A measurement equal to two pints.

queen |kwēn| *n., pl.* **queens** **1.** A woman who is the ruler of a country. **2.** A large female that lays eggs in a group of bees, ants, or termites.

quick |kwĭk| *adj.* **quicker, quickest** Very fast; rapid; not slow: *I turned on the light with a quick movement of my hand.*

quick·ly |kwĭk′ lē| *adv.* In a quick way; rapidly; not slowly: *Come here quickly!*

quit |kwĭt| *v.* **quit, quitting** To stop doing: *I quit work at five o'clock.*

rab·bit |răb′ ĭt| *n., pl.* **rabbits** A burrowing animal with long ears, soft fur, and a short, furry tail.

ran·ger |rān′ jər| *n., pl.* **rangers** A person who patrols or watches over a forest or park: *The ranger helped visitors at the national park.*

ranger

rare |râr| *adj.* **rarer, rarest** Not often found or seen: *Gina collects rare stamps.*

raw |rô| *adj.* **rawer, rawest** Uncooked: *I made a salad of raw vegetables.*

re- A prefix that means "again": *refill.*

re·cess |rē′ sĕs′| *or* |rĭ sĕs′| *n., pl.* **recesses** A short time for rest or play: *We played hopscotch at recess.*

re·make |rē māk′| *v.* **remade, remaking** To make again.

re·pair |rĭ pâr′| *v.* **repaired, repairing** To fix.

re·peat |rĭ pēt′| *v.* **repeated, repeating** To say or do again: *Please repeat your last question.*

re·place |rĭ plās′| *v.* **replaced, replacing** **1.** To put back in place: *I replaced the dishes in the cupboard.* **2.** To take or fill the place of: *Cars replaced the horse and buggy.*

re·tell |rē tĕl′| *v.* **retold, retelling** To tell again; repeat.

re·use |rē yo͞oz′| *v.* **reused, reusing** To use again.

Pronunciation Key

ă	pat	ō	go	th	thin
ā	pay	ô	paw, for	hw	which
â	care	oi	oil	zh	usual
ä	father	o͝o	book	ə	ago,
ĕ	pet	o͞o	boot		item,
ē	be	yo͞o	cute		pencil,
ĭ	pit	ou	out		atom,
ī	ice	ŭ	cut		circus
î	near	û	fur	ər	butter
ŏ	pot	*th*	the		

re·view |rĭ vyo͞o′| *v.* **reviewed, reviewing** To study again; check: *Let's review the chapter before we take the test.*

re·ward |rĭ wôrd′| *n., pl.* **rewards** Something that is given in return for a worthy act or service: *You deserve a medal as a reward for your bravery.*

re·write |rē rīt′| *v.* **rewrote, rewritten, rewriting** To write again: *She rewrote her messy paper.*

riv·er |rĭv′ ər| *n., pl.* **rivers** A large stream of water that is often fed by smaller streams flowing into it.

roar |rôr| *n., pl.* **roars** A loud, deep cry or sound, such as a lion makes: *We heard the roar of a huge tiger.*

round |round| *adj.* **rounder, roundest** Shaped like a ball or circle: *An orange is round.*

row |rō| *v.* **rowed, rowing** To move a boat with oars: *Do you want to row across the lake?*

rub |rŭb| *v.* **rubbed, rubbing** To move back and forth against a surface: *The cat rubbed its head against my arm.*

ruf·fle |rŭf′ əl| *n., pl.* **ruffles** A strip of pleated material, such as ribbon or lace, used as a decoration: *The curtains had ruffles at the bottom.*

311

sad·ly |săd′ lē| *adv.* In a way that shows sorrow or unhappiness: *Carlo waved sadly to his grandparents as they left.*

said |sĕd| *v.* Past tense and past participle of **say**: *Did you hear what he said?*

sail |sāl| *n., pl.* **sails** A piece of strong cloth that is stretched out to catch the wind and move a boat or ship through the water. *v.* **sailed, sailing** To travel on a ship or boat with sails.
♦ *These sound alike* **sail, sale.**

sail

sale |sāl| *n., pl.* **sales** A selling of things at less than usual prices.
♦ *These sound alike* **sale, sail.**

same |sām| *adj.*
1. Exactly alike: *These books are the same size.*
2. Being the very one or ones: *This is the same seat that I had yesterday.*

sand·box |sănd′ bŏks′| *n., pl.* **sandboxes** An enclosed area filled with sand for children to play in: *Darla made a castle in the sandbox.*

Sat·ur·day |săt′ ər dē| *or* |săt′ ər dā| *n., pl.* **Saturdays** The seventh day of the week.

save |sāv| *v.* **saved, saving 1.** To rescue from danger. **2.** To keep from wasting or spending.

saw |sô| *n., pl.* **saws** A tool that has a thin metal blade with sharp teeth for cutting hard material.

say |sā| *v.* **said, saying 1.** To speak: *Sandy always says hello to me.*
2. To state: *The newspaper says that it will rain tonight.*

scald |skôld| *v.* **scalded, scalding** To burn with a very hot liquid: *She spilled boiling water and scalded her hand.*

scare |skâr| *n., pl.* **scares** A feeling of fear: *I got a scare when I went into deep water in swim class. v.* To frighten or become frightened. **2.** To frighten or drive away.

scarf |skärf| *n., pl.* **scarfs** or **scarves** A piece of cloth that is worn around the neck or head.

scene |sēn| *n., pl.* **scenes 1.** A place as seen by a viewer; view. **2.** The place where an action or an event occurs: *The tow truck arrived at the scene of the wreck.* **3.** The place in which the action of a story or play occurs. **4.** A short section of a play or a movie.
♦ *These sound alike* **scene, seen.**

school |sko͞ol| *n., pl.* **schools 1.** A place for teaching and learning. **2.** The students and teachers at such a place.

score·board |skôr′ bôrd′| *or* |skōr′ bōrd′| *n., pl.* **scoreboards** A large board for showing the score of a game: *The winners' names were shown on the scoreboard.*

scratch |skrăch| *n., pl.* **scratches** A thin, shallow cut or mark made with or as if with a sharp tool: *The thorns on the rose bush made a scratch on my arm.*

scream |skrēm| *v.* **screamed, screaming** To make a long, loud cry or sound; yell.

screen |skrēn| *n., pl.* **screens 1.** A frame covered with wire mesh, used in a window or door to keep out insects: *Put a screen in the window to keep out the flies.* **2.** A flat surface on which slides or movies are shown.

seam |sēm| *n., pl.* **seams** The line formed by sewing two pieces of material together.
♦ *These sound alike* **seam, seem.**

search |sûrch| *v.* **searched, searching** To look carefully: *We searched along the beach for seashells.*

second¹ |sĕk′ ənd| *n., pl.* **seconds** A unit of time equal to 1/60 of a minute.

Pronunciation Key

ă	pat	ō	go	th	thin
ā	pay	ô	paw, for	hw	which
â	care	oi	oil	zh	usual
ä	father	o͞o	book	ə	ago,
ĕ	pet	o͞o	boot		item,
ē	be	yo͞o	cute		pencil,
ĭ	pit	ou	out		atom,
ī	ice	ŭ	cut		circus
î	near	û	fur	ər	butter
ŏ	pot	*th*	the		

second² |sĕk′ ənd| *adj.* **1.** Coming after the first: *Elena won second prize.* **2.** Another: *May I have a second chance?*

see |sē| *v.* **saw, seen, seeing** To take in with the eyes: *I see my socks under the bed.*

seek |sēk| *v.* **sought, seeking** To try to find or get; look for: *We are seeking directions.*

seem |sēm| *v.* **seemed, seeming** To appear to be: *You seem worried.*
♦ *These sound alike* **seem, seam.**

seen |sēn| Past participle of **see**: *Have you seen my hat anywhere?*
♦ *These sound alike* **seen, scene.**

sell |sĕl| *v.* **sold, selling** To exchange something for money: *I sold my bike for $50.00.*

send |sĕnd| *v.* **sent, sending 1.** To cause to go: *They sent me home.* **2.** To mail: *Grandma sends me a letter every week.*

Sep·tem·ber |sĕp tĕm′ bər| *n.* The ninth month of the year. September has 30 days.

serve |sûrv| *v.* **served, serving** To present or offer food for others to eat: *Dad served dinner to the family.*

sew |sō| *v.* **sewed, sewn** *or* **sewed, sewing** To make, repair, or fasten a thing with stitches made by a needle and a thread.

shake |shāk| *v.* **shook, shaken, shaking** To move back and forth or up and down with short, quick movements: *Shake the orange juice to mix it up.*

shal·low |shăl′ ō| *adj.* **shallower, shallowest** Not deep.

sham·poo |shăm pōō′| *n., pl.* **shampoos** A liquid soap used to wash hair.

share |shâr| *v.* **shared, sharing** To have, use, or do together with another or others: *Let's share this last orange.*

she's |shēz| Contraction of "she is" or "she has": *She's my sister.*

shin·y |shī′ nē| *adj.* **shinier, shiniest** Bright: *We polished the car until it was shiny.*

shoe |shōō| *n., pl.* **shoes** An outer covering for the foot: *His left shoe hurts his big toe.*

shook |shŏŏk| *v.* Past tense of **shake**: *The strong winds shook our house.*

short |shôrt| *adj.* **shorter, shortest** **1.** Not long: *Short hair is now in style.* **2.** Not tall. **3.** Covering a small distance or taking a small amount of time: *We took a short walk.*

should·n't |shŏŏd′ nt| Contraction of "should not": *We shouldn't leave the party too late.*

shut |shŭt| *v.* **shut, shutting** **1.** To close: *Shut the door.* **2.** To stop entrance into: *Dad shut the beach house for the winter.*

side |sīd| *n., pl.* **sides** **1.** A line or surface that forms an edge: *A triangle has three sides.* **2.** One of the surfaces of an object that connects the top and the bottom: *Let's paint that side of the house first.*

sight |sīt| *n., pl.* **sights** **1.** The ability to see. **2.** Something seen or worth seeing: *The baby whale was a wonderful sight.*

sing·er |sĭng′ ər| *n., pl.* **singers** Someone who performs a song.

skin |skĭn| *n., pl.* **skins** The outer covering of a human or animal body.

skip |skĭp| *v.* **skipped, skipping** To move forward by stepping and hopping lightly: *We held hands and skipped in a circle.*

skit |skĭt| *n., pl.* **skits** A very short play: *We put on a skit for the first graders.*

skunk |skŭngk| *n., pl.* **skunks** An animal that has black and white fur and a bushy tail. A skunk can spray a bad-smelling liquid when it is frightened.

skunk

sky·scrap·er |skī′ skrā′ pər| *n., pl.* **skyscrapers** A very tall building: *From the top floor of the skyscraper, we could see the whole city.*

sleet |slēt| *n.* Rain that is partly frozen into ice: *When the temperature dropped, the sleet turned into snow.*

sling |slĭng| *n., pl.* **slings** A band of cloth looped around the neck to support an injured arm or hand: *The doctor put Maria's broken wrist in a sling.*

slip·per |slĭp′ ər| *n., pl.* **slippers** A light shoe that is easily slipped on and off. Slippers are usually worn indoors: *She got out of bed and put on her warm slippers.*

slow |slō| *adj.* **slower, slowest** Moving or going at a low speed; not quick.

slow·ly |slō′ lē| *adv.* In a slow way; not quickly: *A turtle moves slowly.*

small |smôl| *adj.* **smaller, smallest** Little.

smart |smärt| *adj.* **smarter, smartest** Having a quick mind; bright.

smell |smĕl| *v.* **smelled** *or* **smelt, smelling** To notice the odor of something by using the nose: *I smell smoke. n., pl.* **smells** Odor; scent: *The smell of roses came from the perfume.*

smile |smīl| *n., pl.* **smiles** A happy look on the face. A person makes a smile by curving the corners of the mouth upward. *v.* **smiled, smiling** To have or make a smile.

smoke |smōk| *n.* The mixture of gases and carbon that rises from burning material: *Smoke rose from the burning wood.*

snarl |snärl| *v.* **snarled, snarling** To growl with the teeth showing.

soak |sōk| *v.* **soaked, soaking** To make or become completely wet: *The rain soaked our clothes and hair.*

soap |sōp| *n., pl.* **soaps** A substance that is used for washing: *Use that bar of soap and a washcloth to wash your face.*

Pronunciation Key

ă	pat	ō	go	th	thin
ā	pay	ô	paw, for	hw	which
â	care	oi	oil	zh	usual
ä	father	o͝o	book	ə	ago,
ĕ	pet	o͞o	boot		item,
ē	be	yo͞o	cute		pencil,
ĭ	pit	ou	out		atom,
ī	ice	ŭ	cut		circus
î	near	û	fur	ər	butter
ŏ	pot	*th*	the		

soap·suds |sōp′ sudz′| *n.,pl.* Suds from soapy water: *The washing machine was filled with soapsuds.*

sock |sŏk| *n., pl.* **socks** A short covering for the foot that reaches above the ankle and ends below the knee.

soft |sôft| *adj.* **softer, softest** Not hard or firm: *The pillow is soft.*

soil |soil| *n., pl.* **soils** The loose top layer of the earth's surface in which plants can grow; dirt.

sold |sōld| *v.* Past tense and past participle of **sell**: *We sold the old car and bought a new one.*

some·one |sŭm′ wŭn′| *pron.* Some person; somebody: *I hoped that someone would answer the phone, but no one did.*

some·thing |sŭm′ thĭng| *pron.* A thing that is not named: *I bought something for my parents.*

some·times |sŭm′ tīmz′| *adv.* Now and then; at times: *I see them sometimes but not often.*

soon |so͞on| *adv.* **sooner, soonest** Within a short time: *We'll soon know the answer.*

sought |sôt| *v.* Past tense and past participle of **seek**: *We sought a way to make our sick cat feel better.*

sound |sound| *n., pl.* **sounds**
Something that is heard: *The sound of the drum was very loud.*

sour |sour| *adj.* **sourer, sourest**
Having a sharp taste: *Lemons, limes, and grapefruit are sour.*

space |spās| *n., pl.* **spaces**
1. The area without limits where the stars, planets, comets, and galaxies are. **2.** The open area between objects: *Leave a space for my chair.*

spark |spärk| *n., pl.* **sparks** A small bit of burning matter: *The burning logs crackled, and sparks flew everywhere.*

speak |spēk| *v.* **spoke, spoken, speaking** To say words; talk: *Mom will speak to our doctor about my fever.*

speak·er |spē′ kər| *n., pl.* **speakers**
A person who speaks: *The speaker told his listeners about his trip to Chicago.*

splint |splĭnt| *n., pl.* **splints** A device that is used to hold a broken bone in place: *He had a splint on his broken finger.*

spoil |spoil| *v.* **spoiled** *or* **spoilt, spoiling** **1.** To make less perfect or useful: *A storm spoiled our picnic.* **2.** To become unfit for use; ruin: *The meat spoiled.* **3.** To hurt people by giving them too much: *Don't spoil your younger brothers and sisters.*

spoon |spo͞on| *n., pl.* **spoons** A piece of silverware with a shallow bowl at the end of its handle. Spoons are used for measuring, serving, or eating food: *I need a spoon to eat my soup.*

spot |spŏt| *n., pl.* **spots 1.** A small mark or stain: *Red spots on your body may mean you have measles.* **2.** A place or location: *We found our favorite spot on the beach.*

spray |sprā| *v.* **sprayed, spraying** To make water or another liquid come out of a container in many small drops: *We sprayed the garden with water from the hose.*

spread |sprĕd| *v.* **spread, spreading** To open out wide or wider: *I spread the cloth on the table.*

spring |sprĭng| *n., pl.* **springs** The season of the year between winter and summer when plants begin to grow.

sprout |sprout| *v.* **sprouted, sprouting** To appear as new growth: *The corn sprouted after the rain.*

sprout

square |skwâr| *n.* **1.** A rectangle having four equal sides. **2.** Something shaped like a square. *adj.* Having the shape of a square: *Vannie kept his CDs in a square box.*

squeak |skwēk| *v.* **squeaked, squeaking** To make a high, thin noise such as a mouse makes.

squeak·y |skwē′ kē| *adj.* **squeakier, squeakiest** Making a high, thin noise: *The rusty hinges are squeaky.*

squeeze |skwēz| *v.* **squeezed, squeezing** 1. To press together with force: *The baby squeezed the rubber toy.* 2. To force by pressing: *We squeezed through the door.*

stage |stāj| *n., pl.* **stages** The raised platform in a theater on which actors perform.

star |stär| *n., pl.* **stars** 1. A body that appears as a very bright point in the sky at night. 2. A performer who plays a leading role in a play or movie.

start |stärt| *v.* **started, starting** 1. To begin to move, go, or act: *We started for the lake early in the morning.* 2. To have a beginning: *Camp will start in June.*

step |stĕp| *n., pl.* **steps** An action taken to reach a goal: *We have taken the first step toward cleaning up the school grounds.*

stick |stĭk| *n., pl.* **sticks** A long, thin piece of wood, as a branch cut from a tree. *v.* **stuck, sticking** To fasten with something, such as glue: *I am sticking a stamp on the envelope.*

stick·er |stĭk′ ər| *n., pl.* **stickers** A small piece of paper with glue on the back.

stick·i·ness |stĭk′ ē nĕs| *n.* The quality or condition of being sticky: *I can't get the stickiness of the honey off my hands.*

stick·y |stĭk′ ē| *adj.* **stickier, stickiest** Tending to stick: *Glue is sticky.*

sting |stĭng| *v.* **stung, stinging** To hurt with a small, sharp point: *A bee stung me on the foot.*

Pronunciation Key

ă	pat	ō	go	th	thin
ā	pay	ô	paw, for	hw	which
â	care	oi	oil	zh	usual
ä	father	ŏŏ	book	ə	ago,
ĕ	pet	ōō	boot		item,
ē	be	yōō	cute		pencil,
ĭ	pit	ou	out		atom,
ī	ice	ŭ	cut		circus
î	near	û	fur	ər	butter
ŏ	pot	*th*	the		

stir |stûr| *v.* **stirred, stirring** To mix by moving in a circle again and again: *I stirred the vegetables into the soup.*

stop |stŏp| *v.* **stopped, stopping** 1. To end moving, acting, or operating: *Dad stopped at the red light.* 2. To bring or to come to an end: *The rain finally stopped.*

storm |stôrm| *n., pl.* **storms** A strong wind with rain, hail, sleet, or snow.

sto·ry |stôr′ ē| *n., pl.* **stories** A tale made up to entertain people: *I have just read an adventure story.*

straight |strāt| *adj.* **straighter, straightest** 1. Not curving, curling, or bending; not crooked: *I have straight hair.* 2. Without a break: *It snowed for five straight days.*

straw |strô| *n., pl.* **straws** 1. Stalks of grain, as wheat or oats, whose seeds have been removed: *Some straw is used as bedding for animals, and some is used to weave hats and baskets.* 2. A thin tube, made of paper or plastic, through which a person can drink a liquid.

stream |strēm| *n., pl.* **streams** A small body of flowing water; a brook: *That stream flows into the river by our house.*

street |strēt| *n., pl.* **streets** A road in a city or town: *I live on this street.*

strength |strĕngkth| *n., pl.*
strengths The quality of being strong;
power: *Elephants have great strength.*

stretch·er |strĕch′ ər| *n., pl.*
stretchers A movable bed or cot on
which a sick or injured person can be
carried.

string |strĭng| *n., pl.* **strings 1.** A
cord for fastening or tying: *Tie the pile
of newspapers with string.*
2. A series of things or events: *A
string of accidents have happened at
that corner.*

strong |strông| *adj.* **stronger,
strongest** Having much power, energy,
or strength: *A strong horse pulled the
heavy cart.*

strug·gle |strŭg′ əl| *v.* **struggled,
struggling** To make a great effort:
*Chuck and I struggled to climb the
mountain. n., pl.* **struggles** A great
effort: *Getting up at 6:00 A.M. is a
struggle.*

stub·born |stŭb′ ərn| *adj.*
1. Not willing to change in spite of
requests from others: *The stubborn
child refused to wear boots.*
2. Hard to deal with: *I have a
stubborn cold.*

stu·dent |stōōd′ nt| *or* |styōōd′ nt|
n., pl. **students** A person who studies,
as in a school: *The students studied
for the test.*

stur·dy |stûr′ dē| *adj.* **sturdier,
sturdiest** Strong: *The workbench has
sturdy legs.*

style |stīl| *n., pl.* **styles** A special way
of dressing, looking, or acting: *She
dresses in an old-fashioned style.*

sub·way |sŭb′ wā′| *n., pl.* **subways**
An underground train in a city: *We
rode the subway all the way
downtown.*

sud·den |sŭd′ n| *adj.* **1.** Happening
without warning: *We were caught in
a sudden snowstorm.* **2.** Rapid; quick:
*With a sudden movement, I caught the
falling vase.*

suit·case |sōōt′ kās′| *n., pl.*
suitcases A piece of luggage: *I put
clothes for my trip in my suitcase.*

suitcase

sum·mer |sŭm′ ər| *n., pl.* **summers**
The hottest season of the year.
Summer is between spring and
autumn.

Sun·day |sŭn′ dē| *or* |sŭn′ dā| *n., pl.*
Sundays The first day of the week.

sway |swā| *v.* **swayed, swaying** To
swing back and forth or from side to
side: *The willow trees were swaying in
the wind.*

ta·ble |tā′ bəl| *n., pl.* **tables** A piece
of furniture that has legs and a flat
top: *Carl put plates and silverware on
the table.*

talk |tôk| *v.* **talked, talking 1.** To
say words; speak. **2.** To have a
conversation.

tap |tăp| *v.* **tapped, tapping** To strike gently: *I tapped my friend on the shoulder.*

taught |tôt| *v.* Past tense and past participle of **teach:** *The teacher taught us a new song that she had learned.*

tax·i |tăk' sē| *n., pl.* **taxis** A car that carries passengers wherever they want to go for a fare: *We asked the taxi driver to take us uptown.*

teach |tēch| *v.* **taught, teaching** To give lessons in: *Our teacher taught the class another dance.*

teach·er |tē' chər| *n., pl.* **teachers** A person who teaches or gives instruction.

teeth |tēth| *n.* Plural of **tooth:** *Please brush your teeth.*

test |tĕst| *n., pl.* **tests** Questions or problems used to measure knowledge: *We had an arithmetic test yesterday.*

thank·ful |thăngk' fəl| *adj.* Showing or feeling thanks; grateful: *We were thankful that no one was hurt in the fire.*

their |*th*âr| *pron.* Belonging to them: *They put their boots in the closet.*

♦ *These sound alike* **their, there, they're.**

there |*th*âr| *adv.* **1.** At or in that place: *Set the package there on the table.* **2.** To or toward that place: *I bicycled there and back. pron.* Used to start a sentence in which the verb comes before the subject: *There are several kinds of dogs.*

♦ *These sound alike* **there, their, they're.**

Pronunciation Key

ă	pat	ō	go	th	thin
ā	pay	ô	paw, for	hw	which
â	care	oi	oil	zh	usual
ä	father	ŏŏ	book	ə	ago,
ĕ	pet	ōō	boot		item,
ē	be	yōō	cute		pencil,
ĭ	pit	ou	out		atom,
ī	ice	ŭ	cut		circus
î	near	û	fur	ər	butter
ŏ	pot	*th*	the		

ther·mom·e·ter |thər **mŏm'** ĭ tər| *n., pl.* **thermometers** An instrument that shows how hot or cold it is: *The thermometer showed that the temperature was zero.*

they |*th*ā| *pron.* The persons, animals, or things last talked about; those ones: *Elephants are large, but they move quickly.*

they're |*th*âr| Contraction of "they are."

♦ *These sound alike* **they're, their, there.**

thick |thĭk| *adj.* **thicker, thickest** Having much space between opposite sides; not thin: *A thick board does not break very easily.*

thin |thĭn| *adj.* **thinner, thinnest** **1.** Having little space between opposite sides; not thick: *The sun is shining through the thin curtains.* **2.** Not fat.

think |thĭngk| *v.* **thought, thinking** **1.** To use one's mind to form ideas and make decisions: *I think that I should leave now.* **2.** To believe: *Pam thinks that it is too cold to go swimming.*

third |thûrd| *adj.* Coming after the second: *They picked the first two TV shows to watch, and I picked the third one.*

though |*th*ō| *adv.* However; nevertheless: *The shirt is pretty; it doesn't fit, though.*

thought |thôt| *v.* Past tense and past participle of **think**: *I thought about what you said.*

three |thrē| *n., pl.* **threes** The number, written *3*, that is equal to the sum of 2 + 1. *adj.* Being one more than two.

threw |thr$\overline{oo}$| *v.* Past tense of **throw**: *Todd threw his model plane into the air.*

♦ These sound alike **threw, through.**

through |thr$\overline{oo}$| *prep.* In one side and out the other side of: *We walked through the park to the bus stop.*

♦ These sound alike **through, threw.**

throw |thrō| *v.* **threw, thrown, throwing** To send through the air by moving the arm quickly: *I will catch the towel if you throw it to me.*

Thurs·day |**thûrz'** dē| *or* |**thûrz'** dā| *n., pl.* **Thursdays** The fifth day of the week.

tie |tī| *v.* **tied, tying** To fasten with a cord or rope: *Wrap the package, and tie it with a string. n., pl.* **ties** A narrow band of cloth worn around the neck and tied in front; necktie.

tight |tīt| *adj.* **tighter, tightest** **1.** Held firmly in place; not loose: *I tied a tight knot.* **2.** Leaving no extra room or time; crowded: *My schedule is tight today.*

tooth |t$\overline{oo}$th| *n., pl.* **teeth** One of the hard, bony parts in the mouth that is used to chew and bite: *I broke a tooth when I bit into some taffy.*

tor·na·do |tôr **nā'** dō| *n., pl.* **tornadoes** or **tornados** A twisting, dangerous storm. A tornado has a funnel-shaped cloud that comes down from a thundercloud.

tor·toise |**tôr'** təs| *n., pl.* **tortoises** A turtle, especially one that lives on land.

tortoise

tough |tŭf| *adj.* **tougher, toughest** Strong; not likely to break or tear.

town |toun| *n., pl.* **towns** A place where people live that is larger than a village but smaller than a city.

toy |toi| *n., pl.* **toys** Something that children play with.

trace |trās| *v.* **traced, tracing** To copy by following lines that have already been drawn or printed: *Jack traced the picture of the puppy from a magazine.*

track |trăk| *n., pl.* **tracks** A path or course made for racing or running: *The runners practiced on an indoor track in the gym.*

train·er |**trā'** nər| *n., pl.* **trainers** A person who coaches sports players or show animals: *The trainer taught the seal to bounce a ball.*

trav·el |trăv′ əl| v. **traveled, traveling** To go from one place to another: *The whole family traveled around the world.*

tried |trīd| v. Past tense and past participle of **try**: *Carol tried to telephone Jeff, but no one was home.*

trim |trĭm| v. **trimmed, trimming** To make neat or even, especially by cutting: *Trim my bangs, so that I can see.*

trou·ble |trŭb′ əl| n., pl. **troubles** A cause of unhappiness or difficulty: *We had trouble with our homework, so we asked for help.*

try |trī| v. **tried, trying** To make an effort; attempt: *She tried to win the prize.*

Tues·day |tŌŌz′ dē|, |tyŌŌz′ dē|, *or* |tyŌŌz′ dā′| n., pl. **Tuesdays** The third day of the week.

tu·lip |tŌŌ′ lĭp| *or* |tyŌŌ′ lĭp| n., pl. **tulips** A garden plant that grows from a bulb and has cup-shaped flowers: *Some tulips are light colors, while others are bright red.*

Pronunciation Key					
ă	pat	ō	go	th	thin
ā	pay	ô	paw, for	hw	which
â	care	oi	oil	zh	usual
ä	father	ŌŌ	book	ə	ago,
ĕ	pet	ŌŌ	boot		item,
ē	be	yŌŌ	cute		pencil,
ĭ	pit	ou	out		atom,
ī	ice	ŭ	cut		circus
î	near	û	fur	ər	butter
ŏ	pot	th	the		

tune |tŌŌn| *or* |tyŌŌn| n., pl. **tunes** The musical part of a song: *I was so happy that I whistled several tunes.*

turn |tûrn| v. **turned, turning** To move or cause to move around a center; rotate: *I heard the key turn in the lock.*

two |tŌŌ| n., pl. **twos** The number, written 2, that is equal to the sum of 1 + 1. adj. Being one more than one: *I have two sisters.*

U

un- A prefix that means: **1.** Not: *unhappy.* **2.** Opposite of: *untie.*

un·clear |ŭn klîr′| adj. Not clear; not well organized: *The report is unclear.*

un·der |ŭn′ dər| prep. **1.** Below: *A boat passed under the bridge.* **2.** Beneath and covered by: *I hid the kitten under my coat.* **3.** Beneath the surface of: *The plumber laid a pipe under the ground.*

un·fair |ŭn fâr′| adj. **unfairer, unfairest** Not fair; not right: *We think the decision is unfair.*

un·hap·py |ŭn hăp′ ē| adj. **unhappier, unhappiest** not happy; sad.

tulip

un·hurt |ŭn **hûrt′**| *adj.* Not hurt; not injured: *The driver was unhurt in the accident.*

un·im·por·tant |ŭn′ ĭm **pôr′** tnt| *adj.* Not important; having little meaning or value.

un·kind |ŭn **kīnd′**| *adj.* **unkinder, unkindest** Not kind; harsh or cruel.

un·like |ŭn **līk′**| *prep.* **1.** Not like; different from: *I had heard a sound unlike any other.* **2.** Not usual for: *It's unlike you not to say hello.*

un·tie |ŭn **tī′**| *v.* **untied, untying**
1. To loosen or undo: *I could not untie the knots in my shoelace.* **2.** The opposite of **tie**.

un·til |ŭn **tĭl′**| *prep.* **1.** Up to the time of: *They studied until dinner.* **2.** Before: *You can't have the bike until Monday. conj.* **1.** Up to the time that: *They studied until it was time for dinner.* **2.** Before: *You can't go out until you finish your homework.* **3.** To the point that: *They played soccer until they were tired.*

un·wrap |ŭn **răp′**| *v.* **unwrapped, unwrapping** To open by removing the wrapper from; to open a present: *May I unwrap my gifts, or must I wait until tomorrow?*

use·ful |yo͞os′ fəl| *adj.* Being of use or service; helpful; not useless: *Our map of Chicago was useful when we visited there.*

ver·y |vĕr′ ē| *adv.* **1.** To a high degree; extremely: *I am a very happy person today.* **2.** Exactly: *I said the very same thing.*

vi·o·let |vī′ ə lĭt| *n., pl.* **violets** A low-growing plant with tiny flowers that are bluish purple, yellow, or white.

vis·it |vĭz′ ĭt| *v.* **visited, visiting** To stay with as a guest: *I am visiting an old friend for a week.*

walk |wôk| *v.* **walked, walking** To move on foot at an easy, steady pace. *n., pl.* **walks 1.** An act of walking: *We took a walk on the beach.* **2.** A distance covered in walking: *The walk to school is less than a mile.*

wall |wôl| *n., pl.* **walls** A solid structure that forms a side of a building or room.

wal·rus |wôl′ rəs| *n., pl.* **walrus** or **walruses** A large sea animal that has tough, wrinkled skin and large tusks. Walruses live in the Arctic.

walrus

want |wŏnt| *v.* **wanted, wanting** To wish or desire: *They wanted to play outdoors.*

was |wŏz| *or* |wŭz| *v.* First and third person singular past tense of **be**: *He was late.*

wash·er |wŏsh′ ər| *or* |wô′ shər| *n., pl.* **washers** A machine for washing clothes.

was·n't |wŏz′ ənt| *or* |wŭz′ ənt|
Contraction of "was not": *My friend wasn't home.*

watch |wŏch| *v.* **watched, watching**
1. To look at with care: *People stopped to watch the parade.* **2.** To be alert and looking: *Watch for the street sign. n., pl.* **watches** A small device for telling time that can be worn on the wrist or carried in a pocket.

weak |wēk| *adj.* **weaker, weakest**
Not strong: *My left hand is weaker than my right hand.*
♦ These sound alike **weak, week.**

weak·ly |wēk′ lē| *adv.* In a weak way.
♦ These sound alike **weakly, weekly.**

weak·ness |wēk′ nĭs| *n., pl.*
weaknesses The feeling of being weak: *The weakness in my ankle is due to a sprain.*

wear |wâr| *v.* **wore, worn, wearing**
To have on the body: *I wear mittens on cold days.*

Wednes·day |wĕnz′ dē| *or* |wĕnz′ dā| *n., pl.* **Wednesdays** The fourth day of the week.

week |wēk| *n., pl.* **weeks 1.** A period of seven days: *We will be home in a week.*
2. The period from Sunday through the next Saturday.
♦ These sound alike **week, weak.**

week·end |wēk′ ĕnd′| *n., pl.*
weekends The time from Friday evening through Sunday evening.

week·ly |wēk′ lē| *adv.* Once a week or every week: *My aunt visits us weekly.*
♦ These sound alike **weekly, weakly.**

Pronunciation Key

ă	pat	ō	go	th	thin	
ā	pay	ô	paw, for	hw	which	
â	care	oi	oil	zh	usual	
ä	father	ŏŏ	book	ə	ago,	
ĕ	pet	ōō	boot		item,	
ē	be	yōō	cute		pencil,	
ĭ	pit	ou	out		atom,	
ī	ice	ŭ	cut		circus	
î	near	û	fur	ər	butter	
ŏ	pot	*th*	**the**			

weigh |wā| *v.* **weighed, weighing 1.** To find out how heavy something is: *He weighed himself on a scale.* **2.** To have a certain heaviness: *The car weighs 2,800 pounds.*

well |wĕl| *adv.* **better, best** In a way that is good, proper, skillful, or successful: *Tammy skis well.*

were |wûr| *v.* **1.** Second person singular past tense of **be**: *You were in school yesterday.*
2. First, second, and third person plural past tense of **be**: *We were there too.*

weren't |wûrnt| Contraction of "were not": *Sam and I weren't sick yesterday.*

where |hwâr| *adv.* At, in, or to what or which place: *Where is the telephone? conj.* At, in, or to what or which place: *I am going to my room, where I can study.*

whis·tle |hwĭs′ əl| *n., pl.* **whistles** A device that makes a high, clear sound when air is blown through it: *The coach blew her whistle, and the game began.*

who's |hōōz| Contraction of "who is" or "who has": *Who's knocking at the door?*

wide |wīd| *adj.* **wider, widest** 1. Taking up a large amount of space from side to side; broad: *We live on a wide street.* 2. Fully open: *The little child's eyes were wide with surprise.*

wild |wīld| *adj.* **wilder, wildest** Not grown, cared for, or controlled by people; not tame: *The polar bear is a wild animal.*

will |wĭl| *helping v.* **would** Something that is going to take place in the future: *They will arrive tonight.*

win·dow |wĭn' dō| *n., pl.* **windows** An opening in a wall with a frame and panes of glass to let in light.

win·ter |wĭn' tər| *n., pl.* **winters** The coldest season of the year, between fall and spring.

wis·dom |wĭz' dəm| *n.* Good judgment in knowing what to do and being able to tell the difference between right and wrong; knowledge.

won't |wōnt| Contraction of "will not": *She won't forget to meet us.*

word |wûrd| *n., pl.* **words** A sound or group of sounds that has meaning: *Do you know how to say that word?*

work |wûrk| *n., pl.* **works** 1. The effort that is required to do something; labor: *Cleaning the house is hard work.* 2. A job: *Our neighbor is looking for work as a teacher.* 3. A way by which a person earns money. *v.* **worked, working** 1. To put out effort to do or make something: *I worked hard raking leaves while my little sister played on the swing.* 2. To have a job: *My parents work in a hospital.*

wor·ry |wûr' ē| *v.* **worried, worrying** To feel or cause to feel uneasy: *Your bad cough worries me.*

would |wŏŏd| *helping v.* Past tense of **will**: *They said that they would help.*

would·n't |wŏŏd' nt| Contraction of "would not": *The sick cat wouldn't eat.*

wrap |răp| *v.* **wrapped, wrapping** To cover by winding or folding something: *Wrap the baby in a towel.*

wreath |rēth| *n., pl.* **wreaths** A circle of flowers or leaves: *She wore a wreath of daisies in her hair.*

wren |rĕn| *n., pl.* **wrens** A small brown songbird: *A wren was singing in the tree.*

wren

wrench |rĕnch| *n., pl.* **wrenches** A tool for turning: *She used a wrench to loosen the bolts.*

wring |rĭng| *v.* **wrung, wringing** To twist or squeeze: *Wring out the wet mop when you finish washing the floor.*

write |rīt| *v.* **wrote, written, writing 1.** To make letters or words with a pen or pencil. **2.** To communicate by writing: *I wrote the good news to my friend.*

wrong |rông| *adj.* **1.** Not correct. **2.** Bad: *It is wrong to lie.* **3.** Not working correctly. **4.** Not fitting or suitable: *You picked the wrong time to call.*

x-ray *or* **X-ray** |ĕks' rā| *n., pl.* **x-rays** *or* **X-rays 1.** A machine that takes pictures of parts of the body, such as organs and bones, that cannot be seen from the outside. **2.** A photograph taken by an x-ray machine: *The x-ray showed where the bone was broken.*

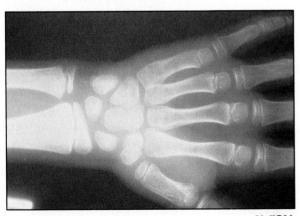

x-ray

Pronunciation Key					
ă	pat	ō	go	th	**th**in
ā	pay	ô	paw, for	hw	**wh**ich
â	care	oi	**oi**l	zh	u**s**ual
ä	father	ŏŏ	b**oo**k	ə	**a**go,
ĕ	pet	ōō	b**oo**t		it**e**m,
ē	be	yōō	c**u**te		penc**i**l,
ĭ	pit	ou	**ou**t		at**o**m,
ī	ice	ŭ	c**u**t		circ**u**s
î	near	û	f**u**r	ər	butt**er**
ŏ	pot	*th*	**th**e		

yel·low |yĕl' ō| *n., pl.* **yellows 1.** Having the color of the sun. **2.** Something having this color, as the yolk of an egg. *adj.,* **yellower, yellowest** Of the color yellow: *He wore a yellow shirt.*

Content Index

Numbers in **boldface** indicate pages on which a skill is introduced as well as references to the Capitalization and Punctuation Guide.

Credits

Illustration **28** Lehner & Whyte **34** Fred Schrier **91** Annie Gusman **94** Lehner & Whyte **99** Annie Gusman **100** Jennifer Harris **134** Lehner & Whyte **145** Jennifer Harris **146** Lehner & Whyte **170** Lehner & Whyte **184** Jennifer Harris

Assignment Photography **53** (t), **64** (tl) (mr), **70** (cl) (c) (cr), **83** (b), **85** (cr), **97** (b), **121** (lr), **124** (tr), **125** (tl) (tr), **128** (br), **145** (lr), **147** (c), **157** (b), **160** (tr), **181** (cr), **193** Allan Landau **164, 175, 176, 200** (lr), **217, 227** (b) Parker/Boon Productions **50** (b), **82–83, 95** (c), **104, 113** (c), **133, 201** (c), **203** (c), **206** (c), **208** (c), **226–227** Tony Scarpetta **134** John Supanic **14** (c), **19** (b), **20** (b), **25** (lr), **32** (lr), **38** (tr) (c) (b), **67** (b), **73, 103** Tracey Wheeler

Photography **6** Image Copyright © 1997 PhotoDisc, Inc. **10** David Epperson/Tony Stone Images **23** (b) Johnny Johnson/Animals Animals **26** Eric Kamp/Phototake/PNI **27** Steve Bly/Tony Stone Images **29** (b) D.J. Ball/Tony Stone Images **35** (inset) Private Collection, Paris, France/Giraudon, Paris/SuperStock **35** (frame) Image Copyright © 1997 PhotoDisc, Inc. **37** Dennis O'Clair/Tony Stone Images **41** (b) David Madison/Tony Stone Images **41** (r) Image Copyright © 1997 PhotoDisc, Inc. **47** (t) David Stoecklein/The Stock Market **47** (b) Lori Adamski Peek/Tony Stone Images **49** © 1994 Lawrence Migdale **52** (l) Image Copyright © 1997 PhotoDisc, Inc. **52** (b) Joseph Sohm/Tony Stone Images **53** (b) Corbis-Bettmann **59** (b) Paul S. Howell/Liaison International **61** (t) Jose Azel/Aurora/PNI **61** (b) Peter Menzel/Stock, Boston/PNI **62** John DeWade/Stock, Boston/PNI **64** (bl) Cosmo Condina/Tony Stone Images **65** (t) (l) Images Copyright © 1997 PhotoDisc, Inc. **65** (b) The Granger Collection **71** (b) Sara Gray/Tony Stone Images **76** (m), **77** (b) Images Copyright © 1997 PhotoDisc, Inc. **76** (r) Renne Lynn/Photo Researchers, Inc. **89** (t) Herb Schmitz/Tony Stone Images **89** (b) NASA **95** (b) Tate Gallery, London/Art Resource **101** (b), **107** (l) Images Copyright © 1997 PhotoDisc, Inc. **107** (b) Corbis-Bettmann **110** Dave Desroches **111** (r) Andy Sack/Tony Stone Images **113** (b)

Charles Krebs/Tony Stone Images **122** © Classic PIO Image **124** (l) (m) Images Copyright © 1997 PhotoDisc, Inc. **125** © Roberto Soncin Gerometta, 1994/Photo 20-20/PNI **131** (l) Image Copyright © 1997 PhotoDisc, Inc. **131** (b) Will & Deni McIntyre/Tony Stone Images **139** © Art Wolfe/Allstock/PNI **143** © Mark Moffett/Minden Pictures **147** Kathi Lamm/Allstock/PNI **148** Images Copyright © 1997 PhotoDisc, Inc. **149** (b) John Cancalosi/Peter Arnold, Inc. **155** (t) David Hanover/Tony Stone Images **155** (inset) Image Copyright © 1997 PhotoDisc, Inc. **161** Stephen Studd/Tony Stone Images **167** (t) Charles Thatcher/Tony Stone Images **167** (b) The Granger Collection **179** Corbis Corporation/Corbis **183** John Terence Turner/FPG International **185** (b) Alan Schein/The Stock Market **185** (l) © Jasmine, 1996/PNI **185** (r) © Rhoda Sidney/Stock, Boston/PNI **197** (m) Matthew Nagy Meyers/Tony Stone Images **197** (b) Peter Vandermark/Stock, Boston/PNI **202** Comstock **203** (b) Julie Bidwell/Stock, Boston/PNI **209** Ariel Skelley/The Stock Market **213, 215** (l) Images Copyright © 1997 PhotoDisc, Inc. **221** Mitch York/Tony Stone Images **282** Frank Herholdt/Tony Stone Images **284, 287** Images Copyright © 1997 PhotoDisc, Inc. **286** © M. Doolittle: A. Doolittle, 1990/Rainbow/PNI **288** John Henley/The Stock Market **291** Image Copyright © 1997 PhotoDisc, Inc. **292** Michael Furman/The Stock Market **294** Daniel J. Cox/Tony Stone Images **296** Peter Correz/Tony Stone Images **298** Rob Crandall/Stock, Boston/PNI **299** Richard Dunoff/The Stock Market **300** Image Copyright © 1997 PhotoDisc, Inc. **303** Gary Braasch, 1992/Allstock/PNI **304** Image Copyright © 1997 PhotoDisc, Inc. **305** David Smart, 1992/Stock South/PNI **307** Kennan Ward/The Stock Market **310** James Randkley/Tony Stone Images **311** James Sugar/Black Star/PNI **312** Jim Corwin/Allstock/PNI **314** Roy Morsch/The Stock Market **316** Phil Schermeister/Allstock/PNI **318, 320, 321** Images Copyright © 1997 PhotoDisc, Inc. **322** Kennan Ward/The Stock Market **324** Tim Davis/Allstock/PNI **325** © Keith/Custom Medical Stock

Handwriting Models

a b c d e f g h i
j k l m n o p q r
s t u v w x y z

A B C D E F G H I
J K L M N O P Q R
S T U V W X Y Z

a b c d e f g h i
j k l m n o p q r
s t u v w x y z

A B C D E F G H I
J K L M N O P Q R
S T U V W X Y Z

Words Often Misspelled

You use many of the words on this page in your writing. Check this list if you cannot think of the spelling for a word you need. The words are in ABC order.

A
again
a lot
always
am
and
another
anyone
anyway
around

B
beautiful
because
before
brought

C
cannot
can't
caught
coming
could

D
didn't
different
don't
down

E
every

F
family
favorite
for
found
friend
from

G
getting
girl
goes
going

H
have
here
his
how

I
I'll
I'm
into
it
its
it's

K
knew
know

L
letter
like
little

M
might
morning
mother
myself

N
now

O
off
other
our

P
people
pretty

R
really
right

S
said
school
some
started
sure
swimming

T
than
that's
their
them
then
there
they
thought
through
to
today
too
tried
two

V
very

W
want
was
where
whole
would
write

Y
you
your
you're